THE POLITICS OF ATTACHMENT

THE POLITICS OF ATTACHMENT

Towards a Secure Society

Edited by

Sebastian Kraemer and Jane Roberts

Preface by Patricia Hewitt

FREE ASSOCIATION BOOKS • LONDON

Published in 1996 by
Free Association Books Ltd
57 Warren Street, London W1P 5PA
and 70 Washington Square South,
New York, NY 10012–1091

ISBN   1 85343 343 8 hardback
       1 85343 344 6 paperback

A CIP catalogue record for this book is available from the
British Library.

Printing history: 99 98 97 96   4 3 2 1

Produced for Free Association Books Ltd by
Chase Production Services, Chadlington, OX7 3LN
Printed in the EC by J.W. Arrowsmith Ltd, Bristol

Contents

Acknowledgements

The idea for this book arose out of a conference of the same name held at the Tavistock Clinic, London, in March 1995, and earlier discussions between the editors, with each other, and with various academics and politicians. We are grateful to the Tavistock Clinic for hosting the conference, and to the Tavistock Foundation and the Faculty of Social Sciences at the University of East London for their generous contributions towards transcription of the proceedings. Although all but one of the authors attended the conference, each chapter has been specially written for the book. We are particularly grateful to them for their forbearance through several revisions of their texts.

Notes on Contributors

John Benington is currently Professor of Public Service Management and Director of the Local Government Centre in the Business School at the University of Warwick. He and his colleagues have been developing programmes of research and development work with a consortium of leading local authorities throughout the UK. He was previously Director of Economic and Employment Development with Sheffield City Council in the 1980s, and Director of the Community Development Project with Coventry City Council in the 1970s. He lived and worked in Moss Side, Manchester, in the 1960s, where he was involved in various forms of community action. [email: lgcjb@wbs.warwick.ac.uk]

Beatrix Campbell is a journalist and broadcaster. Her television documentaries include 'I shot My Husband and No-one Asked me Why' and a Dispatches film about the Nottingham ritual abuse case. Her books include *Wigan Pier Revisited* (Virago, 1984), retracing George Orwell's journey around Britain; *The Iron Ladies* (Virago, 1987), about women and the Conservative tradition; and *Unofficial Secrets* (Virago, 1988) about the Cleveland child abuse controversy. Her most recent book is *Goliath* (Methuen, 1993), about communities, crime and riots in Britain. She writes for the *Guardian* and is visiting Professor of Women's Studies at the University of Newcastle upon Tyne.

Jonathan Gosling is a Senior Fellow at Lancaster University Management School, where he is responsible for several 'executive' programmes, including the MPhil in Critical Management, which offers managers the opportunity to consider the philosophical underpinnings of their practice. He is a partner in the IMPM, a worldwide management education consortium of business schools and corporations, and is organiser of an annual 'working conference' (in the tradition of the Tavistock Institute Group Relations Conferences) on Trans-European Management. Before coming to Lancaster in 1989 he spent six years founding and directing 'the Newham Conflict and

Change Project', specialising in conflict transformation in the East End of London. [email: J.Gosling@lancaster.ac.uk]

Jeremy Holmes is Consultant Psychotherapist at North Devon District Hospital. He was previously a Consultant at University College, London. Educated at Cambridge and London, he then worked in Tanzania, East Africa, before training in psychiatry at the Maudsley Hospital. His publications include *The Values of Psychotherapy* (with R. Lindley, Oxford University Press, 1989), *Between Art and Science: Essays in Psychotherapy and Psychiatry* (Routledge, 1992), *John Bowlby and Attachment Theory* (Routledge, 1993), *Introduction to Psychoanalysis* (with A. Bateman, Routledge, 1995), *Attachment, Intimacy, Autonomy: Using Attachment Ideas in Adult Psychotherapy* (Jason Aronson, 1996) and many papers related to attachment theory and psychotherapy. [email: aaj64@dial.pipex.com]

Tessa Jowell has been the Member of Parliament for Dulwich since April 1992 and since 1994 has served in the Opposition Whips Office where she had responsibility for Trade and Industry, then as Shadow Women's Minister and currently as Shadow Health Minister. Before her election to Parliament she was extensively involved in community care, having directed the pioneering Birmingham Community Care Special Action Project and the Joseph Rowntree Foundation's community care programme. She was a visiting Fellow at the Policy Studies Institute and the King's Fund Institute. She also has extensive experience of the voluntary sector, having been assistant director of MIND for 13 years. She was for 15 years an elected Councillor in the London Borough of Camden and was Chair of several committees including the Social Services Committee. She was also Chair of the Social Services Committee of the Association of Metropolitan Authorities. She is a visiting Fellow of Nuffield College, Oxford, and a Trustee of the Employment Policy Institute.

Helena Kennedy QC is Chancellor of Oxford Brookes University. She is a Commissioner of the National Commission on Education. A frequent broadcaster and journalist, she chairs the Howard League's Inquiry into Violence in Penal Institutions for Young People. She is Chair of the Further Education Funding Council's Widening Participation Committee. She is on the British Council's Law Advisory Committee and Chair of Charter '88. She also chairs the London International Festival of Theatre and is a Fellow of the Royal Society of Arts. Her book *Eve was Framed*, on women and

THE POLITICS OF ATTACHMENT

the criminal justice system, was published in 1992 by Chatto. She won the UK Woman of Europe Award in 1995.

Sebastian Kraemer has been a Consultant Child and Adolescent Psychiatrist at the Tavistock Clinic and at the Whittington Hospital, London, since 1980. He came into medicine after a first degree in philosophy, specialising in paediatrics and later in psychiatry. His principal interests and publications are in family therapy and psychosomatic disorders, the training of child and adolescent psychiatrists, and the origins and roles of fatherhood. Besides lectures and contributions to the media he has also been adviser to think tanks, civil servants and politicians on the clinical and research base for family policy, and the need for a political understanding of attachment throughout the lifecycle. He is married, with two school-age sons. [email: sebastian@kraemer.demon. co.uk]

Oleg Liber spent ten years teaching in London schools and in higher education, during which he was an early proponent of the use of learning technology. His belief in a collaborative model of education led to his involvement in both the design of new computer-based communications systems for use in education, and the application of management cybernetics to education, spending the next ten years with an educational information technology centre where he managed a range of innovative development projects as Director of Research and Development. In 1994 he moved to Anglesey where he is managing a large Europe-wide telematics project for the University of Wales, Bangor, developing an internet-based system for teacher education. [email: o.liber@bangor.ac.uk]

Peter Marris currently teaches in the Department of Sociology at Yale University. For 20 years he was based at the Institute of Community Studies in London. From 1976–91 he was a Professor of Social Policy and Planning in the Urban Planning Programme at the University of California at Los Angeles (UCLA). He has undertaken research on housing, local economic development in Africa, and, in Britain, on higher education, community action and widowhood. He has developed a lifelong concern with the way people cope with loss and social change, which underlies all his work. His books include *Loss and Change* (Routledge, 1974), *Dilemmas of Social Reform* (with Martin Rein, University of Chicago Press, 1982), *Meaning and Action* (Routledge and Kegan Paul, 1987) and, most recently, *The Politics of Uncertainty* (Routledge, 1996).

Marjorie (Mo) Mowlam PhD, Labour MP for Redcar, was promoted to Shadow Northern Ireland Secretary following the Shadow Cabinet elections of October 1994. Her political interests are wide-ranging and include education, the media, trade and industry and, more controversially, Royal architecture. She was elected to the Shadow Cabinet for the first time in 1992 when she was given responsibility for Women's issues and for shadowing the newly created Office of Public Service and Science. Appointed Shadow Heritage Secretary in 1993 she mastered another new and extensive brief covering the arts, broadcasting, the press, the National Lottery, museums and galleries, libraries, sport, leisure and tourism. A member of the Labour Party since 1969, Marjorie Mowlam is also a member of the Transport and General Workers' Union (TGWU). She is patron of the Women's Engineering Society and Patient Power and is Vice President of the British Resorts Association.

Lynne Murray holds a Research Chair in Child Development at the University of Reading, and is Co-director of the Winnicott Research Unit which has bases in the Universities of Reading and Cambridge. Over the last ten years she has conducted prospective longitudinal studies of the mother–child relationship and child development. Together with her colleague Peter Cooper, she has researched the personal and social factors associated with postnatal depression and is now undertaking research funded by the NHS into its prevention. She is married, with three sons and one step-son.

George Nicholson is the Policy and Research Officer for Communities and Homes in Central London (CHiCL). He has written extensively about community and neighbourhood planning, most recently *Place and Local Identity* (with D. McLean-Thorne and S. Pile, London Planning Advisory Committee, 1994). He was Founder of the Peckham Urban Studies Centre, a Southwark Councillor from 1978–82 and a member of the Greater London Council (GLC), Inner London Education Authority (ILEA) from 1981–86 and Chairman of the GLC Planning Committee 1983–86. He is also Vice Chair of Labour Planning and Environment Group, a Director of Coin Street Community Builders and Chairman of the London Rivers Association.

Paul Ormerod is Chair, Post-Orthodox Economics Ltd (35 The Avenue, Kew TW9 2AL). He is the author of *The Death of Economics* (Faber, 1994), translated into German, Italian, Dutch, Spanish,

Portuguese, Turkish, Korean and Japanese, and also published in the US. He was Economic Forecaster and Modeller, National Institute for Economic and Social Research 1973–80 and Director of Economics at the Henley Centre for ten years until 1992. He was visiting Professor of Economics at Queen Mary and Westfield College from 1983 until 1991, a post which he now holds at the University of Manchester. [email: pormerod@mail.bogo.co.uk]

Ray Pahl is a Research Professor at the Economic and Social Research Council (ESRC) Research Centre on Micro-social Change at the University of Essex. Previously he had been Professor of Sociology at the University of Kent at Canterbury, since 1972. He was a member of the Archbishop of Canterbury's Commission which produced the controversial report *Faith in the City* (1985). He has written extensively on work, family and households. His publications include *Divisions of Labour* (Blackwell, 1988), *On Work* (Blackwell, 1988) and *After Success: Fin-de-siècle Anxiety and Identity* (Polity Press, 1995). He is currently collaborating with colleagues in a new project on the 'downsizing' and undermining of the 'psychological contract' in organisations. [email: ray.pahl@essex.ac.uk]

Andrea Pound is Head of Psychology Services in Tower Hamlets, London. She was trained at the Maudsley Hospital and the Tavistock Clinic, London. She has been involved in research on the effect of maternal depression on pre-school children and on the evaluation of New Parent–Infant Network (NEWPIN) and was also a member of the Attachment Seminar which met with John Bowlby over a number of years. For much of her career she practised as a child psychologist but is now involved mainly in psychotherapy.

Jane Roberts qualified as a doctor in 1980, specialising first in paediatrics and later in psychiatry at the Maudsley Hospital and the Tavistock Clinic. She is now Consultant Child and Adolescent Psychiatrist with the Camden and Islington Community Health Services NHS Trust and at the Whittington Hospital, London. Elected a Councillor in the London Borough of Camden in 1990 she has been Deputy Leader of the Council since 1994. She has a six-year-old son, Jack.

Michael Rustin is Professor of Sociology and Dean of Faculty of Social Sciences at the University of East London. He has recently been co-ordinating joint work between the Tavistock Clinic and University of East London to provide academic recognition for many postgraduate courses taught at the Tavistock. Michael Rustin's books include *For a Pluralist Socialism* (Verso, 1985), *The Good Society and the Inner World* (Verso, 1991) and (with Margaret Rustin) *Narratives of Love and Loss: Studies in Modern Children's Fiction* (Verso, 1987). He is currently working on a book on theatre, psychoanalysis and society, and on social theory.

Ian Taylor is Professor of Sociology at the University of Salford. In the 1970s he was best known as co-author of *The New Criminology* (Routledge, 1973) – a sociological critique of orthodox disciplinary criminology, and a series of associated texts – but also for some analytic work on soccer hooliganism. In 1981 he published *Law and Order: Arguments for Socialism* (Macmillan), helping to launch the programme of left realist criminology in Britain. In the 1980s, he was Professor of Sociology at Carleton University, Ottawa, Canada, returning to the UK and his present position in 1989. His most recent publication (written with Karen Evans and Penny Fraser) is *A Tale of Two Cities: Global Change, Local Feeling and Everyday Life in the North of England: A Study in Manchester and Sheffield* (Routledge, 1996). He is also writing a new monograph, *The Criminology of the Free Market* (Polity Press). [email: I.R.Taylor@sociology.salford.ac.uk]

David Utting is a writer, researcher and co-author of *Crime and the Family*, published in 1993 by the Family Policy Studies Centre, London. He is an adviser to the Joseph Rowntree Foundation and author of its 1995 report, *Family and Parenthood: supporting families, preventing breakdown*.

Preface

Patricia Hewitt

Across the industrialised world, the left has been struggling to come to grips with change – to find out 'what's left'. For two decades, globalisation, individualisation, the economic and social revolutions summed up in the metaphor of post-industrialism have provided the conditions for the apparently unassailable intellectual triumph of the right.

But now, and none too soon, a different voice can be heard. The free marketeers forgot something which Adam Smith himself never forgot: that markets depend upon non-market institutions, on trust, on relationships between people and within communities, on norms of good behaviour, on social capital. Destroy that and not only do you damage efficiency, you also destroy the conditions for a good life.

The neo-liberal account of individuals – rational, self-interested, atomised – also turns out to be less than the whole story. The left has always had a different, more optimistic view of human nature, knowing people to be selfless as well as selfish, altruistic as well as self-interested. The rich tradition of developmental psychology and attachment theory – particularly well developed in this country since the 1950s – brings to an impoverished political debate the fundamental insight that we are, each of us, necessarily social beings, individuals created through relationships with others. The need for attachment, for an identity rooted in belonging, is about as far from 'no such thing as society' as it is possible to be.

Thus, developmental psychology can deepen the theoretical basis of the left's new project. But the insights offered in this collection of essays are intensely practical too. Think of the problems which confront people daily and which must, therefore, be confronted by politicians. The 20-year-old son with no chance of ever following his father into the mines, the steel factory or the army. The 20-year-old mother bringing up her child on income support. The manager in his 40s, six months redundant, told by the Job Centre to take a job as a mini-cab driver. The teenage boy who rapes a woman old enough to be his grandmother. The dislocation of economies and communities; the fear of crime and apparently senseless violence; the changing roles of men and women; the apparent fragility of families ... none can be understood, or seriously tackled, unless we also understand the conditions which enable individuals to fulfil their potential for good – or ill.

Ironically, business leaders may be more comfortable than politicians with the 'soft stuff' of psychology. Amongst leading global businesses – the emblem, surely, of cost-cutting Thatcherism – we find a new preoccupation with the networks of employees, suppliers, customers and retailers whose loyalty must increasingly be won rather than assumed. For the growing number of businesses whose product requires creativity, imagination and inventiveness, building effective relationships between 'knowledge workers' becomes the key to success.

These days, we are all too aware of the limits on governments' power to do things for people. This volume, however, stresses the conditions in which people can do things for themselves and for others. If the left understands that the central purpose of national and local governments must be to help build the capacity of individuals, families and communities to fulfil their best potential, then there need be no limit to our imagination – or to our achievement.

.   *Patricia Hewitt*
Deputy Chair,
Commission on
Social Justice

Introduction: Holding the Thread

Jane Roberts and Sebastian Kraemer

Exactly 50 years ago Bertrand Russell noted that the most creative periods in Western history have ended when what are seen as the fetters of moral restraint are cast off. In so doing, those societies sowed the seeds of their own destruction; what followed was the dominance of less civilised governments but which were nevertheless 'not so destitute of social cohesion' (Russell 1946). Russell ventured that liberalism with its appeal to more rational values might lead the way forward out of this endless cycle. As the millennium approaches, we too might find the dazzling uncertainties of the post-modern world brushed away under regimes offering simple solutions to insoluble problems. Maybe, however, we need something more than a liberal analysis. The purpose of this book is to add to the prevailing political language an account of what we know about fundamental human needs and so renew our confidence in the possibility of more complex yet more cohesive societies. 'There is no such thing as society' was perhaps the most provocative statement of the 1980s. We want to join in the refutation of that view. In our support there is now accumulating knowledge of the conditions under which co-operativeness may flourish as well as a richer understanding of how humans may turn against themselves and others. This book is not a manifesto, although implications for policy there most certainly are. Rather, it describes how ordinary human life is both influenced by, and can influence, the process of politics.

Political thought, like fashion, moves in mysterious ways. Yet it has a common thread, the tension between social and individual needs, which can be traced from ancient times to the present. This argument has been brought into sharp relief in recent political history in the UK. With the swing away from the collective solutions of post-war times, came an emphasis, not only from the right, on the importance of individual liberty, freed from the shackles of the state. But there is unease across the political spectrum at where that move has taken us, and an uncertainty as to what route we should now follow. Indeed, in our post-modernist or 're-flexive' (Giddens 1991) maelstrom, there is doubt that any defined way forward is possible. The certainties of the post-war world have gone, particularly the oppositions on which they were based – east and west, male and female – leaving bewilderment in their wake. To whom or what do we belong? With whom or what do we identify? It is a matter of regret and nostalgia to many that we have left behind the age of deference, when people knew their place and behaved properly – at least in public. Now we know that public order, however desirable, can conceal many ills. Knowing this gives us little comfort, however. It serves only to unnerve us and shift the sands yet more. Insecurity abounds – jobs, housing, hierarchies, familiar family structures, our rulers' perceived compe-tence, are all dissolving – and is no longer confined to any one class. Quite how do we make sense of it all?

Since Marx and Durkheim, writers from a phalanx of different 'socio-' disciplines – sociology, social anthropology, social psychol-ogy and social psychiatry – have been preoccupied with the nature of the relationship between the individual and society. Though Marx began: 'In total contrast to German philosophy, which de-scends from heaven to earth, here it is a matter of ascending from earth to heaven ... of setting out from real, active human beings, and on the basis of their real life processes demonstrating the development of the ideological reflexes and echoes of this life proc-ess' (Marx 1846), he ended up with a view of industrial society in which individuals were little distinct from one another except by virtue of their place in the social structure, their class. Political writing has continued to be dominated by a social, rather than a psychological view of the world, but because of that, something has been missing. Cohen persuasively argues that social anthropology has suffered from the same defect, its concern with the social bases of relations ignoring the dimensions of self and self-consciousness. He acknowledges 'the irony that we have to approach the funda-mental problem of social cohesion through its apparent opposite, selfhood and personal identity' (Cohen 1994).

In the political domain little attempt had been made, until recently, to examine the more subtle ways in which the individual and society are inextricably bound up with one another, rather than simply being in irreconcilable conflict. The once agonised political search for 'the big idea' is now more exploratory in mood, with many writers and thinkers, not always aware of each other's work, converging on the questions implied by this book – what are the qualities that define good societies and good relationships within and between them? (Ignatieff 1990, Giddens 1991, Nussbaum 1993, Samuels 1993, Midgely 1994, Zeldin 1995). Much of this debate is reminiscent of the philosophies of the Enlightenment, yet our knowledge, particularly about human desires and needs, is far greater now than then.

Many writers have brought in psychoanalysis to bridge the gap between the individual psyche and the social/political domain, from Freud (1961) himself, through Fromm (1963) and Reich (1983), and more recently to Frosh (1989), Richards (1989), Rustin (1991), Gordon (1995) and many others. These attempts have not on the whole broken through into mainstream political thinking. Yet extensive research over the last half-century in the rather different, but related fields of developmental psychology and personality development have a crucial but hitherto neglected contribution to make to political debate. John Bowlby, on whose theory we focus in this book, was well aware of the social implications of his ideas and indeed considered the interplay between psychology and democracy 50 years ago (Bowlby 1946). Around the same time, another eminent practitioner, the psychoanalyst and paediatrician Donald Winnicott, wrote extensively about the roots of anti-social behaviour and delinquency (Winnicott 1964). Despite the determined efforts of Bowlby and Winnicott, the political and the psychological have remained, until recently, resolutely separate.

There are now, however, some tentative moves from the social/political side towards rapprochement. Words such as community, belonging, stakeholding, exchange, gifting, trust are on everyone's lips. Avner Offer, an economic historian, highlights the notion of reciprocity and the economy of regard in non-market exchange. He goes further: 'It is reasonable to assume that the capacity for regard, like the capacity for language, is innate, even if the forms it takes are culturally specific' (Offer 1996). Indeed it is, as this book seeks to demonstrate. From the social sciences, Anthony Giddens emphasises the notions of risk and trust in our current setting of 'late modernity'. He views trust as 'a crucial generic phenomenon of personality development ... directly linked to achieving an early sense of ontological security' (Giddens 1991). Also focusing on trust, but on its role in economic life, Fukuyama (1995) stresses the significant impact of 'spontaneous sociability', by which he means the ability of societies 'to form new associations' (or, as we would say, attachments).

Recent psychological studies show what the conditions for sociability are, and in this book we attempt to connect these with current political thinking. This is not to say that people are really nicer than one might think but to argue carefully, from what we know from psychology and ethology, that our niceness or nastiness is not irretrievably fixed in our genes, but is reciprocally affected by the social and cultural environment. Whilst acknowledging the complex nature of the relationship between biology and the social sciences, the distinguished ethologist, Robert A. Hinde, has argued too that 'the view that characteristics of human social structures and sociocultural structures are rooted in the behavioural propensities of individuals is reasonable, and indeed inevitable' (Hinde 1987). The essential message is that the quality and style of interaction, in government, business, education and so on, has a major impact on the lives of the participants.

Several disclaimers are necessary. First, we are not offering a theory that can explain everything about human behaviour. Although attachment is a concept based in biology and psychology, it has little to do with the sociobiological views of E.O. Wilson and his followers, who were clearly in possession of what they saw as a comprehensive theory of human nature (Wilson 1978). Attachment theory makes no such claims. It sets out a model of healthy development and is at its most powerful in identifying the conditions that promote it. It is less confident when it comes to accounting for the more extreme and perverse forms of human behaviour. The message of sociobiology, in contrast, is that most of what human beings do, whether good or bad, is determined by evolutionary forces beyond anyone's control; differences between people are primarily genetic. Of course, apart from identical twins, we are all genetically different but attachment theory points to a remarkable consistency in patterns of relationship, not only within the human species but in other mammals, and in birds. It shows that variations in the quality of attachment depend far more on the histories of the participants than on their genes. Our purpose is to place this knowledge alongside complementary social and political theories, not to replace them. It also needs to be said that much post-Darwinian theorising has been used to prop up the uses and abuses of social and political power, most notoriously in the work of the Victorian Herbert Spencer, who actually coined the term 'survival of the fittest' and argued confidently that the theory of evolution supported the class and imperial values of his day (see Rose et al. 1984). Not only was his argument logically wrong, but it was also predicated on a still common assumption about the nature of 'untamed' animal life in the wild, that it is essentially cruel and savage; 'every one for himself'. There is a great deal of modern evidence to show how sophisticated and attentive is the social life of wild animals, particularly primates. Even though fierce and violent acts between individual animals take place, chimpanzees, for example, are highly attuned to one another (Dunbar 1996), and exquisitely conscious of the need for peacemaking and the restoration of order after struggle (de Waal 1996). Midgley neatly sums it up: 'The reality of affectionate bonds among social animals is now fully documented by ethologists. Their sociability is not just a means to an end' (Midgley 1994).

Second, this book is not an appeal to sentiment; quite the reverse. Because attachments are rooted in the earliest intimate relationships, there is a serious risk that some readers will recoil from the argument, as if it were merely an invitation to 'love thy neighbour'. Not so. Human relationships, public as well as intimate, depend as much on conflict as upon co-operation for their vitality, but to manage either requires social and emotional skills which have to be learned. Such skills are all the more vital if we are to be able to cope with and manage the uncertainties and risks that lie ahead. Rather than an exhortation to virtue, this book is an attempt to outline the conditions in which the learning of these skills can most effectively take place.

We have deliberately set out to assemble a group of contributors from disparate fields, from psychology and psychiatry to the social sciences, but taking in economics, politics, law, journalism and cybernetics on the way. As editors, this is something of a double-edged enterprise: a challenging venture but fraught with risks. The attempt to forge a common thread of understanding between different disciplines may be seen as brave but essentially misguided. Undaunted, however, we have persisted in trying to bring together the different contributions in such a way that a genuinely fresh and useful perspective emerges.

Our starting point is an understanding of personal and social well-being, based on attachment theory, which is widely accepted amongst child mental health workers, such as ourselves, but remains little known elsewhere, even amongst some of the most learned people. (Witness, for example, the reactions of many media commentators to the perpetrators of some particularly foul crimes in recent years.) An inescapable truth of human and other higher mammalian relationships is that those who are respectfully treated are more likely to be respectful to others. How this comes to be so is not self-evident and will not be understood simply by seeking recourse to sentimentality, religious ethic or, the last refuge of the desperate, 'common sense'. Our contention is that the ideas underlying attachment theory have a significant contribution to make in understanding the links between one generation and the next, and between the individual and the social. Hard-headed stuff. Yet if the notion of attachment means anything at all to the general reader, it tends to conjure up a rather syrupy picture of loving content-ment, such as a mother and baby enjoying each other's company. Intimate moments like these are vital for healthy development, but attachment is not always sweet; in cases where children are de-pendent upon abusive and neglectful caregivers, it is painfully raw and confused (Main 1995). The idealisation of motherhood in two millennia of Christian iconography has contributed to our collective ignorance of the lives of real babies. What do they actually need? John Bowlby defined and redefined attachment theory from 1939 until his death in 1991 and was for many years scorned because he dared to spell it out, although many parents (mostly mothers, of course) instinctively knew. The answer is that babies need looking after, both physically and emotionally. Most people know about the former but are vague about the latter. As Jeremy Holmes describes in his chapter, attachment theory proposes that we all have a biological need to be in proximity to our caregivers in our earliest years so that we can be not only physically protected but emotion-ally contained, responded to, held in mind and stimulated. In such 'good enough' (Winnicott 1974) conditions, we can then grow and develop in sufficient security to feel good about ourselves, more confident in ourselves and others (see Murray, this volume). It is no accident, from an evolutionary perspective, that the most in-tense proximity-seeking behaviour, at 18 months, is seen in normal development at the time when mobility begins. Furthermore, it is in the first 18 months, before weaning, that the most rapid and critical brain growth occurs, a crucial time of preparation for humans and other primates, for the long period of steady childhood development before puberty and sexual maturation. Indeed it is important to note that the attachment process probably determines not only emotional and social development, but also the stability of physiological variables. There is strong evidence from animal stud-ies to show that early separation from mother, for example, has profoundly disturbing effects on the maintenance of body systems such as the circulation and blood pressure, immunity from infec-tion, hormone levels, temperature control and so on (Hofer 1995; see also Kraemer 1992).

The key to good attachment, as both Jeremy Holmes and Lynne Murray show, is consistency, sensitivity and responsiveness. What has all this got to do with our adult lives, let alone politics?

Although the theory begins with observations of mother–infant pairs in both human and non-human species, it readily extends to include other relationships, such as between children and their fathers, grandparents and others important in any individual's life. Under 'good enough' conditions, the quality of those relationships becomes internalised and so coalesces into a coherent personality – one who feels sufficiently good about him or herself, and can then turn out to meet the world with trust and confidence. It is also important to emphasise, as Holmes and Utting do in their chapters, that a secure attachment is more likely to develop if intense states of mind in infancy are emotionally contained; the setting and maintenance of clear boundaries later on, crucial for continuing healthy development, is thus made easier. In such circumstances, an individual can feel safe to explore and venture further afield. The capacity to trust is enhanced. Note that a secure attachment facilitates creativity, independence and autonomy, rather than encouraging dependency. On the other hand, an insecurely attached child may cling on desperately to a familiar figure, effectively imprisoned by anxiety. There are intriguing parallels here with the notion put forward by the anthropologist James W. Fernandez, that individuals struggle continuously against uncertainty, insecurity, 'the dark at the bottom of the stairs' and reach out for familiarity and certainty. Only then, he argues, can individuals behave competently (Fernandez 1986). Nor is all this only in the realm of speculation; from no less an authority than the eminent child psychiatrist, Sir Michael Rutter, 'most of the key components of attachment concepts have received empirical support' (Rutter 1995). As Holmes details, there is robust empirical research which links the conditions which make for security of children with a number of characteristics in which society has a legitimate and growing interest, such as self-esteem, sense of agency, problem-solving ability and social competence. The story can now be tracked still further with the revealing work on adult attachment which emphasises not just the content of our life experiences, but, crucially, the way in which those experiences are construed, how individuals make sense (or not) of what has happened to them and therefore how their narrative hangs together. Even amongst those who have had adverse experiences and been traumatised, those who can bring coherence to their histories (and thus have a capacity for 'reflexivity') have a far better chance of 'breaking the cycle' – and of making secure attachments to their own children (Fonagy et al. 1994).

Jeremy Holmes concludes his chapter with some thoughts about the application of attachment theory to the political domain and argues for 'a new rallying call: security'. This echoes the issues raised by Mo Mowlam, MP. One of two national politicians contributing to this book, she sets the political context for thinking about insecurity both on an individual level (including Members of Parliament themselves) and at community level. Throughout her chapter, the demoralisation and humiliation of those who cannot find work resounds; if we are serious about addressing the rampant insecurity in our society, we must do all that we can to enable people to find a job in which they are paid and treated decently. Attachment theory can usefully inform our understanding of the social and psychological effects of unemployment. Indeed, the response to unemployment is akin to that of any other situation in which a loss is sustained (Fagin and Little 1984). Studies since the 1930s consistently report the significantly poorer mental health, including loss of self-esteem and reduced social contact, in those who lose their jobs (Bhugra 1993). This is hardly surprising given the importance that work has for self-identity. More recently, ill-effects from the anticipation of job loss, before employment status has changed, have been convincingly demonstrated (Ferrie et al. 1995).

Mowlam goes on to draw on her current portfolio – Shadow Secretary of State for Northern Ireland – to warn of the dangers in communities which, though tightly knit, can be exclusive and, indeed, repressive. We would argue that the intolerance displayed in some communities which appear to be strongly bound together against a common adversary is evidence of an insecure base, which relies on mistrust and 'projection' to keep its boundaries intact. As Michael Rustin and Bea Campbell argue in their chapters, attachment theory is not sufficient on its own to account for the depth of fear and viciousness of certain divisions, notably of ethnicity and gender, in modern society. As Rustin makes clear, 'the need for security and membership is such that psychic health may be sought ... within fragments held together by antagonism to what lies outside their imaginary boundaries. Thus, a gang projects its vulnerabilities on to its victims ...' From the different perspective of social anthropology, Cohen (1994) proposes that at times of uncertainty we are more likely to assert our belonging to collective identities such as nationality, gender and sexuality. Indeed, when the struggle for identity is most acute, the 'battle between the civic and the ethnic nation' (Ignatieff 1994) is heavily weighted in favour of the latter. Disastrous consequences may flow, as the international scene bears witness in all too many countries. Even then, strenuous attempts may be made by an abusing power to obliterate all traces of their dead victims. Derek Summerfield, a psychiatrist working with those who have been tortured, argues for 'the politics of memory', an acknowledgement and naming of the dead and 'disappeared' so that survivors can begin to make sense of their losses. Then at least some repair of the social fabric may be possible (Summerfield 1995). His plea has a powerful resonance with the theme of this book.

It may be easier to understand the qualities that underlie a secure or insecure attachment by seeing what happens when attentiveness, sensitivity and responsiveness are absent. Lynne Murray's studies show that with the best will in the world, some parents fail to be attuned to the changing moods of their children, who are then deprived of the ordinary help that they need to become generous people, curious about and interested in what is going on around them. The resulting deficits are both social and intellectual and may well persist into adulthood. Murray painstakingly examines the writings of Amitai Etzioni and the tenets of communitarianism, drawing out comparisons with recent 'New Labour' ideas about stakeholding. Although communitarianism has captured the imagination of some commentators, it is found profoundly wanting; nowhere is addressed the crucial issue of the conditions in which parents can promote the well-being of children. The focus on parenting and morality is welcome, indeed overdue, but the analysis lacks any theory of moral development. It is merely prescriptive, a behaviourist model and inevitably therefore, incomplete. In general – not only in families – the regulation of behaviour is not determined as much by rules or contracts, necessary though they are, as by a host of other, less rigid means, one of which is the way in which citizens are attached to each other and to the organisations and communities that make up the whole.

Whilst this book is not intended primarily to outline a policy for child care, that inevitably is implied in several chapters, notably those by Andrea Pound and David Utting. Both describe some of the pitfalls that may lie in wait for us all as parents. Pound highlights the pioneering, preventative work being done by voluntary sector organisations, such as the New Parent–Infant Network (NEWPIN), which attend to the isolation felt by often desperate mothers. Here the focus is on the younger age group, particularly the under-fives. Utting succinctly summarises the known risks for later delinquency but acknowledges the difficulties in tracing causation in such a tangled web. He nevertheless points the way towards a considered strategy to reduce delinquent behaviour. He highlights the thesis that the quality of attachments formed by children and adolescents is the key to healthy social behaviour. Securely attached children are more likely to be socially active, sought out by other children, peer leaders and sympathetic to peer distress (Waters et al. 1979). Such attachments may be formed not just with family members but with other significant figures including teachers and friends, and also, by extension, with social institutions, notably schools, whose ethos has the capacity to foster a respect for others (Rutter et al. 1979).

The links with the importance of friendship follow on seamlessly. In our moral panic over the perceived disintegration of the family, friendship has been quietly neglected as a major player in our lives, as Ray Pahl so elegantly demonstrates in his chapter. He highlights the crucial distinction between individualism and individuality, emphasising the importance of the latter for communities in which fraternity can flourish. With the trend towards smaller families and increasing numbers of women choosing to remain childless, friendship links will become ever more important for us all. What then makes for mutually beneficial, trusting friendships? Whilst there is much research still to be done, there are positive associations between secure attachment in children and later friendship quality (Dunn and McGuire 1992). The evidence is available too in the findings quoted by both Lynne Murray and Andrea Pound in their chapters of the modifying effects on mothers' parenting skills, of friendship or its more formal sibling, befriending. We know also that despite entreaties from yesteryear to 'get on yer bike', few of us ever do; of those who move house, 22 per cent move only within two miles and a further 41 per cent within five miles (Bob Tyrell, personal communication). Perhaps we all instinctively know of the importance for psychological health of social support networks, a conviction which is now supported by empirical research in the field of social psychiatry. Brugha (1993) stresses that it is 'the specific "personal" provisions of social relationships and particularly their more subjective components, e.g. confiding, intensity, and reciprocity of interaction and reassurance of worth' that should further be explored rather than the material value of the support, crucial though that may be.

We know that men and women, indeed girls and boys, have different patterns of friendship. Girls have more emotionally intimate same-sex friendships than boys and invest heavily in trust and loyalty, with high expectations in return (Graham and Rutter 1985). What implications might these have for the way in which different communities, whether neighbourhood, parent and toddler group or boardroom, function? We know that gender demarcates much of our public space. As Bea Campbell, in her chapter, trenchantly points out, it is women, particularly mothers, who take on the job of bringing together fractured, despairing communities and interdigitating private and public domains. That task goes on, day in, day out, though, of course, it is rarely acknowledged and is hidden from the political spotlight. Unacknowledged too, she continues, is the glaringly obvious fact that the overwhelming majority of delinquents and criminals are male: 'the problem with no name'. These young men 'hijack the public space they share with their community'. Attachment theory helps us to understand the conditions in which deviancy takes root (see Utting, this volume) but it does not purport to offer an explanation of how the two sexes then go on to express differently the pain of their insecure attachments: why, for example, women are more likely to internalise their pain and become depressed while men beat the living daylights out of each other (and their partners). Men too are thought to be more vulnerable to the effects of unemployment because of the centrality of work to their identity. There is no NEWPIN or its ilk for them, however; on the contrary, contacts by those in 'blue collar' jobs with their social network decrease as unemployment continues (Atkinson et al. 1986).

Friendship and other social support networks flourish in known, well-worn and familiar communities which still can be open and trusting. A statement of the obvious, perhaps, even tautological. What is far more testing, however, is the maintenance of such communities at times of change and their evolution anew, where none previously had existed. George Nicholson, in his chapter, gives a thoughtful overview of the planning processes in London in the last half-century. He outlines the tensions that almost inevitably exist between residents on the one hand, and policy planners and property developers, on the other. Planning authorities have not only to mesh the conflicting demands, but more subtly to reinforce a sense of place (or, in attachment terms, 'a secure base'), a connection to our environment in space and time such that we are able to grow and develop. Our sense of place and connection with now often sadly neglected public spaces has, however, been sorely tested; urban parks best exemplify the descent into public squalor, with women and children driven out first. Yet public parks are of essence places of 'communality'; where different people's needs are met in very different ways, where strangers make glancing, subtly negotiated contact and where personal and community meanings can be embodied (Burgess 1994). Although undoubtedly the growth of 'non-places' – airports, motorways, supermarkets, for example, where individuals are supposedly all uniformly connected and where no organic social life is possible (Auge 1995) – strains our ability to make sense of the world,

Nicholson demonstrates our remarkable persistence in hanging on to our sense of place, whether defined by neighbourhood or by community of other interests.

Ian Taylor continues the theme of the loss of a sense of place and mastery but over a wider terrain. (In so doing, he points wryly to the discovery of a sense of place for all those avid anthropologists and commentators of supermodernity.) He does nevertheless complete a full circle to draw on three aspects of life in England, (note: not UK, Celts beware) – football, differences between and within regions, and 'the Corporation' – which give shape and identity to our lives. Such attachments depend on intense attunement to even small differences (or 'local distinctiveness' (Clifford and King 1993)), so important is the sense of identity that flows from it. This echoes Nicholson's emphasis, in this volume, on the importance in the planning process of the recognition of difference rather than the pursuit of similarity, for local identity. There is a sense of optimism, grittiness and humour in Taylor's contribution, qualities which themselves inform the affectionate (and playful) processes of attachment.

As we know, however, attachments are not always so healthy, especially when they are principally defined by the exclusion of other, hated, groups, as Michael Rustin powerfully demonstrates in his chapter. He sets the development of attachment theory in its historical context; it was very much the creature of its post-war period. He goes on to argue cogently, nevertheless, that ideas about attachment are germane to the changed circumstances in which we find ourselves at the end of the century. Communities may be experienced more 'as symbolic, even imaginary entities' rather than merely in face-to-face encounters; such a complex society will inevitably now be composed of widely different sub-groups. The crucial issue though, is 'to ensure that dialogue, mediation and movement of individuals between them is possible'. This theme reverberates throughout this book.

Attachments may be fostered in local geographical communities or within organisations of work or interest, but, as Jonathan Gosling portrays, there is a blurring round the edges of differences between 'community' and 'organisation'. Employers especially are increasingly using the rhetoric of community to engender loyalty and commitment from their workers whilst communities are moving into more formal structures and procedures in the name of efficiency and effectiveness. In both, however, processes of attachment have significance. Both communities and organisations involve a quid pro quo: work/interest/commitment/duty put in, for satisfaction of some sort and, at minimum, a wage extracted. The more intense the sense of belonging and ownership, the more both sides of the equation benefit. Attention therefore to reciprocity pays dividends (perhaps literally).

Reciprocity is a word that has not been fashionable in local government circles until recently. Local government has been much maligned in the last 20 years, an object by some of contempt and derision. Yet as both Ian Taylor and John Benington in their chapters make clear, municipal government in times gone by was a leading force for the betterment of its citizens, proud, civilising and unbowed. The relentless, fragmenting sweep towards the introduction of internal markets, the contract culture, quangos and privatisation, together with the crushing blow to the self-esteem of many local authorities at the loss of political autonomy in the 1980s, has led to an uncertainty, even floundering, about the way forward. Benington describes the stirrings of a local government movement, increasingly sure of its role but defined now in terms of 'community governance' rather than simply in the provision or the enabling of services. The essence of the notion of community governance is that communities defined by locality (here, district, county or borough) should have representation on all matters of interest to its citizens, that the council should act as advocates for its constituents. In so doing, a local authority can be seen not only to restore some sense of agency to its citizenry but in pulling together disparate strands, to facilitate social networks and encourage a sense of belonging and cohesion. In Britain, it appears that we strongly associate the notion of citizenship with membership of a community rather than, as in the US, with the endowment of legal rights and responsibilities (Crewe 1996) or, as promulgated by the Conservative right, with the acquisition of consumer status. There is a resurgence in the idea of citizenship which is rooted in 'the context of social networks bound together by the ties of membership, loyalty and mutual obligation ... Relationships between individuals are based upon reciprocity, interdependence and commitment rather than market exchange' (Prior et al. 1995). We seem, nevertheless, increasingly reluctant in practice to engage in even the most minimal community activity, preferring instead to retrench into the atomised, televised and private world behind our front doors. Civic bonds are weakening, journalists proclaim, 'the single most important issue of our time' (Kettle 1996). Who better, then, to foster, cajole or even provoke the regeneration of our civic connectedness than local authorities? They are of course not the only bodies who play a part in the complicated, delicate web of their locality, but their elected position confers on them a degree of legitimacy that is unique. Local authorities should, however, keep their side of the bargain, to earn the respect and trust of the populace, they must engage with their citizens responsively, respectfully and in a spirit of openness. Councils have a crucial role to play in making sense of what goes on at a local level, relating this in a meaningful way to the national context. Jeremy Holmes emphasises the importance of process in government, central as much as local: 'we should expect of our politicians respect for persons, the capacity to listen, acknowledgement of pain, acceptance of the need of legitimate expressions of anger, and above all to strive for security so that exploration and growth can take place'. These themes hark back to the significant relationship between the coherence of adults' narratives of their childhood and their own style of parenting. It is not just what happens (the content) that is important, but the way in which it is construed and made sense of (the process) that determines its impact on our daily lives.

Whilst we make more, or at least different, demands of our politicians, we should be mindful of the intense load already placed on councillors and MPs alike. Even the securest attachments are likely to be tested, as one of the editors – Jane Roberts – is all too aware. Tessa Jowell, MP, takes up this theme and asks whether politicians can ever be normal people. She portrays the intricate juggling act required of all MPs who will inevitably have an intense attachment to their political values, to their parliamentary party and to their constituency, but who must also nurture their attachments to intimate figures in their own lives. Not only must they do this for their personal survival but, paradoxically also, for their effectiveness as politicians, connected to the real struggles of ordinary people.

Economics has, however, traditionally taken little heed of such dilemmas. In a more provocative vein (for many readers of this volume, perhaps), Paul Ormerod unequivocally affirms the fruits of capitalism. He makes clear, however, that there is a choice to be made between social cohesion and economic performance, at least as conventionally defined. Ormerod illustrates the point with the experience of the US. Others, however, have argued that despite high crime rates and many other social ills, the US is a country where trust, co-operation and mutual respect are still highly valued in commerce (Fukuyama 1995, Kay 1996). In Britain, high unemployment has played a significant part in the disintegration of our social fabric, but has been justified, with crocodile tears, on the grounds of its painful necessity on the road to higher growth. Rates of unemployment, however, as Ormerod demonstrates, show little correlation with medium-term economic growth. He challenges the notion (expressed elsewhere and by other contributors in this book) that national governments are rendered helpless by the onslaught of globalisation. Other countries have maintained relatively low rates of unemployment despite a slowdown in economic growth. Unemployment is therefore essentially a political matter. The issue then becomes whether or not support can be garnered for the inevitable financial cost of reducing unemployment – either from work sharing, higher taxation or higher prices – and under what conditions is this support most likely. Our contention in this book is that if we can understand the conditions which promote a cohesive society then we are better able to make informed choices about the relative merits of the different approaches to it, rather than settle by default for the (incalculable) costs of social disorder. As Michael Rustin reminds us in this volume, there is a progressive breakdown in understanding and relationship across the social spectrum, the forerunner of social disorder, as economic inequality grows. And it is not just social disorder, alarming as that may be, which may result from a less cohesive society, but possibly also a reduced life-expectancy. There is evidence, even from developed countries, that widening inequality in income reduces life-expectancy across all income groups, not just that of the more deprived groups (Wilkinson 1994, Davey Smith 1996). The mechanism of such an effect is open to speculation, but Richard Wilkinson suggests that it is not only poverty, damp housing and other social ills that determine health inequalities but the 'feelings of failure, insecurity, depression, anxiety, low self-esteem'. There is then almost certainly a psychological twist to the tale.

Aneurin Bevan knew a thing or two about attachment theory when he wrote: 'The assertion of anti-socialists that private economic adventure is a desirable condition stamps them as profoundly unscientific. You can make your home the base for your adventures, but it is absurd to make the base itself an adventure' (Bevan 1978). The gadarene rush towards demutualisation of building societies is but one example of our tendency to retreat into our own lairs at times of insecurity, when our homes almost literally are no longer a secure base. Peter Marris carries forward this theme with his description of how power is used above all to protect against uncertainty. Uncertainty is then bundled down towards those who are the most vulnerable, with the least power. This concentration of uncertainty amongst the most disadvantaged will in turn have repercussions on the quality of their emotional attachments, marginalising them still further.

Uncertainty is of course no longer confined to the working class (hence, many argue, all the fuss and maybe this book). New technology has swept away many middle and senior manager posts and radically changed the working environment for those remaining; known and familiar hierarchies flattened, the once 'secure base' of the firm's headquarters metamorphosing into satellites of digital home-working. What does that mean for those men, especially, whose friendships and self-esteem have traditionally been forged in the camaraderie of the shopfloor or office? Whilst these are undoubtedly thorny issues, new technology enables us to communicate in innovative ways and hence opens up the possibility of different sorts of communities, as Oleg Liber describes in his chapter. His plea for us not to shirk from this challenge, but instead to pursue with vigour the opportunities offered by technology for a more participative democracy, echoes the cry from very different quarters for a practice of citizenship based on increased participation in the political process (Prior et al. 1995).

Helena Kennedy, in her chapter, takes further the case for citizenship as she delivers a sweeping critique of the British government of the last two decades. She vigorously asserts that the roots of citizenship are nurtured within the socialist ethic of solidarity and fellowship, but they then depend for their sustenance on a political system in which people can have trust. On this count, our political system has failed most spectacularly; the plummeting fall in ethical standards of some prominent politicians is only the most visible example of how our political process has come to be so mistrusted. Kennedy brings the work of the sociologist, Robert Putnam into the debate; his insistence on the importance of 'social capital' – mutual trust, reciprocity, strong local networks – has an obvious resonance with the theme of this book. Kennedy presses further for a model of citizenship which has, as a prerequisite, radical constitutional reform. Anything less simply will not do.

So where does all this leave us? Do the ideas underlying attachment theory really have any relevance for the political world? Or should we psychiatrists know our place and return to the metaphorical couch? We argue here that politicians must now give credence to such ideas. They cannot afford not to. Cynicism in our political masters is rampant, though perhaps not always justified. Unless politicians are able to engage with the electorate in a more meaningful way, they are complicit in their own demise.

The arguments marshalled in this book point to three broad ways in which the political domain could benefit from incorporating some of the tenets of attachment theory, a politics of attachment. First, the theory itself, grounded in biology, ethology and psychology, provides a coherent underpinning for the current preoccupations with 'community', 'stakeholding', 'solidarity', themes which all skirt around the same sort of issues, but somehow remain anchorless, doomed to float away with apple pie and motherhood. Second, a politics of attachment could usefully influence the content of policy in a number of areas other than family policy: for example, the criminal justice system, housing (to ensure, at the very least, an obligation to house those who are most vulnerable, which could not be discharged by temporary accommodation), the organisation of the workplace, planning and regeneration, environmental issues, the role of the voluntary sector, local government. Crucially too, it underlines the priority that should be given to a sustained reduction in unemployment. Many of these areas are examined in the following chapters, but this book is not intended to be a policy document, merely to hint at what the policy implications of a collaborative approach between the psychological, sociological and political, might be. Attachment theory too can enable politicians to have a more sophisticated understanding of the unforeseen impact of policies already enacted. The absence of the 'feel good factor' is perhaps the most obvious example but, more specifically, the outrage and grief caused to many elderly people forced to sell their own homes in order to pay for their care could so easily have been predicted. Third, ideas from attachment theory could very significantly influence the process of policy implementation. In the frantic scrabble to press the right electoral button, politicians ignore process at their peril. It is what you do, but it is also how you do it. In spite of the inevitable coarsening of thoughtful ideas as they metamorphose into public policy, there is a crying need for politicians to make sense of our complicated, tangled world and to acknowledge the importance of authenticity, responsiveness and trust. As with attachment theory, though, it takes two to tango; this message therefore applies equally to our responsibilities as citizens, as the Canadian philosopher, Jean Tronto makes clear: 'the qualities of attentiveness, of responsibility, of competence, or responsiveness ... can also inform our practices as citizens' (Tronto 1993).

We should here make a final bid for humility. We are not arguing that attachment theory offers a complete account either of normal development or of psychopathology, nor indeed that a psychological explanation provides a comprehensive framework for all political endeavour. That would be truly omnipotent. We do, however, believe passionately that the psychological in general, and ideas based on attachment theory in particular, have much to inform the debate, yet have hitherto been sadly neglected. A message which is a little too close to home for some, perhaps. Politics is, however, about life, avers John Cole (1995). So it is. How then can we ignore what we know about the ways in which we humans grow, develop and relate with others: an ordinary yet fundamental part of life?

REFERENCES

Atkinson, T., Liem, R. and Liem, J.H. (1986) 'The social costs of unemployment: implications for social support', *Journal of Health and Social Behaviour* 27: 317–33.

Auge, M. (1995) *Non-Places. Introduction to an Anthropology of Supermodernity*. London/New York: Verso.

Bevan, A. (1978) *In Place of Fear*. London/Melbourne/New York: Quartet Books.

Bhugra, D. (1993) 'Unemployment, Poverty and Homelessness' in D. Bhugra and J. Leff (eds), *Principles of Social Psychiatry*. Oxford: Blackwell Scientific Publications.

Bowlby, J. (1946) 'Psychology and Democracy', *The Political Quarterly* XVII 61–76.

Brugha, T.S. (1993) 'Social Support Networks' in D. Bhugra and J. Leff (eds), *Principles of Social Psychiatry*. Oxford: Blackwell Scientific Publications.

Burgess, J. (1994) *The Politics of Trust: Reducing Fear of Crime in Urban Parks*. London: Comedia/Demos Working Paper No. 8.

Clifford, S. and King, A. (1993) *Local Distinctiveness. Place, Particularity and Identity*. London: Common Ground.

Cohen, A.P. (1994) *Self Consciousness. An alternative anthropology of identity*. London/ New York: Routledge.

Cole, J. (1995) *As It Seemed To Me*. London: Weidenfield and Nicolson.

Crewe, I. (1996) 'Citizenship and Civic Education'. Lecture given at the Royal Society of Arts, London, 21 May.

Davey Smith, G. (1996) 'Income inequality and mortality: why are they related?', *British Medical Journal* 312: 987–8.

de Waal, F. (1996) *Good Natured: The Origins of Right and Wrong in Humans and Other Animals*. Cambridge, MA: Harvard University Press.

Dunbar, (1996) *Grooming, Gossip and the Evolution of Language*. London: Faber.

Dunn, J. and McGuire, S. (1992) Sibling and Peer Relationships in Childhood, *Journal of Child Psychology and Psychiatry* 33(1): 67–105.

Fagin, L. and Little, M. (1984) *The Forsaken Families*. Harmondsworth: Penguin.

Fernandez, J.W. (1986) *Persuasions and Performances. The Play of Tropes in Culture*. Bloomington: Indiana University Press.

Ferrie, J.E., Shipley, M.J., Marmot, M.G., Stansfeld, S. and Davey Smith, G.

(1995) 'Health effects of anticipation of job change and non-employment: longitudinal data from the Whitehall II study', *British Medical Journal* 311: 1264–9.

Fonagy, P., Steele, M., Steele, H., Higgitt, A. and Target, M. (1994) 'The Emanuel Miller Lecture. The Theory and Practice of Resilience'. *Journal of Child Psychology and Psychiatry* 35(2): 231–57.

Freud, S. (1961) 'The Future of an Illusion' (1927) and 'Civilisation and its Discontents' (1930) in J. Strachey (ed.), *The Standard Edition of the Complete Psychological Works of Sigmund Freud*, 24 vols. London: The Hogarth Press, vol. 21.

Fromm, E. (1963) *The Sane Society*. London: Routledge and Kegan Paul.

Frosh, S. (1989) 'Melting into Air. Psychoanalysis and social experience', *Free Associations* 16: 7–30.

Fukuyama, F. (1995) *Trust; The Social Virtues and the Creation of Prosperity*. London: Hamish Hamilton.

Giddens, A. (1991) *Modernity and Self-Identity. Self and Society in the Late Modern Age*. Oxford: Polity Press.

Gordon, P. (1995) 'Private practice, public life: is a psychoanalytic politics possible?', *Free Associations* 5(3) 275–88.

Graham, P. and Rutter, M. (1985) 'Adolescent Disorders' in M. Rutter and L. Hersov (eds), *Child and Adolescent Psychiatry. Modern Approaches*. Oxford: Blackwell Scientific Publications.

Hinde, R. (1987) *Individuals, Relationships and Culture: Links between Ethology and the Social Sciences*. Cambridge: Cambridge University Press.

Hofer, M. (1995) 'Hidden Regulators: Implications for a New Understanding of Attachment, Separation, and Loss' in S. Goldberg, R. Muir and J. Kerr (eds), *Attachment Theory: Social, Developmental and Clinical Perspectives*. Hillside, NJ: The Analytic Press.

Ignatieff, M. (1990) *Needs of Strangers*. London: Hogarth Press.

Ignatieff, M. (1994) *Blood and Belonging*. London: Vintage.

Kay, J. (1996) 'The Good Market', *Prospect* (May) 39–43.

Kettle, M. (1996) 'Passive observers in our own front rooms', *Guardian*, 25 May.

Kraemer, G.W. (1992) 'A psychobiological theory of attachment', *Behavioural and Brain Sciences* 15: 493–541.

Main, M. (1995) 'Discourse, Prediction, and Recent Studies in Attachment: Implications for Psychoanalysis', in T. Shapiro and R.N. Emde (eds), *Research in Psychoanalysis: Process, Development, Outcome*. Madison CT: International Universities Press.

Marx, K. (1846) *The German Ideology*. London: Lawrence and Wishart, 1970.

Midgely (1994) *The Ethical Primate. Humans, Freedom and Morality*. London/New York: Routledge.

Nussbaum, M. (1993) 'Non-Relative Virtues: An Aristotelian Approach' in M. Nussbaum and A. Sen (eds), *The Quality of Life*. Oxford: Clarendon Press.

Offer, A. (1996) *Between the Gift and the Market: the Economy of Regard*. Discussion Papers in Economic and Social History, University of Oxford.

Prior, D., Stewart, J. and Walsh, K. (1995) *Citizenship: Rights, Community and Participation*. London: Pitman Publishing.

Reich, W. (1983) *The Mass Psychology of Fascism*. Harmondsworth: Penguin.

Richards, B. (ed.) (1989) *Crises of the Self. Further Essays on Psychoanalysis and Politics*. London: Free Association Books.

Rose, S., Lewontin, R.C. and Kamin, L.J. (1984) *Not in Our Genes: Biology, Ideology and Human Nature*. Harmondsworth: Penguin.

Russell, B. (1946) *History of Western Philosophy*. London: George Allen and Unwin.

Rustin, M. (1991) *The Good Society and the Inner World. Psychoanalysis, Politics and Culture*. London/New York: Verso.

Rutter, M. (1995) 'Clinical implications of attachment concepts: retrospect and prospect', *Journal of Child Psychology and Psychiatry* 36(4): 549–71.

Rutter, M., Maughan, B., Mortimore, P. and Ouston, J. (1979) *Fifteen Thousand Hours*. London: Open Books.

Samuels, A. (1993) *The Political Psyche*. London: Routledge.

Summerfield, D. (1995) 'Raising the dead: war, reparation, and the politics of memory', *British Medical Journal* 311: 495–7.

Tronto, J.C. (1993) *Moral Boundaries: a Political Argument for an Ethics of Care*. New York: Routledge.

Waters, E., Wippman, J. and Sroufe, L.A. (1979) 'Attachment, positive affect, and competence in the peer group: two studies in construct validation', *Child Development* 50: 821–9.

Wilkinson, R. (1994) 'Health, Redistribution and Growth' in A. Glyn and D. Miliband (eds), *Paying for Inequality: The Economic Cost of Social Injustice*. London: IPPR/Rivers Oram Press .

Wilson, E.O. (1978) *On Human Nature*. Cambridge, MA: Harvard University Press.

Winnicott, D.W. (1964) *The Child, the Family and the Outside World*. London: Penguin.

Winnicott, D.W. (1974) *Playing and Reality*. London: Penguin.

Zeldin, T. (1995) *An Intimate History of Humanity*. London: Minerva.

1 The Political Context

Marjorie Mowlam

I am driven as a politician by my desire to see people have the opportunity of a better life, whether by means of a job, education or more security in old age. To achieve that end, I need to be part of a government with specific policies to address the many problems in our society. I am after all often able to do very little about the catalogue of social problems with which I am presented in my surgery in Redcar, week in, week out. Like many other Members of Parliament, I do, nevertheless, find my constituency surgery one of the most satisfying parts of the job. It satisfies our desire to be needed, to be wanted and our belief that we can make a difference. Just look at the data on MPs' backgrounds: the number who come from dysfunctional families in which one parent may have died or left is well above the national average.

Such early difficulties can leave their mark with a trail of insecurity in the Palace of Westminster. Can the MPs who love the sound of their own voice, who cannot be kept off television and radio and who can act in such a pompous way really be insecure? Well, in my experience, they most certainly can. To suggest, however, that the insecurities of our childhood may help to account for our standing for election in the first place and then to explain some of our actions as MPs, is not at all popular. But I offer this view because I think that an acknowledgement of these possible links enables us to understand both ourselves and others more, as well as to take such factors into account in policy making.

The formulation of policy in all British political parties has been through a time of tremendous flux. In the 1970s the right stressed the supremacy of the individual over the state. Under Mrs Thatcher, personal responsibility was extolled as responsibility not just for yourself but to yourself alone. Outside of a duty not to break the law, the Thatcher philosophy appeared to exclude the broader notion of a duty to others. It became narrowly acquisitive and ultimately destructive. Its emphasis on the individual in an unregulated, privatised world created greater inequality and uncertainty. Whilst Thatcherism did bequeath a strong belief amongst many – especially young – people of the importance of individual freedom, it is notable that many now are coming to realise that freedom with a high degree of uncertainty, feels less like freedom and more like repression. The battle rages in the Conservative Party now, between the individualist creed on the one hand, and the more embracing idea of one-nation Toryism on the other.

There have been sea changes too within the Labour Party. During the early 1980s we had constitutional aims which could not be implemented and a set of policy proposals which were no longer in line with our values. Since then, we have broadened our base of support from representing specific interest groups to a majority in our society. The political consequences which follow are, however, radical. We are acknowledging that a straightforward class-based analysis is no longer adequate either to explain society's functioning or to offer a clear policy direction. Obviously there are still important divisions in a capitalist economy: principally between those who have power and those who do not. The relationship between the powerful and the powerless is, however, increasingly complex, demanding more innovative responses from national governments. The globalisation of the economy, the subsequent changing structure of work, differences in family structure and the ability of the state to deliver responsive services have called into question the simplistic left/right divisions of the past. Many of us in the Labour Party have argued that we need to go back to first principles and focus on the relationship between the individual and the community. This relationship is at the heart of our thinking – the need for a strong and cohesive society in which everyone has a stake, enabling individuals to prosper and develop to their full potential. The relationship between the individual and the community is interdependent, involving duties from society to the citizen as well as the other way round.

Tony Blair has led the new debate in the Labour Party, exploring the crucial balance between individual rights and responsibilities. Whilst Labour has always been very clear about the centrality of individual rights, there must also be an emphasis on the parallel importance of responsibilities. The debate has drawn on thinking which is loosely described as communitarianism. Without some understanding of individuals' states of mind – their fears and emotions, their many and differing needs – the communitarian vision (especially in the form espoused by the American sociologist, Amitai Etzioni (1993)) can seem mechanistic, excluding and exclusive. For many, nevertheless, there is a sense that our social fabric is being unpicked; that the attachments that bound communities together are disintegrating. This, coupled with the destruction of a sense of self for those who have not only lost their job but also any prospect of a future one, has sapped the confidence of all too many. This is well illustrated by some snapshots of people that I speak to in my Redcar constituency: for example, a 48-year-old man, off work from stress, is sacked after 23 months and 3 weeks at work. He has therefore no rights to redundancy. He has always worked hard, often overtime including weekends, and flexibly for his boss. He cannot understand why he has been treated like dirt. He will, at his age, probably never work again. He can only sit and cry.

There is undoubtedly a widespread, profound sense of insecurity. There is increasing uncertainty about jobs, housing, education and old age. Despite low inflation, price and tax levels career about wildly. One moment, your job seems secure, the next, redundancy looms. One moment, your NHS hospital is providing a first-class service, the next it is threatened with closure. One moment, you have a home to pass on to your children, the next it has all disappeared in fees for residential care in your old age. The Labour Party's understanding of the depth of personal insecurity that exists was well illustrated at our conference last year; over 300 people attended a fringe meeting to discuss how the ideas contained in this book can provide a response. I view *The Politics of Attachment* – an interesting amalgam of psychology, ethics and politics – as a useful addition to the body of democratic socialist thinking for the turn of the century. It helps us to understand more about communities and the people who make them, and it can sit comfortably under a political umbrella dominated by an analysis of power and macro-economic thinking.

My understanding is that attachment theory concerns initially how children relate to their parents, how they develop emotional attachments and so create meaning, and how they are then equipped to deal with unfamiliarity and uncertainty. Meaning evolves as past experiences are organised into an increasingly coherent whole, which then plays an important part in determining the response to new experiences. Those experiences and meanings are brought into adulthood and affect how we interpret the world and relate with one another.

We can take this thinking further to help us with our analysis of political systems. We might do well to consider more carefully how individuals may react to society rather than simply imposing a philosophical system from above. This is what one might call an organic way of looking at society rather than the more eighteenth-century rationalist approach which has tended to dominate political and economic theory from Marx to monetarism.

Uncertainty is both subjective and objective and can also translate to organisations and institutions. Small maintenance firms, competing for business from a multinational that dominates a regional economy, face a much more uncertain future than the multinational because the multinational can use its power to shift the uncertainties of the future on to these smaller firms. In the past, in organisations, big or small, people could use collective bargaining in order to achieve their goals and to have their voices heard. This led in some cases to inflexible organisations. Most firms now are organisationally very flexible. Their flexibility is, however, gained in part by sub-contracting to smaller firms those aspects of production which are most at risk to changes in a vulnerable market – an example of how the powerful pass on uncertainty and fear to those who have the least power (see Marris, this volume).

Let me focus on young people for a moment. We know that they have far less security than did the previous generation in terms of family structure, education and future job prospects. We know too that young people feel little sense of belonging to their local community: only 23 per cent did so in a recent MORI poll. There are, however, some communities where the ties are very strong and yet insecurity persists on an exaggerated scale. One example is Northern Ireland. Here the insecurity of the individual is reflected in the insecurity felt by whole communities.This is partly a function of the 'ordinary' problems of high unemployment and job insecurity, insecurity about welfare provision and old age and other social changes. But for many people these issues are swamped by overriding concerns about discrimination and political identity.

The divisions between the two traditions – unionist and nationalist – allow for stronger communities, it is true. A child in Northern Ireland can grow up in a community composed entirely of one tradition that impacts on their play, their schooling and all their contact with adults. Identity – be it religious, cultural or political, or all three – is a force that binds people together. But, as the experience of the people in Northern Ireland shows, strong communities of this kind can be exclusive and they can be repressive of minority views and identities. The sense of responsibility to 'your' community can swamp your commitment to the rights of others, particularly minorities (see Gosling, this volume). That is why a new settlement is needed in Northern Ireland that fully respects both identities and sets of aspirations. And it is why a proper balance of rights and responsibilities has to be established across both communities.

Whether in Northern Ireland or elsewhere in the UK, our ability as politicians to understand the nature of social problems could be enhanced by examining them in terms of the politics of attachment. What is interesting about the arguments presented in this book is that they reinforce ideas that have been at the core of socialist thought since its inception. The concept of alienation, for example, is not far removed from the focus on uncertainty in the politics of attachment.

What we do not want is a nanny state – that would not ensure greater security. As attachment theory has shown, children with secure attachments are more likely to have the confidence to move away from a secure base. They can deal with uncertainty, use the resources around them to better effect, become more independent and are more willing to take risks. This line of thought should be applied to government policy in areas such as the welfare state where the benefit system should be a hand up, not a handout.

The most constructive way to tackle individual insecurity would be on an economic level – to provide work for people. Paid work, at a fair wage, is the most effective way of tackling poverty and increasing security. We need a skills revolution to switch the emphasis in the workplace away from a cheap, unskilled and inherently insecure labour market to a skilled, educated and valued workforce. Employment rights for all, especially those in the growing part-time sector are essential both for improving job security and for acknowledging the value of employees. A minimum wage along with the introduction of the European Union Social Chapter will give people more choice, more motivation to succeed, help reduce poverty traps and help stop taxpayers subsidising bad employers.

Returning to my focus on young people, there has been a breakdown in their relationship with government. At the last general election, over two and a half million young people did not vote. Nearly one in five are not even on the electoral register. Some thinking needs to be done urgently to reconnect the two, young voters and government. We can draw from attachment theory that individual citizens need to have the sense that they can genuinely have a meaningful impact on government (see Liber, this volume). In this context, a Bill of Rights, more open government and a return to stronger local democracy will help. It would make a difference if government was at a level that people could identify with, perhaps through Scottish and Welsh devolution. Reform of our electoral system (which would hopefully be the outcome of a referendum) would mean people's votes would mean more to them.

I think, however, that at the heart of the problem is people's lack of a sense of belonging. The meaning and the nature of the nation-state is changing. Historically our sense of nationhood was epitomised by the monarchy, and our status in the world was symbolised by the empire. But public scrutiny of the monarchy has undermined its status as an institution and the days of empire are long gone. Tony Blair has identified the need for a new, stronger sense of nationhood, to enhance a stronger sense of self. That is why the UK needs symbols of national identity which are relevant in today's society and for the decades ahead rather than just the past. Remembering our history is important, but we cannot live in it. There is no reason in today's changing world why we cannot identify with regions closer to home. Attachments at that level do not negate the importance of our connection to the UK or, for that matter, to Europe. An acknowledgement of the different levels at which decisions are made makes sense. At a European level, we need to address issues which are supranational, which need not acknowledge national boundaries, such as competition policy in industries, environmental issues and openness in European institutions. At national level we must serve the interests of these islands for defence, for security, for the economy and transport. And at regional level and below, there must be the implementation of policies that should be made closer to the public, such as housing. There must be co-ordination between regional, national and European levels of government; people must feel that they belong, that they are attached to all three.

The relevance of political structures is being questioned and politicians will have to think laterally and creatively about the direction in which British politics is going to move. That is what Tony Blair has been doing and that is why we have refined and modernised the Labour Party. Whilst the politics of attachment clearly cannot stand alone in understanding the state of our society, I do believe that it can bring a refreshing new perspective that can help in our overall understanding of social problems and in policy formulated in response. The world is changing rapidly – radical changes are going to be needed in social, economic and constitutional areas to respond to these changes. Understanding how human beings will cope with this change is crucial.

REFERENCE

Etzioni, A. (1993) *The Spirit of Community*. New York: Crown.

2 Attachment Theory: A Secure Base For Policy?

Jeremy Holmes

And so the coyotes are out there earnestly trying to arrange their lives to make more coyotes possible, not knowing that it is my forest, of course. And I am in this room from which I can sometimes look out at dusk and see them warily moving through the barren winter trees, and I am, I suppose, doing what they are doing, making myself possible, and those who come after me. At such moments I do not know whose land this is that I own, or whose bed I sleep in. In the darkness out there they see my light and pause, muzzles lifted, wondering who I am and what I am doing here in this cabin under my light. I am a mystery to them until they tire of it and move on, but the truth, the first truth, probably, is that we are all connected, watching one another. Even the trees. (Miller 1987, p. 599)

Connection, watchfulness and ecological awareness – these could be the starting points for a psychologically-informed twenty-first century politics. Security rests on recognising and valuing our connections, locally, nationally, internationally and interspecifically. But coyotes are predatory as well as fellow earth-dwellers. They need watching, just as we do by them. So security depends on watchfulness, a gaze that is the essence of curiosity and triumphant scientific and artistic exploration, but also of defensiveness and paranoia. As comfortable assumptions of ever-expanding productivity seem less and less tenable, a central issue for contemporary politics has become security itself, which, as well as being the precondition for a good society, can, in one of capitalism's cruel ironies, also be a commodity to be bought, sold, hoarded, seized or expropriated.

Psychotherapy and politics are alike in that, although buttressed by scientific argument, the one from psychological science, the other from the social sciences, both are essentially moral discourses (Bradley 1991). Both put forward a view about what it is to lead a good life, and what conditions are required for this to be possible, each concentrating on its chosen sphere, but rarely (with honourable exceptions – Reich, Marcuse and, more recently, Samuels) on both, or their connections.

The notion of security is a useful meeting place for psychological and political dialogue, and among psychotherapeutic discourses attachment theory has especially emphasised security as a central human need. In this chapter I shall try to show how the basic ideas and findings of attachment theory can act as a point of entry for psychotherapy into the social debate, as a contribution to a more psychologically informed politics. This enterprise is, however, not without its dangers. There can be something faintly absurd about the psychoprofessions straying out of their sphere to comment on social events, a kind of attention-seeking in what is still largely a marginal profession, handfuls of gravel thrown against advancing tanks. Conversely, however, social comment on psychological matters often seems, to the professional, inept, or far too general to be of much practical use. But ideas *can* turn back tanks as well as set them rolling. The times demand it, and, as W.H. Auden mischievously said: 'private faces in public places/ are much nicer than/ public faces in private places'.

ATTACHMENT THEORY

Attachment theory starts from the vulnerability and helplessness of the newborn baby. Unlike classical psychoanalysis, its roots lie in ethology and biology. Bowlby saw that parent–infant bonding was universal in mammalian species, and wanted to develop a psychology that took account of these biological roots. In this he was both similar and very different from Freud. He was similar in that Freud's project was also in origin biological, but rooted in the nineteenth-century notions of the struggle for survival based on drives and reflexes. Bowlby's biology was that of twentieth-century ecology and neo-Darwinism, with an emphasis on co-operation and the fit between an organism and its environment. Bowlby saw that attachment was essential for survival in the 'environment of evolutionary adaptiveness' in which humans evolved, and was the only sure protection against predation by hostile species or unfavourable conditions. Thus adults and infants are programmed to bond to one another for survival's sake.

A baby that was not so programmed would have soon died from predation. Hence Winnicott's famous phrase, 'there is no such thing as a baby – only a mother and baby together' (Khan 1958). Like coyotes, we are intensely social animals: without 'community' we could not survive. Mrs Thatcher's even more famous reversal of Winnicott – 'there is no such thing as society' – was, to view it charitably, an attempt to emphasise the importance of individual choice and responsibility. But individuality and the capacity to choose are end products of the psychological growth within the societies of the family and school which her policies have done so much to stunt for so many in present-day Britain.

How then do adults and infants become attached to one another? Infant research has revealed how exquisitely aware of one another mother and baby are: within hours of birth a mother can pick out her own child's cry from those of others (just as ewes choose their own lamb's mews from others in the flock); a newborn baby turns preferentially towards the smell of its own mother's milk, and will often imitate her mouth, tongue, and facial movements in the first week or two of life. Parent and child are aware of each other from the start – Trevarthen (1984) calls this 'primary intersubjectivity'. Mother and baby are no strangers: already in the uterus the child has absorbed the rhythms of the mother's heartbeat and speech patterns. Stern uses the word 'attunement' to describe the emotional alignment of parent and child that lays the foundations for secure attachment (Stern 1985).

Attunement implies an intimate knowledge of and responsiveness to the baby's individual patterns of feeling and behaviour. To be attuned is to acknowledge the child as a separate yet utterly dependent being, and to be able to enter into a variety of cooperative activities – feeding, bathing, changing, playing, lulling to sleep, stimulating when bored, soothing when overstimulated – that depend for their success and pleasure on getting on the child's wavelength, via 'imaginative identification'.

In the early days the mother stands for the whole world – her face, her feel, her warmth, her smell, her capacity both to satisfy and frustrate. Gradually the child begins to turn outwards, to encounter James' (1890) 'buzzing booming' world of sensations with which she is bombarded, to discover for herself the place and the people – father, grandparents, siblings, friends – which are 'hers'. The relationship with the mother usually provides the primary platform from which this outward turning can occur, although it is a job which fathers, grandparents and others can also do. In Bowlby's and his collaborator Mary Ainsworth's phrase, the primary caregiver provides a 'secure base' which makes it safe to begin to explore the world. Around seven months an important change occurs when the child begins to distinguish those she knows from those whom she does not. Stranger anxiety makes her turn inwards to the mother in the face of novel faces and sounds. But as her confidence grows, so, working collaboratively with the mother, she uses visual cueing to check whether a new situation is safe or not.

Gradually the child will extend her radius of exploration away from the secure base, returning abruptly when threatened, tired or ill. Of course the mother is much more than a secure base, also providing food, warmth and playful enjoyment. A key feature of the secure base is 'separation protest'. Any attempt to part the child from the caregiver at times of stress will provoke furious protest, clinging, searching, and if separation is prolonged, bitter despair. It was the heart-rending recording of these responses in his films of children going into hospital, made with James and Joyce Robertson (1952), that made Bowlby's ideas so widely known, and which led to a radical change in attitudes towards parental visiting in children's wards.

There is some irony in the fact that, despite his vilification from some feminist critics, Bowlby's central mission was the rehabilitation of childhood and the valuation of parenthood as a vital contribution to society:

> Man and woman power devoted to the production of material goods counts as a plus in all our economic indices. Man and woman power devoted to the production of happy, healthy, and self-reliant children in their own homes does not count at all. We have created a topsy turvy world ... the society we live in is ... in evolutionary terms ... a very peculiar one. There is a great danger we shall adopt mistaken norms. For, just as a society in which there is a chronic insufficiency of food may take a deplorably inadequate level of nutrition as its norm, so may a society in which parents of young children are left on their own with a chronic insufficiency of help take this state of affairs as its norm. (Bowlby 1988, p. 2)

In this late passage he is careful to say *man and* woman power, whereas in his early writings he was mainly concerned with women's role in bringing up children. The impact of his best-selling *Child Care and the Growth of Maternal Love* (Bowlby 1953) was ambiguous: it helped to raise the status of those delivering child care, and undoubtedly transformed paediatric practice, but a generation of working mothers felt guilty about leaving their children, and even those who did not, felt bad about their inability to live up to the high standards of devotion Bowlby seemed to advocate. Winnicott (1958) with his sanctioning of 'good enough' mothering was the great liberator.

Bowlby's view that continuous maternal care for the first five years of life was essential for subsequent mental health has often been misunderstood, for three reasons. The first is a simple semantic confusion between the meaning of continuous and continual. Continuity is essential, but that does not mean the mother must be ever-present. Second, he was wrong about what he called monotropism, that is, the view that a secure base can only be provided by one attachment figure alone. This was an ethnocentric error, as Margaret Mead insisted, since in most societies and at most periods of history infants are cared for by groups of adults, rather than one on her own. There is usually a hierarchy of attachments of whom the mother is only one, albeit usually the most important. Here lies further support, if any is needed, for the importance of nursery and pre-school provision.

Third, the quality of parent–child interaction matters just as much as its quantity. This extends even to parental loss in childhood. Most evidence suggests that the loss of a parent by death or divorce predisposes subsequent depression in adult life mainly by virtue of the disruption and impoverishment that follows, rather than the loss per se, which, in favourable circumstances can be adequately mourned and coped with (Rutter 1985). Here too is a message for family policy makers, especially in view of the sinister trend towards scapegoating of single mothers by the right-wing press and politicians.

Bowlby at times gave the impression that the recipe for happiness was the complete avoidance of such separations and therefore of the need for protest. It is now clear that pain, occasional desperation, and loss are universal phenomena in childhood – Bradley (1991) ironically posits a 'basic misery' to stand alongside Erikson's 'basic trust'. Babies fuss, cry, suffer colic, won't sleep, refuse food, get cold and wet, just as much as they smile, coo, giggle, gurgle, feed passionately, sleep satiatedly, and sweep adults off their feet with their adorableness. It is not the absence of unhappiness that is important, but how it is responded to and resolved. The psychoanalyst Wilfred Bion saw the mother's role as that of containing such unhappiness, being unfazed by it, holding it inside herself, acknowledging it, and 'detoxifying' it. The acceptance of healthy protest, without retaliation, while retaining the capacity to set state- and phase-appropriate boundaries – for example, putting the child to bed when she is obviously tired – is a vital ingredient leading to secure attachment.

Patterns of Secure and Insecure Attachment

Attachment theory suggests that the roots of insecurity are to be found in the early years of life. Bowlby contrasted 'secure attachment', which he found in about two-thirds of children he first studied, with 'insecure attachment'. Three main patterns of insecurely attached infants have now been defined, classified by their response to separation from, and reunion with, their parents.

'Avoidant' children seem detached from their parents, suppressing protest when separated, and hovering nervously near them when reunited, apparently unable either to be reassured by being cuddled, or to play contentedly. 'Ambivalent' children by contrast cling desperately to their parents, unwilling to let them out of their sight, and when reunited after separation cannot be pacified despite physical contact. These patterns can be related to parental handling in the first year of life. The parents of avoidant infants tend to ignore their child's bids for comfort, concentrating on efficiency rather than playfulness. Parents of the ambivalent group tend to be inconsistent, sometimes ignoring the child when it is obviously in need of attention, at other times intruding when it is playing happily.

A third, highly significant group of babies has more recently been described. This is the 'disorganised' group whose response to separation is inconsistent, showing episodes of behavioural collapse or 'freezing'. The 'avoidants' and 'ambivalents' have at least found a survival strategy: they have achieved a measure of security and remain in touch with its source, albeit at the cost of uninhibited exploration and playfulness. Children showing disorganised responses, however, seem to have no consistent route to feeling psychologically safe. Their parents themselves may well have been abused, so that attachment itself becomes entirely problematic, either by its lack or by its association with extreme confusion and pain (Bretherton 1991). In high-risk populations of socio-economic deprivation, as many as 80 per cent of infants show disorganised patterns.

An important finding in the attachment literature is the relative independence of attachment ratings between fathers and mothers. A given child may be securely attached to one parent and insecurely attached to another. Presumably there is survival value in this, in that it provides the child with a wider range of options depending on her future life circumstances. In a related vein, Rutter found that resilience to adversity in deprived children was associated with good relationships with extra-familial figures like teachers or sports coaches. Similarly it has been found that in areas of famine, families more likely to survive are those with diversity of investments and talents. The political significance of this might be the need always to extend citizens' options for security, rather than relying exclusively on either the state or private enterprise.

Once established, these dyadic patterns of attachment tend to persist. Children shown to be secure at one year are, at school entry four or five years later, usually still showing signs of self-confidence and an ability to relate appropriately compared with their insecurely attached counterparts. These five-year-olds already show the germs of good citizenship: generosity and co-operativeness based on self-confidence and the capacity to communicate and to stand their ground when necessary. By contrast those with insecure patterns of attachment contain the seeds of social pathology. The 'avoidants' often tend to be rather isolated and show unprovoked aggression, while the 'ambivalents' are frequently nervous, hover near their teachers and cannot easily initiate activities. The contrast here is between security as a 'contested' commodity, as opposed to the freely achieved and offered security of the securely attached group of children – one child acquiring it only at another's expense.

There are even suggestions that these patterns carry through into adolescence and adult life and affect the ways in which we make sense of and ascribe meaning to our world. Follow-up studies on the disorganised group are awaited, although it is likely that some of them at least will be vulnerable to extreme behavioural disorder and personal distress, manifest in problematic behaviours such as social disaffection, substance abuse, persistent relationship difficulties, and chronic physical and mental ill-health. Some of these 'borderline' individuals seem to be attached almost to the idea of disorder itself. Secure attachment appears to be mediated by brain opioids – securely attached primates have higher levels of these substances in their brain fluids. They are also released at times of extreme stress, presumably as an adaptive response to mental pain. De Zulueta (1993) links the increasing social prevalence of self-injury, addiction and social violence with insecure attachment and the desperate search for endogenous opiate release through the repetition – actually or in symbolic form – of traumatic events in childhood.

The Importance of Attachment in Adult Life

Most of the studies we have mentioned have focused on the behaviours of infants and small children. Research is beginning to reveal significant connections between these early behaviours and the themes of later life. The most striking of these come from looking at the ways in which older children and adults talk about their past experience. Children classified as secure at one year, ten years later often show the beginnings of 'autobiographical competence' (Holmes 1992) – the ability to talk coherently about oneself and one's life, including painful experiences – while those who were classified as avoidant tend to be monosyllabically dismissive when asked about their past ('can't remember', or 'fine'), and ambivalents are bogged down or enmeshed in past pain, often weeping inconsolably when asked to recall their early childhood. These 'stories' people tell about themselves reflect internal models of attachment which serve as templates for intimate relationships in adult life. A number of studies have now demonstrated inter-generation transmission of attachment patterns. Parents-to-be can be classified on the basis of their narrative style in the Adult Attachment Interview, and their infants subsequently tested in the Strange Situation Test at one year. These studies show that parents classified as dismissive tend to have avoidant infants, while free-autonomous adults have secure children (Fonagy et al. 1995), thus providing vivid evidence of the reality of cycles of deprivation. These cycles are not irremediable however. Some mothers who themselves had difficult childhoods do not produce avoidant infants. These women have the capacity for what Fonagy calls 'reflexive self-function' (RSF) – the capacity to stand back from one's difficulties and talk freely about them. Other evidence (Rutter 1985) suggests that RSF may arise if children, otherwise deprived or abused, achieve a good relationship with someone outside their immediate family, such as a grandparent or teacher. This provides a strong argument, if it is needed, for the pastoral as well as narrowly pedagogic role of the educational system.

These findings suggest significant links between the 'private' space of the family and infant–parent bonds on the one hand, and the 'public' domain on the other. A particular social order inscribes itself though the security or otherwise of its children. The capacity of parents to provide security for their children will depend in part on the felt security of their world: the labour market, housing, health and welfare. When their children grow up, if they have primarily internalised an insecure model of the world, they will perceive the public domain as inherently insecure, and respond to political strategies that chime with those feelings of insecurity. Insecurity breeds insecurity, and vice versa.

Attachment is not something that is grown out of once adulthood is achieved. We seek and try to maintain a secure base throughout life. If a secure base is not available then an insecure one is better than no base at all. Faced with stress or threat, adults seek out intimate attachments no less vigorously than a separated infant. Our capacity to be autonomous and deal with anxiety is dependent on an 'internal' secure base comprising a gestalt of experiences, affects and beliefs which G.W. Kraemer (1992) calls the 'attachment icon'. The typical patterns of attachment – secure, avoidant, ambivalent, disorganised – seem to correlate with the way in which young adults approach intimate relationships. While two-thirds are relatively comfortable with their partners and can cope with both closeness and separation, some find real intimacy intensely threatening, while others are made anxious or 'traumatised' by any hint of distance or separation. We can easily imagine how political perceptions may also be coloured by attachment models. Right-wing views can be related to avoidance, seen by the Frankfurt school of sociology as the 'authoritarian personality'. Clearly some left-wing policies have an ambivalent feel, perpetuating rather than helping to overcome dependency. The emergence of extreme political disaffection and banditry can perhaps be related to the increasing prevalence of disorganised patterns of relationship in childhood.

POLITICAL IMPLICATIONS

Can we use these ideas and findings to illuminate contemporary political debate? I will comment briefly on three key areas: violence and inequality, the environment, and nationhood.

Violence and inequality

Bowlby was a passionate advocate of democracy which he saw as an extension of the benign patriarchy he approved of in family life: responsive parents, prepared to listen to and take seriously the views of their children. His was essentially an Enlightenment view of man as inherently good, co-operative and free, perverted by social insecurity and defective parenting. For him violence was a response to trauma in early life, a manifestation of separation pro-test, or, in De Zulueta's (1993) phrase, 'attachment gone wrong'. He saw the capacity to express healthy protest and to have it listened to as a mark of a well-functioning family.

If the state is to be seen as a 'good parent' then it needs to take its citizens seriously, to be attuned to the reality of their lives and their needs, although not necessarily in the patriarchal way in which Bowlby conceived it. Violence in the family is only possible when adults dehumanise children, failing to see them as capable of feeling pain or having separate minds. 'Respect for persons' begins in the cradle. Political 'yobbism' – viewing citizens as 'scum', 'scroungers', 'rentacrowd', 'animals', 'sick', and so on – contributes to the very violence it deplores, since the greater the alienation from a secure base, the more unresponsive and unattuned the 'parent', the greater will be the tendency to avoidance and unpro-voked violence. Here, too, perhaps, we see how 'narrative style' reflects attachment patterns, the typical unelaborated argot of yob-bism being a direct expression of avoidant attachment.

Bowlby did not, perhaps, realise the full extent to which de-structive violence could overwhelm both individuals and societies (see Rustin, this volume). He resisted the prevailing psychoanalytic view which sees envy and hatred as inherent properties of the human infant, no less than love and gratitude. But with the disad-vantage of our late-twentieth-century hindsight we can see that any social philosophy which fails to take account of these dark forces is bound to fail. Even within a more environmentalist vision, psycho-social trauma can, via the neurobiological mechanisms mentioned, lead to 'wired in' destructiveness at an early age that is hard to eradicate by simple ameliorist measures.

Personal and political maturity implies the ability to distinguish and differentiate. Violence as healthy protest needs to be separated from destructive violence that is analogous to deliberate self-harm. In both cases the underlying pain needs to be acknowledged and listened to. Violence needs to be seen as arising out of a context, even if instrumental measures are needed to contain it. An atmos-phere of trust needs to be built up, while at the same time making it clear that certain kinds of behaviour are not tolerable. Attach-ment theory cuts across the sterile nature–nurture debate, showing how social forces can reach into the psychic heart and neurobiology of individuals.

Violence and inequality are intimately linked at a soiological level. I have suggested that the origins of this can in part be found in the childhood experience of avoidant individuals whose feelings have been brushed aside and thus not treated as 'equal', in the sense of having their emotions respected as being no less valid and powerful than those of adults. Hutton's (1994) 'thirty-thirty-forty' society is one built around insecure attachment, in which the possibility of community is constantly undermined by the struggle for resources, of which security itself is one. Secure parents can provide a secure base for all their children, dealing fairly and bringing out the unique potential of each. The inherent inequality of Western societies means that the state is forced to support the most disadvantaged, much as parents may appear always to side with the youngest and weakest of their offspring. When the state itself appears weak and threatened, as it does currently in the US, this may unleash triumphal victimisation of the weak by the strong, as appears to be happening in the assault on welfare in most Western societies.

The Environment

Attachment theory is a systemic theory in that it sees the individual not in isolation, but in reciprocal relationship; first to a primary attachment figure, then to subsidiary attachment figures within the family, then to the wider society, of whose workings politics is a major expression. Each level of these concentric circles can provide security or insecurity for that which it contains. Thus, as I have argued, does social insecurity via joblessness, homelessness and hopelessness percolate down to personal feelings of insecurity and resultant anger and destructiveness.

Until fairly recently the left has tended to ignore the silent outer circle of this system – the environment – except, perhaps, via nostalgic arcadian communitarian yearnings far removed from the cloth cap and the barricade. Capitalism, urbanisation and the mobility of people in search of resources has broken the intimate bond between person and place, so, like a military bomber command we can attack alien locations so long as they are felt as 'not-me' . But modern science, as well as giving us the potential to destroy this final attachment, also enables us to understand the earth as a whole, as opposed to our little corner of it, giving us an ecological perspective from which to unite in mutual solidarity to secure a mother earth whose children we all are.

Behind this polemic lies a serious point about attachment and post-modernism. Attachment starts as the link between a particular parent and child in a specific house, flat, or hostel in this town, suburb, or village, but, as development proceeds, becomes internalised as a template, phantasy or 'internal working model' for all intimate relationships. 'Me and you' is transformed into 'I and thou', 'My home' becomes 'our world'. Our piecemeal, pluralistic post-modern existence can be integrated at this higher level, providing sufficient maturation of its citizens takes place, which is why education and support for children must be near the top of any political agenda that also takes the environment seriously.

Nationhood

Michael Ignatieff ends his magnificent foray into contemporary nationalism with the pessimistic conclusion:

> I began the journey as a liberal and I end as one, but I cannot help thinking that liberal civilisation – the rule of laws not men, or argument in place of force, of compromise in place of violence – runs deeply against the human grain and is only achieved and sustained by the most unremitting struggle against human nature. The liberal values – tolerance, compromise, reason – remain as valuable as ever, but they cannot be preached to those who are mad with fear or mad with vengeance ... What's wrong with the world is not nationalism itself. Every people must have a home, every such hunger must be assuaged. What's wrong is the kind of nation, the kind of home that nationalists want to create ... A struggle is going on ... between those who still believe that a nation should be a home to all, and that race, colour, religion and creed should be no bar to belonging, and those who want their nation to be home only to their own. It's a battle between the civic and the ethnic nation. I know which side I'm on. I also know which side, right now, happens to be winning. (Ignatieff 1994, p. 189)

A battle, one might say, between secure and insecure attachment. The stumbling blocks in this argument are the phrases 'human nature', 'the human grain'. Liberalism is easily caught between an ironic relativistic stance – whose practical expressions are pluralism, devolution and an openness to self-deconstruction – and the wish to proclaim liberal values as universals (Rorty 1991). Science, as one of the highest expressions of liberalism, can help to tease out what is intrinsic to 'human nature', and what, in contrast, is socially derived. Attachment theory suggests that the potential for both insecure and secure attachment exists within the human repertoire, and can point to the kinds of conditions in which one or the other is likely to predominate.

The nation is as fictional and as necessary a notion as the self. Both are composite entities, comprising diversity often subordinated and repressed for the sake of survival. The state has similarly to hear and find some way to integrate the legitimate aspirations of its component members, with their regional, ethnic, class- and gender-based diversity. If the state acts like the parent of an ambivalent child it will intermittently intrude on and then neglect these voices, leading to a failure to respect boundaries or real differences. If it behaves like the parent of an avoidant child it will turn a deaf ear and try with increasing state power to quell expressions of discontent, leading in turn to disillusionment and sporadic violence. Nationalistic movements can be compared to insecurely attached individuals, clinging desperately to outmoded values, while projecting and attacking the weaker disowned part of the self in 'the enemy'.

The Sicilian writer Gesualdo Bufalino wrote:

Now I know this simple truth: that it is not only my right but my duty to declare myself a citizen of Everywhere as well as of a hamlet tucked away in the Far South between the Iblei Mountains and the sea; that it is my right and duty to allow a place in my spirit for both the majestic music of the universe and that of the jet gushing from a fountain in the middle of a little village square, on the far southern bastions of the West. (Cited in Holmes 1993, p. 208)

The village square and Everywhere; Glasgow and Brussels; the constituency surgery and the Cabinet rooms in Downing Street. A new political system has to be fashioned that will accommodate both these attachments – the one concrete and specific, the other abstract and universal – that can connect local and global security in a meaningful way. The SDLP leader John Hume gave an interesting example of this new perspective when, in discussing the peace process in Northern Ireland, he made the very obvious but politically taboo point that which 'side' you were on in the conflict depended entirely on the accident of your birth.

CONCLUSION

Nostalgic, perhaps, for his days as a neurologist, Freud described psychoanalysis and 'government' as belonging to the 'impossible professions' – because 'one can be sure beforehand of achieving unsatisfying results' (Freud 1937). But if psychotherapy is hard work, politics is surely harder. To try to change the world is more formidable a task than merely interpreting it. Perhaps attachment theory can provide some of the theoretical basis for political choice, if only by making policy makers more aware of the unconscious assumptions about human relationships upon which they base their decisions. Perhaps politicians are much less able to influence events than they would have us (and themselves) believe. Perhaps, like psychotherapists, the best they do is to try to create a climate, or a setting, in which certain kinds of outcomes are more or less likely to happen. That is not to say that there are not moments when a line has to be drawn, a stand has to be taken, a decisive lead given. But for much of the time the style and manner of government are as important as its content, just as the style of psychotherapy or parenting is a crucial determinant of outcome. To add to my opening quote from Arthur Miller: 'Literature has to speak to the the present conditions of man's life, and thus would implicitly have to stand against injustice as the destroyer of life' (Miller 1987, p. 596). As for literature, so for culture generally.

In this chapter I have argued not just for liberty, equality and fraternity, valid though they still are, but also for a new rallying call: security. In conclusion then, a psychologically-informed politics would include among its basic principles respect for persons, the capacity to listen, acknowledgement of pain, acceptance of the need for legitimate expressions of anger and, above all, the provision of a secure base for all citizens as a precondition for exploration and growth.

REFERENCES

Ainsworth, M. (1982) 'Attachment; retrospect and prospect' in C.M. Parkes and J. Stevenson-Hinde (eds), *The Place of Attachment in Human Behaviour*. London: Routledge.

Bowlby, J. (1953) *Child Care and the Growth of Maternal Love*. London: Penguin.

Bowlby, J. (1988) *A Secure Base: Clinical Applications of Attachment Theory*. London: Routledge

Bradley, B. (1991) *Visions of Infancy*. Cambridge: Polity.

Bretherton, I. (1991) 'Roots and growing points of attachment theory' in C.M. Parkes, J. Stevenson-Hinde, and P. Marris (eds), *Attachment Across the Life Cycle*. London: Routledge.

De Zulueta, F. (1993) *From Pain to Violence*. London: Whurr.

Fonagy, P., Steele, M., Steele, H., Leigh, T., Kennedy, R., Mattoon, G. and Target, M. (1995) 'The predictive specificity of Mary Main's Adult Attachment Interview: implications for pschodynamic theories of normal and pathological emotional development' in S. Goldberg, R. Muir, and J. Kerr (eds), *John Bowlby's Attachment Theory: Clinical, Historical and Social Significance*. New York: Academic Press.

Freud, S. (1937) 'Analysis terminable and interminable' in J. Strachey (ed.), *The Standard Edition of the Complete Psychological Works of Sigmund Freud*, 24 vols. London: Hogarth, vol. 23.

Giddens, A. (1992) *Intimacy and the Search for Self*. Oxford: Polity.

Gilbert, P. (1989) *Human Nature and Suffering*. London: Erlbaum.

Goldberg, S., Muir, R., and Kerr, J. (eds) (1995) *John Bowlby's Attachment Theory: Clinical, Historical and Social Significance*. New York: Academic Press.

Grossman, K. and Grossman, K. (1991) 'Attachment quality as an organiser of emotional and behavioural responses in a longitudinal perspective' in C.M. Parkes, J. Stevenson-Hinde, and P. Marris (eds), *Attachment Across the Life Cycle*. London: Routledge.

Hobsbawm, E. (1992) *The Age of Extremes*. London: Methuen.

Holmes, J. (1992) *Between Art and Science: Essays in Psychotherapy and Psychiatry*. London: Routledge.

Holmes, J. (1993) *John Bowlby and Attachment Theory*. London: Routledge.

Holmes, J., and Lindley, R. (1989) *The Values of Psychotherapy*. Oxford: Oxford University Press.

Humphrey, N. (1992) *A History of the Mind*. London: Chatto.

Hutton, W. (1994) *The State We're In*. London: Faber.

Ignatieff, M. (1994) *Blood and Belonging*. London: Vintage.

James, W. (1890) *Principles of Psychology*. New York: Basic Books.

Khan, M. (1958) 'Introduction' in *Through Paediatrics to Psychoanalysis*: D.W. Winnicott. London: Hogarth.

Kraemer, G.W. (1992) 'A psychobiological theory of attachment', *Behavioural and Brain Scence*. 15: 493–541.

Miller, A. (1987) *Timebends, A Life*. London: Methuen.

Robertson, J. and Robertson, J. (1952) Film: A Two-year-old Goes to Hospital. London: Tavistock.

Rorty, R. (1991) *Contingency, Irony, and Solidarity*. Cambridge: Cambridge University Press.

Rutter, M. (1985) 'Resilience in the face of adversity: protective factors and resistance to psychiatric disorder', *British Journal of Psychiatry* 147: 598–611.

Stern, D. (1985) *The Interpersonal World of the Infant*. New York: Basic Books.

Trevarthen, C. (1984) 'Emotions in infancy: regulators of contacts and relationships with persons' in K.Scherer and P. Ekman (eds), *Approaches to Emotion*. Hillsdale, NJ: Erlbaum.

Winnicott, D. (1958) *Through Paediatrics to Psychoanalysis*. London: Hogarth.

3 Personal and Social Influences on Parenting and Adult Adjustment

Lynne Murray

INTRODUCTION

We are poised at a critical point in British Politics, when it is acknowledged by contemporary commentators of diverse political persuasions that the issue of the relationship between the individual and society is being recast, and when the Labour Party in particular is redefining its values and agenda. Until recently, on both sides of the political divide, the individual has been taken as the starting point: on the right this has taken the form of the argument that individuals should be self-reliant and free to strive for themselves, along with a denial, embedded in an unregulated, global, free market economy and most clearly expressed in Thatcher's rhetoric, of the interdependency inherent in the individual's relation to society. On the left there has also been a focus on individual rights, over and above one on obligations, both from those emphasising the state's role in granting individual rights, and from those on the neo-liberal left favouring policies of social individualism (see Gray 1994). (Strangely, both these formulations are at odds with the original philosophies of each of these movements.) Now, however, the tide is turning, and the word 'community' is upon everybody's lips. This seemingly common agenda of the moment does, however, belie persistent fundamental divisions; the way in which community is conceived, and the individual's relation to it varies, with old traditions of left and right grafting on to it their own particular emphasis. One recent and influential formulation of community and the individual's place in it is that developed in the US by the sociologist, Amitai Etzioni. In contrast to the previous emphasis on individual rights, this communitarian doctrine stresses individual duties and responsibilities, and in this respect the communitarian approach has much in common with that recently expounded by New Labour. This chapter gives a brief critique of communitarian and New Labour positions, and pays particular attention to the way in which parental and family functioning are conceptualised. There then follows an account of three British longitudinal studies on the developmental pathways to a number of personal outcomes that are of key concern to a well functioning community. Finally, communitarian and New Labour positions are discussed in the light of the research findings, together with a consideration of the nature of personal and public morality informed by the writings of Bowlby and Winnicott.

COMMUNITARIANISM AND THE PARENTING DEFICIT

The recent publications by the communitarian writer Amitai Etzioni, *The Parenting Deficit* (1995), together with his book *The Spirit of Community* (1995) argue that the ills besetting contemporary society, from delinquency to drug abuse and general lack of decency have, at their roots, a failure of adequate parenting. Etzioni frames the parenting deficit in terms of a lack of moral strength, seeing its principal manifestations in divorce and the fact that parents do not make themselves sufficiently available to their children: 'Fathers and mothers consumed by "making it" and consumerism, or preoccupied with personal advancement, who come home too late and too tired to attend to the needs of their children, cannot discharge their most elementary duty to their children and their fellow citizens' (1995). While Etzioni acknowledges that 'many low income couples and single parents have little or no choice' his main argument is that this *is* a matter of choice, and a moral choice at that – 'a finger should be pointed at those who, in effect, abandon their children to invest themselves whole hog in other pursuits' – parents should consider what is important to them, 'more income or better relationships with their children'. He adds: 'at some level of income, which is lower than *the conventional wisdom would have us believe*, parents do begin to have a choice between enhanced earnings and attending to their children' (1995; my emphasis).

NEW LABOUR AND STAKEHOLDING

Somewhat similar notions that emphasise individual responsibility have recently been aired by Blair (1996a, b) in his formulation of the Stakeholder Society. This account emerged as an attempt to create a more inclusive One-Nation Britain, fostering a sense of national community. As in the communitarian model, the stake-holding idea stresses the role of the individual in making an invest-ment in society through work, family and home which, it is proposed, will in turn lead to a sense of security and financial independence. This is not to be achieved by attempting to recreate the post-war system of dependence on the state, as set up in Britain by William Beveridge. Rather, it is proposed to tackle the legacy of insecurity created by Thatcherism, and in particular that associated with five million redundancies, by strategies principally geared to changing opportunities and conditions in the workplace. A key component of stakeholder policy in this respect is to estab-lish additional worker powers, giving people a sense of inclusion through schemes such as worker ownership of shares, National Insurance schemes like those in Singapore, and, through 'learning accounts', creating opportunity and choice regarding training.

ADVERSE IMPACT OF DIVORCE AND DAY CARE

There can be no argument with the central tenet outlined in the communitarian formulation, and implicit in New Labour's ap-proach, that individual responsibility within the family and good parenting practices are essential to the well-being of children and have beneficial effects in the wider community. Similarly, no one would dispute the fact that divorce and parental neglect are detri-mental to the welfare of children and thus to society at large. With regard to divorce, there is sound evidence that, in comparison to children whose parents remain married, those whose parents di-vorce, from similar social backgrounds, show consistent differences in development throughout childhood and adolescence, and rather different trajectories into adulthood (Richards 1996). In particular these children have, on average, lower levels of academic achieve-ment, poorer self-esteem and higher rates of behaviour problems and other difficulties in psychological adjustment. Moves into het-erosexual relationships are made earlier, as are those to leave home and enter into cohabiting relationships. In young adulthood there is evidence for more changes of job, lower economic status, a greater incidence of divorce and possibly higher rates of depression. Sim-ilarly, prolonged parental absence through work for very young in-fants that is associated with day care programmes where there is little continuity of good quality care and inadequate facilities, is likely to be linked to more insecurity of child attachment to the parents (Belsky and Isabella 1988) and poorer cognitive development in the child (Hennessy and Melhuish 1991).

DIFFICULTIES OF COMMUNITARIAN AND STAKEHOLDING ACCOUNTS

Pressures to Work

Both Etzioni's account of communitarianism and the Stakeholder Society formulation, while attracting considerable interest, are nevertheless open to criticism on a number of fronts. A principal difficulty with both is that in focusing on individual choice and responsibility they fail to identify the conditions that facilitate parental behaviour that is conducive to the well-being of children. Thus, with regard to individual choices in the context of work, neither Etzioni nor Blair adequately addresses the two most important characteristics of current employment: first, there is not that much of it, and, second, what there is does not readily lend itself to the kinds of choices assumed in the communitarian and stakeholding models. As the Joseph Rowntree report on income and wealth in the 1980s (Hills 1995), and the analyses of diverse political economists and philosophers make clear (for example, Gray 1994; 1995a; 1996, Hutton 1995; Mulgan 1996), it is idle to talk of real choice when current economic conditions, and in particular the combination of a general slowing down in the economy, the availability of a large female workforce and the globalisation of economic life, has meant that one-third of the population is excluded from work, and another third lives in chronic job insecurity. In these latter circumstances the kinds of stakes that might in fact be available are not secure ones that can provide a foundation for strong families, but, for example, those in multinational companies with obligations far wider than any to British workers (Gray 1996; see Marris, this volume). In addition, the recent trends for more short-term contracts and jobs relying on commission means that the insecurity that used to be confined to particular groups of manual workers (such as dockers) is now a widespread phenomenon. Together these factors have the consequence that the stakes that could typically be held in the workplace crucially rely on the individual's acceptance of risk, a risk that is beyond their own control, having more to do with 'the influence of distal happenings on proximal events' (Giddens 1991).

The globalisation of the economy has not just brought about job insecurity, but it has also contributed to the rapid growth in wage inequalities, such that the incomes of unskilled workers are driven down to levels that make supporting a family beyond the means of many. The middle classes are not immune to these forces, being just as likely to be faced with both job insecurity and new levels of poverty. The impact of these macro-economic forces on families has been anything but alleviated by recent British fiscal policy which has progressively moved money away from couples with children, and put pressure on women to work outside the home. Specifically, the transfers have been away from those with children to those without, from families with one main earner to couples as two main earners, from two-parent families to lone parents, and from child care in the home to child care outside (Field 1980; Morgan 1995) In this context it is understandable that both parents feel compelled to take what work they can, have less time and energy available for their children, and place their children in day care. Such decisions arise therefore not so much out of a lack of moral strength, a competition between selfish interests and the duties of child care, as from necessity. In fact, most parents would far rather combine work with caring for their children at home. In Hewitt and Leach's report on a recent British social attitudes survey (1993), they note that over half of all employed women, and two-thirds of those with school-age children would prefer to work only while their child was at school. Similarly, the recent research by Catherine Hakim (1996) challenges one feminist orthodoxy that, given the choice, women would opt to work rather than stay at home, finding that only a small number were truly 'career minded'. However, the possibility of giving priority to children and home is in fact little available to the female workforce in Britain; here, the failure to adopt the European Union (EU) Social Chapter has meant that women have, in contrast to those in almost every other industrialised country, failed to benefit from expanding opportunities for part-time work coupled with an increase in employment rights and social security protection.

Pressure on Marriages

Not only do current economic trends make it hard for parents to be available to their children as much as they would like, but the same pressures place considerable burdens on marriages. As Gray (1995b) has argued, the increasing fragility of families cannot be unconnected with the strains imposed by economic policies that put flexibility of labour above any social consideration. In his view it is not accidental that Britain, which has the highest divorce rate in Europe, also has the greatest labour mobility; given that couples with children need two incomes to make ends meet, and both partners are subject to the incessant demands of job insecurity and mobility, it is not surprising that relationships fail.

Pressure on Communities

The impact of current economic forces does, furthermore, extend far beyond experiences within the family and affects life directly at the level of the wider community. In particular, the marked nature of economic inequalities fundamentally weakens community ties, especially in cities where differences in income and jobs result in segregation at every level: different social groups have ceased to make common use of public institutions, and meet in the same public space only rarely (Hutton 1995). Yet despite the impact economic forces exert on the nature of community, both communitarian and stakeholding accounts emphasise the role of the individual, principally acting within the context of the family, to underpin the growth of community. Neither formulation gives proper consideration to the conditions required to facilitate the individual's potential for responsible behaviour in the family and community context, and, with the exception of Tessa Jowell's statements in her former role as Shadow Minister for Women, there has been virtually no discussion of the political strategies that are needed to support individuals in their role as parents.

Absence of a Theory of Morality

Stakeholding and communitarian accounts not only fail to consider the measures that might enable parents to become physically more available to their children, but they neglect an issue that is even more central to their thesis, that of the preconditions for the personal and emotional resources necessary not only for good parenting, but also for a wider concern and commitment to others. Thus, although talk of morality cuts right through Etzioni's writings, and is held to be the key agent of any change in the direction of the communitarian agenda, there is no theory of moral behaviour. Besides being of interest to philosophers (see Introduction) this topic is of course of central concern to those who work in a clinical capacity with families, and to those engaged in research on the intergenerational transmission of difficulties in personal functioning. Here, the direct experience of the forces, both social and economic and those within the individual, that influence human conduct, may fruitfully inform the current political debate. This is perhaps especially so for those who are in a clinical relationship with families. This experience is possibly unique in permitting an understanding of exactly the point at which individuals are genuinely free to make choices, and the point at which either external or inner circumstances render various options more or less possible. The clinical perspective can, for example, usefully inform decisions about the circumstances in which it may indeed be appropriate, as Tony Blair has suggested (1995), to think of taking parents of truanting children to court – when such a strategy would provide some containment and be productive, as opposed to being misplaced. For example, where a more effective strategy might be to focus resources on providing experiences in schools that empower young people, and which could be seen by them to relate in a meaningful way to post-school training and eventual employment (see Utting, this volume). This chapter, by contrast, outlines some research findings from three British longitudinal studies that have traced developmental pathways of central importance when considering both individual well-being and that of the wider community, namely, the routes to delinquency in young men, depression in young women, and the experience of the children of depressed mothers.

DELINQUENCY AND CRIMINAL BEHAVIOUR

David Farrington and Donald West and their colleagues at the Institute of Criminology in Cambridge have conducted an exemplary study of the development of over 400 boys growing up in a working-class area in London (1990). The families were first assessed when the children were eight years old, and the researchers managed to follow up some 95 per cent of the sample up to age 32. One-fifth of the sample were convicted as juveniles, one-third by the time they were 25; and 6 per cent were chronic offenders. Regular assessments conducted throughout the study included reports of the children themselves, their peers at primary school, class teachers and their parents. One of the most striking findings of this study was that, even within this relatively homogeneous population, the worst offenders differed from the rest of the sample on nearly all the variables measured from an early age. Four key factors affected outcome: the first was economic – eventual offenders were, as children, brought up in poor, large families, living in bad housing, with fathers who were unemployed; second, as young as eight, problems were being identified in school, the eventual offenders being seen as troublesome and hyperactive, and having poor concentration, and low IQ and attainment; third, poor parenting was associated with delinquent or criminal outcome, and in particular a combination of neglect (both physical and in terms of poor supervision) and punitive, harsh but erratic discipline. Finally, a culture of criminal behaviour in the family was influential. These factors combined to set up a causal sequence whereby parental mishandling of the child in the context of poverty and insecurity became associated with poor school achievements, then truancy, followed by few or unstable job prospects and eventually adult criminality. Notably, the particular form of parenting deficit identified by Etzioni (that is, absence through work) was not a factor; rather, paternal unemployment was predictive, and maternal work away from home was not associated with poor outcome.

DEPRESSION IN WOMEN

Similar complex causal sequences, involving both early childhood experience of parental care and a range of social and economic factors, are apparent if one looks at the situation of women, where poor outcome, rather than taking the form of criminality, is more commonly manifest as clinical depression. Depression is a matter of public interest, not least because it is costly: the mental health care costs alone for those identified as depressed in 1990 amounted to some £333 million (West 1992). Some of the most important research in this area has been carried out by Tirril Harris, George Brown and Toni Bifulco (1990). Their work is particularly notable in that it has sought to trace the pathways linking early experience to adult depression by taking account of both external or environmental influences, and more internal or psychological processes. In order to be able to study properly the role of early lack of parental care, this research group studied 225 women from General Practice populations in Walthamstow, north London, where about two-thirds were vulnerable in terms of having suffered the loss of a mother, either by death or separation, in childhood. Based on hypotheses deriving from their previous research, detailed interviews were conducted to obtain information in a number of areas: (i) the quality of care experienced in childhood (and in particular neglect, control, and separation); (ii) the experience of premarital pregnancy; (iii) the degree to which the woman felt able to influence events or felt helpless, both as a child and in adulthood, and (iv) the quality of current support, as well as recent stressful circumstances, and information on social class and psychiatric state. The results indicated that women who, as children, had lost their mother through death when they were very young (under five), were likely to have developed a sense of helplessness and low self-esteem, perhaps because, at this age, effective mourning may be less possible. Those whose mothers died later on were rather less at risk of helplessness, even though they tended to receive inadequate subsequent care, and it seemed that they were protected by a previously good relationship with their mother. Girls whose mothers left them were particularly at risk: they too were likely to go on to receive less than adequate care following their mothers' departure, but these children had generally also suffered neglect at the hands of their own mothers before the separation. The helplessness and low self-esteem arising from these childhood difficulties then seemed to launch these girls on a trajectory in which they became easily entangled in unsatisfactory, unstable relationships, often precipitated by premarital pregnancy. This situation in itself further diminishes self-esteem and feelings of control, such that, in the context of some subsequent stressful event, depression is likely.

There is now considerable evidence that depression makes it hard for those looking after children to give appropriate and sensitive care. It is of particular interest therefore in thinking about communitarian concerns with the impact of working mothers on the child's early experience of care, to explore the links between maternal depression and women's employment status. The early work by Brown and colleagues indicated that, far from being beneficial, the lack of any employment when bringing up small children was associated with vulnerability to depression. This finding has subsequently been replicated by this research group in a further sample, where it seemed that the lack of independence associated with not having paid employment rendered women more vulnerable in the face of difficulties with their partners (Brown and Bifulco 1990). However, this later study also indicated that full-time employment, combined with the responsibility for young children posed a similar risk for depression to having no paid employment at all, women in this situation feeling overburdened by their multiple responsibilities. The ideal in terms of women's mental health seemed, therefore, to be the ability to work part-time.

52   THE POLITICS OF ATTACHMENT

PARENTING AND THE DEVELOPMENT OF CHILDREN OF DEPRESSED MOTHERS

Finally we turn to the question of parenting, and some findings are presented from a study conducted by the author and colleagues in Cambridge of first-born children and their mothers who, to date, have been followed up over their first five years. One aim of the study was to examine the influence of the quality of the child's early care on their development, and for this reason, as well as having a number of women who were broadly representative of the local population, the study also included a group of women who, becoming clinically depressed after childbirth, were at increased risk for difficulties in their relationship with their infants. From an initial postnatal sample of more than 700 women, 111 were recruited at two months postpartum, including 56 women who had been depressed after childbirth. The depressed women commonly experienced difficulties with their partners, lacked support from their families and tended not to have relationships with other women in whom they could confide; they also more often experienced financial hardship or housing difficulties. Even among those who were not depressed, however, the practical support received from others amounted to rather little: the infants' fathers, who had precious little, if any, paternity leave, spent on average only 12 hours a week actively caring for their two-month-olds, and were generally absent from home for around 50 hours a week. In spite of regular contacts with the primary health care team, depression was frequently not detected, and when it was, women were generally reluctant to take the antidepressant medication that was normally prescribed. Many felt guilty about their experience, attempted to mask their problems and avoided public situations where they imagined they would be seen as failing. Ironically, then, the depressed women did not avail themselves of the mother and baby clinics set up by health visitors to serve their needs. By two months, those who had become clinically depressed were experiencing a range of difficulties with their infants; for example, they found it hard to settle their infants to sleep, were more likely to have problems breastfeeding, reported their infants to cry for prolonged periods, and experienced significant problems in combining household tasks with caring for the infant.

A particular focus of our study was the quality of play between mother and infant: videotapes of face-to-face engagements were rated by researchers (who were unaware of the mother's mental state) on a series of scales assessing, for example, the mother's sensitivity to the infant's cues, her acceptance and warmth, or the degree to which she was either disengaged and remote, or else intrusive and interfering. The results showed, as one might expect, that the depressed women were, as a group, less responsive and sensitively attuned to their infants, and were more prone to be hostile and critical. However, it is important to note that it was not only in the context of depression that such difficulties arose: although social and personal adversity tended to predominate in the group of women who were depressed, where such difficulties existed in the absence of depression, the mothers' interactions with their infants were similarly insensitive and rejecting (Murray et al. 1996a). It appeared, therefore, that in order to be 'preoccupied' with her infant, to use Donald Winnicott's phrase, the mothers needed to be in an environment that was supportive, both personally and practically.

When the children's development was followed up at eighteen months, by which time the great majority of postnatally depressed women had recovered, continuing difficulties were still apparent: the infants of depressed women were likely to have increased rates of behaviour problems, were more likely to be insecurely attached to their mothers and were more likely to fail on cognitive tasks assessing the infant's capacity to understand that objects and events in the world can exist, independent of the infant's own subjective experience. Strikingly, these cognitive problems shown at eighteen months were strongly predicted by the quality of the mother's engagement with the infant at two months' postpartum, the infants performing well where their mothers had been sensitively engaged with them. This influence was still apparent in the children's cognitive performance at age five; notably, those children who, as infants, had experienced particularly insensitive interactions with their mothers not only had poor cognitive outcome at eighteen months, but their developmental trajectory beyond infancy continued to be constrained by their earlier experience (Murray et al. 1996b).

At five years the study children were also assessed on a range of social and emotional measures: each was observed in school during a period of free play and at a time when the teacher read to the children, and the teachers completed questionnaires on the children's adjustment once they had attended their first term (Sinclair, 1994). The quality of the children's friendships was also assessed, as were their perceptions of their family lives. Mothers were interviewed about the presence of child behaviour difficulties, family circumstances and their own psychiatric state over the intervening three years.

The mothers themselves continued to experience their children as being difficult to manage if they had experienced postnatal depression, and these difficulties applied to the behaviour of both boys and girls. These associations with the mother's early postpartum experience were still found even when taking into account current and recent maternal depression, and the presence of conflict between the parents.

At school the children whose mothers had experienced postnatal depression were reported by their teachers to show significantly raised rates of behaviour problems, and these problems were associated with insecurity in attachment in infancy. The boys were particularly likely to have difficulties, and this usually took the form of hyperactive behaviour, whereas the girls were rated as the least distractible and the most prosocial children. Although this latter finding may not at first glance seem problematic, there is independent evidence (Hay 1994) that extreme expressions of prosocial behaviour are predictive of later depression, possibly reflecting a basic insecurity and an inappropriate concern with others' well-being at one's own expense; and this interpretation seemed to be borne out by the results of other assessments.

When the children were observed during free play differences again emerged according to the mother's experience after childbirth: both boys and girls whose mothers had been postnatally depressed were less likely to engage in creative play than well mothers' children, and were instead more occupied in lower level, mechanical activities. The patterns of social interaction also differed between the two groups. Postnatally depressed mothers' children were generally less well integrated: they showed fewer positive approaches to their teachers, were approached less by other children, and when they were approached they responded less positively.

Finally, the way in which the children themselves described their experience differed according to whether or not their mothers had been depressed early on: here, the children were asked to enact their experience in their families in a dolls' house play scenario: each child was invited to choose doll figures to represent the people in their home, and they were then asked to play out what happened in four situations – a meal time, bed time, a bad and nasty time and their best and favourite time. Transcripts were made of the children's play narratives and these were then scored using a system, a case grammar analysis, designed to describe the way in which the child constructs and organises his or her experience; in particular, the scheme shows the extent to which the child perceives him or herself as being able to influence events, in contrast to feeling that events are out of their control and the degree to which their experience is framed in a negative way (Barnard et al. 1996). The children whose mothers had been postnatally depressed were once again at a disadvantage, being less likely, when they referred to themselves in the dolls' house scenario, to describe themselves as being active agents, influencing the course of events; and they were also more likely than well mothers' children to construct their experience in a negative way. These self schemas were quite unrelated to the quality of the current mother–child relationship, but were, however, significantly predicted by the extent of the mother's hostility towards the child at two months.

IMPLICATIONS OF RESEARCH FINDINGS

It is clear from the research described above that, where the context for parenting is unfavourable, parents may become involved in difficult cycles of relationship with their infants that easily persist, at least into the early school years, and that have an impact on a number of areas of child functioning, including poor cognitive achievements, and a problematic adjustment in school manifest in behaviour problems, poor social relationships and an absence of creativity. All these difficulties in the child seem likely to relate to the fundamental lack of a sense of agency or secure sense of self evident in the children's narrative descriptions of their lives. These early problems observed in the children of mothers who had experienced postnatal depression were strikingly resonant of the those identified in the studies of Farrington and West of the routes to delinquency and criminal behaviour in young men, and in those of Harris, Brown and Bifulco on the routes to depression in women. Thus, the insecurities of the five-year-old boys of depressed women were manifest in hyperactive and disturbed behaviour in class, both of which are risks for future delinquent behaviour, whereas the girls' insecurity was more likely to be reflected in their greater adaptation to others' concerns at the expense of their own interests.

It is important to note that the parenting problems we observed generally had little to do with women selfishly rushing to find fulfilment in the workplace: without exception, the mothers in our research were highly motivated to do the best they could for their children; only a small minority worked more than 15 hours per week, if at all, as is generally true for mothers of children under two in Britain. Indeed, in this sample, there was no relationship between maternal employment and adverse child outcome. How-

ever, it is evident that, without good emotional support and resources, it is difficult for parents to provide an environment in
which children are to flourish; this may be particularly hard to
achieve where the parents themselves have had inadequate care in
their own childhoods, where they are likely to have been launched
on a trajectory that only compounds their initial difficulties.

INTERVENTION STUDIES

The conclusions arising from studies concerning the impediments
to good parenting are reinforced by the results of intervention research that aims to facilitate parental capacities to meet their children's needs. For example, our own research group has recently
explored the possible benefits to depressed mothers and their infants of providing brief psychotherapy, over and above the benefits
of routine primary care (Cooper and Murray 1995). The treatment
in this study was modelled on provision that could feasibly be
provided within the Health Service context, and, from eight weeks'
postpartum, women who were identified as depressed received
weekly, hour-long sessions from a therapist in their homes over a
two-month period. The women's mental state was assessed immediately after treatment and at nine and eighteen months follow-up.
There were clear beneficial effects of the additional support in
terms of the women's depression remitting by 4½ months postpartum. In addition, there were significant benefits in terms of the
mothers reporting fewer difficulties with the infant, both immediately after treatment and at eighteen months follow-up. And although there was no simple effect of treatment on infant attachment, the early remission from depression associated with treatment predicted more infant security at eighteen months.

Treatment in this study had been delivered mainly by qualified
psychologists, and following completion of the trial we extended
the work to mount a local health visitor intervention that involved
an emotionally supportive, counselling approach (Seeley et al.
1996). With only six half days additional training in the detection
and management of depression, health visitors in the Cambridge
district became far more effective in their work with postnatally
depressed mothers; rates of remission within a two-month period
doubled over those prior to the intervention; and what was particularly striking was the benefit in terms of the mother's experience of
caring for her infant, with difficulties in all aspects of care, including the sense of satisfaction and pleasure in the relationship, show-

ing marked improvement over and above the beneficial effect on maternal mood of the extra support.

THE NATURE OF MORALITY AND IMPLICATIONS FOR POLICY

As noted in the Introduction, the communitarian thesis casts the issue of the parenting deficit principally in terms of rational, moral choices – whether to pursue one's own interests or those of one's children. However, the model offers no theory of morality, nor an understanding of the circumstances likely to give rise to the expression of moral or responsible behaviour. At this point it is informative to consider the research findings on adult adjustment and the quality of parenting in the light of evidence on early infant social development, and also the clinical work of John Bowlby and his near-contemporary, the paediatrician and child psychiatrist Donald Winnicott; in particular the latter's writings on the capacity for concern (Bowlby 1953; Winnicott 1963a, b). Studies in developmental psychology have revealed a remarkable capacity in the human infant to engage in personal contacts from the very first day of life. Within hours of birth the infant will attend selectively to human rather than non-human stimulation and, over the first days, will develop preferences for the particular characteristics of the persons involved in their care. By two months, and long before the capacity arises to manipulate objects in the physical world, infants show a wide repertoire of communicative actions and facial expressions in face-to-face interactions that appear responsive to the quality of the adult's behaviour. If this is experimentally disrupted, even in brief and mild ways, the infant becomes rapidly distressed: initially there is often protest, and the infant will appear to try to solicit the unresponsive adult's involvement; if this is not forthcoming the infant eventually becomes dejected and withdrawn. Together these findings attest to a fundamental motivation to be engaged in a world of consistent human contacts, where mutual, interpersonal relations are an end in themselves rather than a means to pursue individual interests. Such behaviour, with its intrinsically affective components tied to the nature of interpersonal relatedness, can be seen as the basis for a genuine morality, arising spontaneously as part of the human condition. However, it is evident from clinical work that this capacity and motivation requires certain conditions if it is to flourish and develop into a mature sense of morality and concern for others. In both Bowlby's and

Winnicott's view, the capacity to feel a sense of responsibility and to be concerned on behalf of others arises through a complex developmental progression. The first stage of this process is the dependent infant's experience of a reliable, caring environment, which over the first six to twelve months or so gradually becomes internalised as a sense of satisfaction, goodness or worth, and which becomes part of the infant's sense of self. What is being fostered is, in effect, a sense of there being something good within the self that will eventually be felt to be worthwhile giving to others. This component of the capacity for concern is not, therefore, the inculcation of a rational sense of duty, a set of learned moral codes, but a felt experience of being of value. The research findings outlined above similarly indicate that the adult expression of concern, like the infant's, is not simply a product of rational decisions based on a cold appraisal of self-interest, nor is it neatly regulated according to some set of moral codes: it is just as much an emotional affair where issues of security, attachments and interdependencies in relationships loom large. In concrete terms it appears, therefore, to be of fundamental importance for good parenting that it is undertaken in conditions where there is emotional support, and where circumstances free the parent to be preoccupied with the infant, rather than with financial worries or the pressure to return to full-time work in order to retain a place in the job market. Clearly a number of policy changes could achieve much on this front, including the provision of longer parental leave (including paternity leave), more flexible employment patterns, and fiscal changes to relieve the taxation burden on parents.

Thus far, it may appear that an argument is emerging for an Old Labour-style welfare state in which responsible and moral behaviour will inevitably occur if certain basic supports are provided. However, Winnicott's account of the development of the capacity for concern suggests that a more complex process is involved. He describes a phase subsequent to the provision of 'good enough' parental care when the infant develops a more holistic appreciation of the parent, becoming aware both of his dependency and of the fact that his behaviour has an impact on the parent. In other words, the infant begins to have a sense that what he or she does matters to the person on whom he or she is dependent, and that harm could be done as well as good, and out of this emerges, in healthy development, the sense of responsibility.

This latter stage of the development of the capacity for concern in infancy, like the initial one, seems to be analogous with adult experience; thus, it seems plausible to argue that in circumstances where support may be adequate, but society is organised in such a way that individuals feel themselves to be irrelevant to events, a kind of moral apathy may ensue. In fact, in the context of parent–infant relationships, good support alone may well be sufficient (for those not too damaged by previous adversity) since, once facilitated, the very process of caring will evidently be important in the infant's response and will thus bring about its own immediate reward. (This phenomenon is, in fact, actively exploited in certain therapeutic approaches that deliberately engage the infant in the clinical process – for example, Fraiberg 1981.) In the wider social context, however, it does appear to be the case that with the ever-growing erosion of local democracy, increasing numbers of people, and particularly the young, are disaffected with the political process and fail to vote or engage themselves actively in mainstream society, their capacity for care being expressed rather in 'alternative' causes where they do feel themselves to be effective, say, in relation to animal rights or environmental protection, where they are literally prepared to lay down their lives. What this suggests is that strategies for decentralisation and more democratically sensitive local control (see Nicholson, this volume) are appropriate policies regarding the expression of concerned and responsible behaviour, provided that they are accompanied by the provision of conditions in which people may feel secure.

REFERENCES

Barnard, P.J., Scott, S.K. and Murray, L. (1996) *Depression, early experience and the development of schematic models of the self.* Manuscript submitted for publication.

Belsky, J. and Isabella, R. (1988) 'Maternal, infant and social-contextual determinants of attachment security' in J. Belsky and T. Nezworski (eds), *Clinical Implications of Attachment.* Hillsdale, NJ: Erlbaum.

Blair, T. (1995) 'Blair shifts on to Tory territory'. *Guardian*, 23 March.

Blair, T. (1996a) 'The Stakeholder Economy'. Speech to public meeting. Derby: Assembly Rooms, 18 January.

Blair, T. (1996b) 'Battle for Britain'. *Guardian*, 29 January.

Bowlby, J. (1953) *Child Care and the Growth of Love.* London: Penguin.

Brown, G.W. and Bifulco, A. (1990) 'Motherhood, employment and the development of depression: a replication of a finding?', *British Journal of Psychiatry* 156, 169–79.

Cooper, P.J. and Murray, L. (1995) 'The impact of postnatal depression on infant development: a treatment trial'. Proceedings of the Cape Town Conference on Infant Psychiatry, January 1995.

Etzioni, A. (1995) *The Spirit of Community. Rights, Responsibilities and the Communitarian Agenda*. London: Fontana Press.

Farrington, D.P. and West, D.J. (1990) 'The Cambridge Study in Delinquent Development: A Long-Term Follow-Up of 411 London Males' in *Criminality: Personality, Behaviour and Life History*. Berlin: Springer-Verlag.

Field, F. (1980) *Fair Shares for Families: the need for a family impact statement*. London: Child Poverty Action Group.

Fraiberg, S. (1981) *Selected writings of Selma Fraiberg*. Columbus: Ohio State University Press.

Giddens, A. (1991) *Modernity and Self-Identity*. Cambridge: Polity Press.

Gray, J. (1994) *The Undoing of Conservatism*. London: The Social Market Foundation.

Gray, J. (1995a) 'Beggaring our own neighbours'. *Guardian*, 17 February.

Gray, J. (1995b) 'Hollowing out the core'. *Guardian*, 8 March.

Gray, J. (1996) *After Social Democracy*. London: Demos.

Hakim, C. (1996) 'The Sexual Division of Labour and Women's Heterogeneity'. *British Journal of Sociology* 46(1): 178–88.

Harris, T., Brown, G.W. and Bifulco, A. (1990) 'Loss of parent in childhood and adult psychiatric disorder: A tentative overall model', *Development and Psychopathology* 2: 311–28.

Hay, D.F. (1994) 'Prosocial Development', *Journal of Child Psychology and Psychiatry* 35: 29–72.

Hennessy, E. and Melhuish, E.C. (1991) 'Early day care and the development of school-age children: a review'. *Journal of Reproductive and Infant Psychology* 9 (2/3): 117–36.

Hewitt, P. and Leach, P. (1993) *Social Justice, Children and Families*. London: Institute for Public Policy Research.

Hills J. (1995) *Inquiry into Income and Wealth. Volume 2: a summary of the evidence*. York: Joseph Rowntree Foundation.

Hutton, W. (1995) *The State We're In*. London: Jonathan Cape.

Morgan, P. (1995) *Farewell to the Family? Public Policy and Family Breakdown in Britain and the USA*. London: IEA Health and Welfare Unit.

Mulgan G. (1996) 'A high-stake society'. *Guardian*, 30 January.

Murray, L., Fiori-Cowley, A., Hooper, R. and Cooper, P.J. (1996a) 'The impact of postnatal depression and associated adversity on early mother–infant interactions and later infant outcome', *Child Development* (In Press).

Murray, L., Hipwell, A., Hooper, R., Stein, A. and Cooper, P.J. (1996b) 'The cognitive development of five year old children of postnatally depressed mothers', *Journal of Child Psychology and Psychiatry* (In Press).

Richards, M.P.M. (1996) 'The Interests of Children at Divorce', in *Families and Justice*. Brussels: Editions Bruylant and Paris: Librairie Generale des Droits et Jurisprudence .

Seeley, S., Murray, L. and Cooper, P.J. (1996) 'Postnatal depression: The outcome for mothers and babies of health visitor intervention', *Health Visitor* 69(4): 135–8.

Sinclair, D.A. (1994) The effects of postnatal depression on the social behaviour of children during the transition to school. Unpublished Ph.D. thesis, Cambridge University.

West, R. (1992) *Depression*. London: Office of Health Economics.

Winnicott, D. (1963a) 'From Dependence towards Independence in the Development of the Individual' in M.R. Khan (ed.) *The Maturational Processes and the Facilitating Environment*. London: Hogarth Press.

Winnicott, D. (1963b) 'Morals and Education' in M.R. Khan (ed.) *The Maturational Processes and the Facilitating Environment*. London: Hogarth Press.

4 Hope in the Inner City: Towards a New Deal

Andrea Pound

INTRODUCTION

Public concern about the current state of the family in the UK has reached a pitch that has been described as a 'moral panic'. Politicians, sociologists, criminologists, psychologists, educators and churchmen have engaged in an intense and often acrimonious debate regarding the links between family breakdown and delinquency. Rising unemployment, especially of unskilled young men, has given rise to anxiety about a 'lost generation' with no valued place in society, alienated, angry and dangerous. From the right come attacks on the 'dependency culture' and concern regarding the growth of an 'underclass', particularly from Charles Murray in the US, who links rising crime and economic dependence with high rates of single parenthood and multiple partners (Murray 1990).

From the left come more anguished voices noting the increased disparities in wealth in our society, the increasing prosperity of the few at the top and increasing poverty of the many at the bottom of the economic order. There is also concern about the loss of a sense of community and responsibility for others and of a growing culture of greed and acquisitiveness which leaves no space for neighbourliness and mutual care. Increasingly there is unease over the capacity of parents to care effectively for their children, linked to the diffusion of extended families and lack of alternative family support. Many of these preoccupations focus particularly on the inner city, where crime is most rife, unemployment and poverty most severe in their effects and rates of child abuse and neglect at their highest levels.

This chapter examines three broad groups of children in the inner city – children of depressed mothers, children whose parents have divorced, and children living in poverty – and goes on to describe a number of parent support schemes that have grown out of attachment research, which may help us to craft policies to avert the escalating cycle of disadvantage for the youngest members of our society (Egeland et al. 1988).

DEPRESSED MOTHERS AND THEIR CHILDREN

As long ago as 1978, Brown and Harris drew attention to the high rates of clinical depression among women in inner-city areas, particularly those with young children and no close confiding relationship. Wolkind (1985) and Richman et al. (1982) confirmed that between 30 and 40 per cent of working-class mothers of young children were depressed at any one time, and their depression was highly associated with disturbance in the children. Richman also found expressive language delay at age three and reading delay at age eight where the mother had been depressed in the pre-school period. A study to explore the mechanisms by which disturbance is transmitted from one generation to the other showed marked child disorder in 61 per cent of the two-year-old children of depressed mothers. Depressed mothers were likely to have a poor relationship with their own mother, to have married and had children before the age of 21, to have conflictual marriages and to have more children than non-depressed controls. They were also much more likely to live in conditions of high environmental adversity, and in bleak, overcrowded and vandalised homes and neighbourhoods (Pound et al. 1988). Observation of the mother–child interaction showed more ignoring, more controlling behaviours, more physical handling of the child and fewer questions, suggestions, explanations and extended conversation in the depressed group. However, some depressed mothers maintained a warm relationship with the child and these children were much less likely to be disturbed (Cox et al. 1987; see also Murray, this volume). Those of us involved in these studies felt considerable concern about what we had seen and heard in the course of our data collection. Some depressed women could hardly get out of their chairs to attend to their children, while others were engaged in an escalating battle of wills with an uncontained and miserable child. Many mothers and children were extremely isolated, with no family or social support. However, despite growing evidence that all was not well for the inner-city family, the public conscience was unstirred and there was little publicity for these findings outside of the child care professions. What has stirred the moral majority is the rising rate of crime, especially among young unemployed men (see Utting, this volume).

CHILDREN OF DIVORCE

After a dramatic rise since the 1960s the divorce rate stabilised, and then increased again (Utting 1995). If present rates continue, more than one in three marriages will be dissolved and one in four children will experience the break-up of their parents' marriage by the time they are sixteen (Haskey 1990). One in three women are dependent on benefits post-divorce compared with one in twenty-five pre-divorce, and nearly half of divorced women with children live on state benefits.

What are the effects of such widespread family breakdown and absence of fathers in the home? Evidence has been steadily accumulating that children of divorce fare worse than their contemporaries from intact homes; they are more likely to leave school early, to be in unskilled jobs and to be depressed as young adults. Two important studies have looked more closely at the effects of divorce on children. Wallerstein and Kelly (1980) conducted a study in the US of 60 children which painted a heartbreaking picture of children continuing to yearn for their absent fathers over many years, afflicted by intense grief, fear and often anger. Young children especially tend to blame themselves for the break-up and have vivid fantasies of bringing about reconciliation. A more recent British study by Hetherington (1988) followed up a group of four-year-old middle-class children six years after divorce. Most experienced considerable disruption in the first two years but then improved, though a number of boys continued to show anti-social behaviour at home and school, difficulty getting on with peers, and lower school achievement than before the break-up and also conflict with their mothers, compared to a control group of stable families.

For some years, nevertheless, there was considerable denial (especially by the women's movement who seemed to see divorce as liberating) that these children faced any adversity other than poverty. Clearly, poverty, with lower family income and poorer quality housing, is a common consequence of divorce, as are changes of home and school. Poverty is, however, by no means the whole story; we need to examine critically all the mechanisms put forward to account for the poorer outcome of children of divorced parents. One review did just this. It compared the evidence for parental loss, economic deprivation and family conflict as mediating factors. Although there was some support for all three mechanisms, the family conflict perspective accounted for the most significant difference in outcome for children of divorce (Amato and

Keith 1991). A further study confirmed that even before separation, chronic marital tensions can have a deleterious effect on the children (Elliott and Richards 1991). There is no doubt that severe marital conflict is deeply disturbing to children, whether in intact or separated families. Children feel torn in loyalty between two parents, both of whom they love but who are tearing each other apart. We know that one-third of children lose touch with a parent on the break-up of the marriage and another third within five years of divorce. Twenty per cent of children experience another marriage of their custodial parent and a proportion of those children also experience a second divorce before the age of sixteen. A recent large-scale study has confirmed many of these findings and noted that the effect was particularly powerful in relation to daughters of middle-class families (Cockett and Tripp 1994). One study found that the effects of divorce are greater than for death of a parent, because it affects the child's sense of self-worth which is 'a very heavy message for children' (Richards 1996).

How do we interpret these findings? From a viewpoint of attachment theory it is unsurprising that children experience distress at their parents' separation. Their sense of security and value derives from their attachment to both of their parents and their parents' attachment to them, and from their observation of the parents' attachment to each other. Loss of a parental attachment figure is always a traumatic event, but when it is voluntary and intentional, as in divorce and separation, it implies that not only the marital partner but also the child is of little value. It also suggests to the child that intimate partnerships are risky ventures, and potentially unstable, with implications for their own, later, love relationships. Given this impact, it is imperative that the absent parent maintain consistent and predictable contact with the child and that both parents work at maintaining a co-operative attitude in the children's best interest (Camara and Resnick, 1989).

CHILDREN AND POVERTY

Next to rising rates of divorce and single parenthood, the poverty of many families, especially those with young children is a source of much public concern. It has been estimated that one-third of all children now live in poverty, three times the number in 1979 (Hewitt and Leach 1993). We are an increasingly unequal society. The richest 1 per cent of the population own 18 per cent of the wealth while the poorest half own only 6 per cent, and the social class differential has widened over the past decade and a half since we discovered that 'there is no such thing as society'.

Rising numbers of unemployed people and others in low-paid jobs, and a sharp rise in homelessness as a direct result of government policy, also account for much of the increased levels of poverty in the past decade. Again, inner-city families are most at risk. The expansion in the numbers of owner-occupiers during the 1980s and the consequent improvement in living conditions for many middle-income families was not reflected in a similar improvement for low-income families, who continue to live in multi-occupied properties or high-rise flats which are often cold, damp, mouldy and difficult to heat. There is a significant correlation between unemployment and child mortality and ill health, and also with higher levels of family breakdown. There has also been a widening differential in educational standards between relatively prosperous areas and deprived inner-city areas in recent years (Kumar 1993).

Homelessness is one of the worst disasters which can befall a family and has increased 100 per cent since the early 1980s. Many more families are in temporary accommodation awaiting rehousing. Conditions for families in bed and breakfast hotels have been described by the Audit Commission (1989) as 'the worst standard of accommodation ... totally unsuitable for family life'. Many families spend several years in such places, spending long hours in tiny rooms with no space for children to play, creating tension between parents and children and leading to impaired child-rearing skills.

Apart from being utterly demoralising and degrading in itself, one of the most pernicious effects of poverty is the enormous stress that it adds to the already difficult job of parenting. The effects of poverty then slide insidiously on to the next generation. Indeed in some families the strain is too much and their children are taken into care. Whilst it will be in some children's best interests to be removed from home, there is a painful and exquisitely sensitive job to be done to help them make sense of the heartbreak of disrupted attachments. The fostering of 'autobiographical competence' (see Holmes, this volume) is a crucial safeguard against the most damaging effects of such separations and Quinton and Rutter (1985) show how those leaving care, who are among the most disadvantaged of young people, may even at this relatively late stage be helped in a relationship with a partner who is able to be supportive and loyal.

CHILD CARE AND FAMILY SUPPORT

In spite of the despair and damage engendered by poverty and loss in families, there are projects that show promise, and lend some justification for the title of this chapter. Much research has been done on early intervention. Pre-school education for three- to five-year-olds has been conclusively shown to help them make better progress in primary school, as in the highly regarded French system. The Ypsilanti study in the US showed huge benefits in educational level, later employment record and lack of criminal record for children of poor black families who had good pre-school education (Schweinhart and Weikart 1983). These benefits were also of course financial in that there are savings on expensive interventions, including punitive ones, directed against delinquency in later years (see Utting, this volume). Good quality day care, nursery education, playgroups, family centres and other neighbourhood projects such as toy libraries would all contribute towards better parental functioning and a richer cognitive and social experience for young children. All such projects need to provide a stimulating programme of structured child activities, encouraging co-operative play and developing skills and creativity. Just as important as the work with the children is the involvement of parents in the organisation and day-to-day running of the project. The ingredients of success in these programmes are consistent with the theme of this book, which is that reciprocity of relationships is more likely to promote confidence, curiosity and generosity.

Over the past 15 to 20 years a number of innovative projects have arisen which aim to support parents and enrich their parenting skills, some aimed at families with particular difficulties such as depression in the mother or an abusive relationship with the child, others at less disadvantaged families who feel the need for some education in parenting. One of the first in Britain was Home-Start, developed in Leicester in the late 1970s and evaluated some years later by Willem Van der Eyken (1982). Home-Start trains volunteers to visit and befriend young mothers who are isolated, depressed or having problems in parenting. Volunteers tended to be slightly older and better-off than client mothers, but as time has passed many clients have overcome their presenting problems, developed more self-confidence and have trained themselves to become volunteers. The evaluation showed varying levels of satisfaction with the project, clients seeing it as most effective, then referring agencies, while volunteers themselves had the most modest view of their success. Home-Start is highly economical, requiring very modest accommodation as most of the work goes on in clients' own homes. There are now 300 or more projects around the country.

NEWPIN (New Parent–Infant Network), a more intensive project particularly suited to the inner city, was founded in 1978 in Walworth in South London, by a group of local professionals who were concerned at the high levels of family distress and child abuse in the district. As in Home-Start, volunteers were recruited and trained to act as befrienders to mothers of under-fives who were experiencing difficulties, again most commonly because of depression or parenting problems. In addition, it provided a drop-in centre and a crèche where mothers could take their children whenever they wished. A small pilot study carried out in 1982 showed that most of the participants were very positive about their experience of NEWPIN. Both referrals and volunteers had suffered much distress in childhood and adult life, with high levels of loss, broken relationships, single parent status and depression. Many currently were experiencing problems in the care of their children and continued to have difficult lives, but almost all had benefited from NEWPIN and expressed their feelings in very eloquent terms:

'When my volunteer started, I was at the end of my tether. I didn't know it was depression I had. I felt suicidal before coming to NEWPIN.'

'I know I can't change everything in people. Sometimes I can't condone or even understand but I try to see their point of view. Now I stop, look, listen and accept.'

'My kid was a little cow. It's lovely now since NEWPIN and we have a lovely household. It was a non-stop battle before.'

'I am a totally different person. I am brighter and can laugh and have a joke. I didn't know what a laugh was before.'

'I had always felt I was on my own, a lonely person, but down there at NEWPIN everyone wants to know you.'

A more substantive study compared a NEWPIN group with a similar group in Tower Hamlets over a six-month period. Both groups commonly suffered from adverse experiences in childhood and adult life, including being in care, being physically and sexually abused and having seen a psychiatrist for mental health problems, mostly commonly for depression. Again the outcomes were in favour of the NEWPIN group, who showed improvements in self-esteem and trust in others and improved relationships with partners. Mother–child interaction and child behaviour changed little in either group, perhaps because of the short time-scale of the study, though well-involved NEWPIN mothers improved the most (Cox et al. 1987). Yet the outcome for women engaged over longer periods of time has been in many cases quite remarkable. Some women who entered the project as clients with major problems have gone on to become volunteers and then very effective co-ordinators of new projects. Many others have gone into further education and moved on to other careers. There seems little doubt that projects such as NEWPIN, using the resources of a community to help that community, can change lives and transform the future for its children.

NEWPIN has a strong ethos of mutual responsibility, with each having something to offer to the group as well as needs for support. Three principles in particular underlie its effectiveness; acceptance, attachment and insight into the mechanisms which underlie blaming and scapegoating of a child. Each member is accepted as someone of value, with all their shortcomings, but there is also a strong expectation of change and growth. Unreasonable blaming of a child is seen as arising from the unbearable pain of feeling the self to be bad, as in the parent's childhood, and shifting the badness on to the child. It is seen as the basis of most child abuse and neglect and 'helping the hurt child within the parent' as the main task with abusing families. Many of NEWPIN's members have suffered multiple losses in childhood and in adult life and a fear of further loss and rejection is a common preoccupation. The patterns of ambivalent and avoidant attachment relationships can be observed and worked on within NEWPIN and every effort is made to secure stable and trustworthy relationships within it. As many women told us, 'Someone is always there for you in NEWPIN', and this is not only figuratively but literally true. Every member has a list of addresses and telephone numbers of all the others and can call on them at any time of the day or night, a privilege which has rarely, if ever, been abused. These are bonds of friendship, deliberately fostered to promote securer attachments (see Introduction, and Pahl, this volume).

There are a number of other services designed to support families with young children. Parent Network, for example, is an organisation which runs courses for parents which combine information about child development, discussion, role-play and other devices to help improve the quality of parenting of the participants. Several years ago

Waltham Forest's education department asked Parent Network to run courses in its nursery and primary schools and so far over 200 parents have taken part. An independent evaluation of the project concluded that the courses have led to significant benefits to parents in terms of confidence, better communication with their children, improved understanding of children's feelings and improved handling of children's behaviour. Exploring Parenthood is another organisation with a more psychoanalytic orientation which has developed very interesting and effective ways of supporting, educating and encouraging parents in their vital role as the nurturers of the next generation, including working with young fathers in prison, who were amazed to find out how important they were to their children's health and development. PIPPIN is an organisation which provides short courses for expectant parents and has been shown to reduce anxiety, increase pleasure in the baby and satisfaction in the couple relationship (Parr 1996). Another parenting programme arising from the NEWPIN research team (Mellow Parenting) has been assessed on a group of 21 mothers, 12 of whose children were on the at-risk (child protection) register maintained by the local social services department. A marked reduction in negative mood and increase in positive mood and an increase in child centredness were found at the end of the four months' intervention (Puckering et al. 1994). This programme is expected to be implemented throughout NEWPIN from now on. Similar interventions in Canada, but more focused on parent training for at-risk populations, have also been shown to be effective as as part of a community provision (Cunningham et al. 1995).

Support for parents must begin at the beginning, however. New family centres, offering child care facilities, are being set up which encourage participation of both mothers and fathers, and are used by families across the social spectrum. Yet these are pioneers in a virtual desert. At present there is little in the way of organised quality child care in Britain. To set up a comprehensive service would cost money, but possibly not as much as it would seem. If employers were to contribute to child care costs, for example, they might well save on retraining new staff to replace those that have to leave. Some parents want to take longer breaks from work to be with their babies, others are keen to return. Either way they will need help. There is no doubt that children do well in the attentive care of people they know best. If they are securely attached to their parents the care provided for children by nurseries and creches will help to develop their social skills. The conditions that are increasingly seen to make for quality in day care are the attentiveness of adults towards the children, their training for this work and their understanding of children's developmental needs; the stability of the relationships between worker and child, the turnover of staff, their status and working conditions and the ratio between them and their charges (Melhuish and Moss 1991). If one adult is responsible for more than about four small children he, or more usually she, is put in a controlling rather than a caretaking role. It is clear that the qualities of good day care are those that also promote secure attachments in families.

Preparation for parenting has never been seen as a high priority for policy makers. It is seen as something everyone, or at least all women, instinctively know how to do and needs no instruction. We now know from animal studies that our close primate relatives brought up in isolation, like the baby monkeys in Harlow's disturbing experiments (Harlow and Harlow 1966), are unable to mother their own babies in adulthood and may even attack them if they are too demanding. Parenting human children, with the requirement not only to provide basic nurture, affection and protection from harm but also for the transmission of the culture to the next generation is an infinitely more complex and precarious enterprise. At present we rely almost entirely on the internalisation of the reciprocal role of the parent in childhood to produce a basis for parenting, with little if any opportunity for learning the day-to-day skills such as feeding the young child, dealing with its distress and rage and with jealousy and rivalry between siblings. We know that change is possible from one generation to the next, but it cannot be left to chance. The family is the crucible of the personality and also, as the image suggests, a cauldron of the most intense passions of love and hate, desire and destructiveness. It requires considerable skill to contain these forces in the developing child and to provide a reasonably integrated and balanced adult individual. Given the lack of opportunity for practising child care skills in later childhood and adolescence in modern societies with small family size, we need to find ways of providing for it within the education system. Several useful programmes for adolescents have been developed which include factual material, observational tasks such as watching a young child at play and role-plays of conflict situations in family life. One such set of materials also includes a course on human development, sexuality and marriage, and financial and time management which could well form part of the National Curriculum (Whitfield 1994). It should be noted that preparation for parenthood is just as necessary for boys as it is for girls, and that other social provisions, such as parental leave from work, are also important initiatives on the European political agenda (see Kraemer, 1996).

CONCLUSION

Support for parents' care for children should be a political priority, to ensure the competence of the next generation of parents. We need a New Deal which takes into account human needs for attachment, of children for their parents, of parents for each other, and of every citizen for their community. It will not happen by chance, but by serious intent on the part of legislators, business, educators, local authorities, architects, planners and every concerned citizen. 'Cultural capital can go to waste no less than physical capital, only when it happens it is more difficult to see' (Dennis and Erdos 1993).

REFERENCES

Amato, P. and Keith, B. (1991) 'Parental Divorce and the well-being of children: a meta-analysis', *Psychological Bulletin* 110(1): 26–46.

Audit Commission (1989) *Housing the homeless: The Local Authority Role*. London: HMSO.

Brown, G.W. and Harris J. (1978) *Social Origins of Depression*. London: Tavistock.

Camara, K. and Resnick, G. (1989) 'Styles of conflict resolution and co-operation between divorced parents: effects on child behavior', *American Journal of Orthopsychiatry* 59: 560–75.

Cockett, M. and Tripp, J. (1994) *The Exeter Family Study – family breakdown and its impact on children*. Exeter: University of Exeter Press.

Cox, A.D., Puckering, C., Pound A., and Mills, M. (1987) 'The impact of maternal depression in young children', *Journal of Child Psychology and Psychiatry* 28(6): 917–28.

Cunningham, C.E., Bremner, R. and Boyle, M. (1995) 'Large Group Community-Based Parenting Programs for Families of Preschoolers at Risk for Disruptive Behaviour Disorders: Utilization, Cost Effectiveness, and Outcome', *Journal of Child Psychology and Psychiatry* 36(7): 1141–59.

Dennis, N. and Erdos, G. (1993) *Families without Fatherhood*. London: IEA Health & Welfare Unit.

Egeland, B. Jacovitz, D. and Sroufe, A. (1988) 'Breaking the Cycle of Abuse'. *Child Development* 59: 1080–8.

Elliott, B. J. and Richards, M. P. M. (1991) 'Children and Divorce: educational performance and behaviour before and after parental separation', *International Journal of Law and the Family* 5: 258–76.

Harlow, H.F. and Harlow, M.K. (1966) 'The effect of rearing conditions on behaviour' in J.F. Rosenblith and W. Allinsmith (eds), *The Causes of Behaviour*. Boston: Allyn and Bacon.

Haskey, J. (1990) 'The children of families broken by divorce', *Population Trends* 61: 34–42.

Hetherington, E.M. (1988) 'Parents, children and siblings: Six years after divorce' in R.A. Hinde and J. Stevenson-Hinde (eds), *Relationships within Families*. Oxford: Oxford Science Publications.

Hewitt, P. and Leach, P. (1993) *Social Justice, Children and Families*. London: Institute for Public Policy Research.

Kraemer, S. (1996) 'Parenting Yesterday, Today and Tomorrow' in *Families and Parenting: Conference Report*. London: Family Policy Studies Centre.

Kumar, V. (1993) *Poverty and Inequality in the UK – The Effects on Children*. London: National Children's Bureau.

Melhuish, E.C. and Moss, P. (1991) *Day Care for Young Children: International Perspectives*. London: Routledge.

Murray, C. (1990) *The Emerging British Underclass*. London: IEA.

Parr, M. (1996) 'Support for Couples in the Transition to Parenthood'. Unpublished PhD Thesis, Department of Psychology, University of East London.

Pound, A., Puckering, C., Mills, M., and Cox, A.D., (1988) 'The impact of maternal depression on young children', *British Journal of Psychotherapy* 4: 240–52.

Puckering, C., Rogers, J., Mills, M., Cox, A.D., and Mattson-Graff M. (1994) 'Process and evaluation of a group intervention for mothers with parenting difficulties', *Child Abuse Review* 3: 299–310.

Quinton, D. and Rutter, M. (1985) 'Parenting behaviour of mothers reared in care', in A.R. Nicol (ed.), *Longitudinal Studies in Child Psychology and Psychiatry*. Chichester: Wiley.

Richards, M.P.M. (1996) 'The Interests of Children at Divorce', in *Families and Justice*. Brussels: Editions Bruylant and Paris: Librairie Generale des Droits et Jurisprudence.

Richman, N., Stevenson, J., and Graham, P. (1982) *Pre-school to School: A Behavioural Study*. London: Academic Press.

Schweinhart, L.J., and Weikart, D.P. (1983) 'The effects of the Perry Preschool Programme on youths through age 15 – a summary' in *As the Twig is Bent ... Lasting Effects of Preschool Programmes*. London and New Jersey: Erlbaum.

Utting, D. (1995) *Family and Parenthood: Supporting Families, Preventing Breakdown*. York: Joseph Rowntree Foundation.

Van der Eyken, W. (1982) *Home-Start: a four year evaluation*. Leicester: Home-Start Consultancy.

Wallerstein, J. and Kelly, J. (1980) *Surviving the Break-up*. London: Pitman.

Whitfield, R., (ed.) (1994) *Life Foundations*. NES Arnold and National Family Trust.

Wolkind, S. (1985) 'The First Years: Pre-School children and their families in the inner city' in J.E.Stevenson (ed.), *Recent Research in Developmental Psychology*. Oxford: Pergamon.

PARENT SUPPORT RESOURCES

NEWPIN, Sutherland House, Sutherland Square, London, SE17 3EE.
Telephone 0171 703 6326.

Home-Start UK, 2 Salisbury Road, Leicester, LE1 7QR.
Telephone 0116 2339955.

The Parent Network, 44 Caversham Road, London, NW5 2DS.
Telephone 0171 485 8535.

Exploring Parenthood, 4 Ivory Place, 20a Treadgold St, London W11 4BP.
Telephone 0171 221 6681.

PIPPIN, Derwood, Toddsgreen, Stevenage, Herts. SG1 2JE.
Telephone 01438 748478.

Parenting Education and Support Forum,
NCB, 8 Wakley St, London EC1V 7QE.
Telephone 0171 843 6009.

5 Tough on the Causes of Crime? Social Bonding and Delinquency Prevention

David Utting

Why is it that some children as they grow up become criminals, while others manage to stay out of trouble and observe the rule of law? The question, in all its deceptive simplicity, addresses what are sometimes described as the 'roots of delinquency'. It has for long been of compelling interest to criminologists, yet it is only of late that it has assumed any prominence in public debates about youth crime and its prevention.

Previous inattention on the part of British policy makers is curious, not least because of the evidence that a high proportion of total crime is attributable to young people. More than four out of ten known offenders are aged under 21 and a quarter are juveniles, aged between 10 and 17. The ages at which individuals are most likely to be cautioned by the police or successfully prosecuted are 18 for men and 14 for women. Moreover, there is every reason to believe that a decline in official statistics for the number of young offenders during the past decade is an illusion created by changes in police and prosecution procedures (Farrington 1996). A recent Home Office survey of 14- to 25-year-olds found that nearly half the males and a third of females admitted having committed at least one crime in their lives. Similar proportions had illegally used drugs. Most young offenders had only broken the law a few times and in relatively minor ways, but it was also apparent that young people whose criminal activities started at an early age (14 and under) were more likely to have grown into recidivist offenders responsible for an altogether disproportionate volume of total crime. As additional cause for concern, the survey provided evidence that young men who would once have been expected to grow out of crime in their late teens are now extending their criminal careers into their mid-twenties (Graham and Bowling 1996).[1]

Crime statistics and surveys seldom lack critics. Disputes regularly arise about whether crime trends are more reliably portrayed by police records, showing that the number of annual offences has doubled since the start of the 1980s, or 'victim' surveys, suggesting a different rate of increase, but an overall level of crime that is three times higher (Mayhew et al. 1995, Barclay 1995). Whatever the 'true' level of offending may be, the most salient question remains why some individuals become criminals and others do not. For if the answers point us towards practical policies that make it less likely that children will turn to crime in the first place then the potential exists for a very powerful crime prevention tool indeed. To coin a familiar soundbite, a genuine opportunity will present itself to be tough on the causes of crime as well as crime itself.

Research and preventive practice have not yet reached the desired state of understanding in the UK. This chapter will argue, nevertheless, that enough pieces of the puzzle have been exposed to justify a much stronger commitment to initiatives whose aim is the prevention of criminality as well as crime. Attachment theorists are among those who must claim due credit for advancing understanding about child development to a point where this is possible. But a much wider construct of social bonding is nowadays brought into play as the theoretical base for interventions that are currently at the cutting edge of crime prevention. Thus, while John Bowlby's very early hypothesis (1946) linking physical separation from parents to later delinquency has been heavily qualified (Rutter 1981), the behavioural contrast that he went on to describe between securely attached infants and those whose emotional needs have been neglected is a cornerstone on which others have successfully built. As currently construed, attachment theory has given rise to an understanding that the quality of relationships between children and their parent(s) at successive stages in their development is one of the most important influences on anti-social behaviour and a future criminal career. It has, for example, been observed that boys who are insecurely attached as infants are more likely than other children to behave aggressively by the time they reach primary school (Renken et al. 1989). But it has also recently been found that the likelihood that young men will desist from crime in their early twenties relates to whether they continue living at home and how well they get on with their parents (Graham and Bowling 1996).

Longitudinal surveys, observing children from an early age

through to adolescence and young adulthood, are the most reliable method of identifying factors that distinguish the background circumstances, behaviour and attitudes of those who become offenders from those of non-offenders. Studies conducted during the past half-century in such varied locations as Britain, Finland, Sweden, the US and New Zealand have shown considerable consistency in suggesting what the most important factors might be (Utting et al. 1993, Farrington 1996). Those supported by the strongest statistical evidence can be grouped together, for convenience, under four main headings:

- Personal risk factors

- Family risk factors

- Educational risk factors

- Socio-economic and community risk factors

PERSONAL RISK FACTORS

The syndrome observed as a combination of hyperactivity, impulsivity and a short attention span in children as young as three has been linked to later offending, including violence. Low intelligence measured as early as ages three or four has also been correlated with later delinquency, but has, unsurprisingly, proved hard to separate from the influence of low achievement in school. Research does, nevertheless, suggest that low scores for non-verbal intelligence are particularly characteristic of recidivists who begin their criminal careers at an early age. It has also been argued that young people who are unable to manipulate the abstract concepts in many IQ tests may also find it harder to foresee the consequences of crime and/or to empathise with their victims (Farrington 1996).

The part that nature, as opposed to nurture, may play is inevitably called into question under this heading. Sir Michael Rutter (1996) is among those who have concluded that genetic factors may be especially important where anti-social behaviour is associated with pervasive hyperactivity in young children. Conversely, he suggests that genetic influences are least likely to be significant in teenage delinquency where there is no previous history of hyperactivity. But in framing these points, he argues persuasively against the notion of a 'gene for crime'. Genes may create an increased propensity for anti-social behaviour, but whether that leads to offending will depend on an individual's upbringing and other social circumstances. Even if certain genes are one day found to be associated with an increased risk of reckless criminal behaviour in some, then it is entirely possible that they may also be linked to restless curiosity and creativity in others. Meanwhile, since this chapter is concerned with the possibility of practical, preventive measures, its focus will be on social and environmental factors affecting children that *can* be altered rather than on genes and biology, that cannot. David Farrington (1996) makes a similar point with regard to the very obvious difference in offending rates between men and women. Changing males into females is not a practicable option, but there may be much to learn from examining differences in the ways the boys and girls are socialised by their families, schools and communities (for example, Phillips 1993).

FAMILY RISK FACTORS

The level of supervision provided by parents and whether children are subject to harsh or erratic discipline or neglect by their parents are recurrent themes in delinquency research. A longitudinal study of boys raised in south London during the 1950s and 1960s found that any of these adverse family circumstances roughly doubled the risk of later juvenile convictions (Farrington 1996). A follow-up study of ten-year-old boys in the West Midlands concluded that lax parental supervision was especially significant in relation to delinquency (Wilson 1987). And from observing family interactions in the home, researchers at the Oregon Social Learning Center have described a vicious, downward spiral in which poor parental monitoring and inconsistent praise and discipline draw children into increasingly coercive and anti-social behaviour (Patterson 1994). Conflict between parents and separation from a biological parent also carry an increased risk of later offending, although the evidence suggests it is the *quality* of parent–child relationships, rather than the quantity of parents (one parent or two) that is the underlying influence (Utting et al. 1993, Graham and Bowling 1996). Children whose parent(s) have criminal records are also at increased risk of criminal involvement: a factor that seems less related to genetic inheritance than whether children are raised in homes where the law and other 'norms' of social behaviour are respected.

One helpful way of understanding how family circumstances and parenting can influence children's behaviour and later delinquency are the four models used by Rolf Loeber and Magda

Stouthamer-Loeber (1986) to gauge the strength of statistical evidence from a range of different studies. In summary, these are:

- **Parental neglect**. Parents do not supervise their children adequately and fail to deal effectively with conduct problems. They only find out about their children's delinquent behaviour from neighbours or the police and even then may go on leaving them to 'do their own thing'. The children are not held in their parents' minds.

- **Family conflict**. A child's chronic disobedience is matched by the parent's inability to exert control in a consistent, non-violent way. The child is not contained, and learns that aggression equals attention and – in extreme cases – replaces its parents as the dominant force within the family.

- **Deviant behaviour and attitudes**. The 'norms' regarding acceptable and unacceptable behaviour within the family are not those of the outside world. Parents fail to label serious misbehaviour as 'wrong' and their own anti-social and criminal acts teach children a contempt for the law. When police or the neighbours report wrongdoing, the parents' reaction is to protect their child from the consequences.

- **Disruption**. Chronic conflict between parents and/or separation mean they become preoccupied, irritable, and turned-in on their own problems. Because they are under stress they do not supervise their children sufficiently or exert discipline in an effective way. Once the crisis is reduced or resolved – but only perhaps after a number of years – the children's conduct may improve to pre-stress levels.

Loeber and Stouthamer-Loeber found that all four of these models achieved a positive fit with research findings regarding conduct problems and delinquency. It is worth recording, however, that the first three were supported by statistically stronger evidence than the fourth.

EDUCATIONAL RISK FACTORS

Once children are of school age, it becomes apparent that their success in the classroom, or lack of it, is another factor closely related to the risks of later offending. Indeed, families and schools can be viewed as institutions that, together, have the power either to make or break a criminal career (Graham and Utting 1996). As already noted, the effects of low school attainment and low intelligence are difficult to separate, but there is no doubt that children who perform poorly in primary school are at greater risk of becoming delinquent. An even stronger indication of risk has been obtained from ratings by teachers of the way that children behave in class. For instance, in the study of south London boys, four out of ten boys who acquired juvenile convictions had been rated 'troublesome' in primary school by their teachers and classmates (West 1982). But although there are very obvious differences between the offending rates of pupils attending different schools, the question of how far this relates to the schools themselves is complicated. Bullying, truancy and exclusion from school are known risk factors for delinquency, but the dividing line between home and school influences is unavoidably blurred. The recent rapid growth in the number of exclusions is particularly worrying given a strong association that surveys have found with offending. It is, however, also necessary to remember that exclusion can be a consequence as well as a cause of juvenile crime (Graham and Bowling 1996). Even so, where it was once thought that schools were relatively unimportant compared with individual and family factors, it is now widely acknowledged that the quality of teaching and organisation in schools does have a considerable impact on pupils' progress, classroom behaviour and attendance (Rutter et al. 1979, Mortimore et al. 1988). Hence the growing interest among education policy makers in tackling bullying, truancy and classroom disruption through measures designed to improve the ethos and effectiveness of the 'whole school' (Smith and Sharp 1994, Learmonth 1995).

SOCIO-ECONOMIC AND COMMUNITY RISK FACTORS

Although standard classifications of parental occupational status have not proved particularly reliable as guides to the risks of children's delinquency, more specific measures of low family income and poor housing reveal significant connections (Wadsworth 1979, Farrington 1996). In the longitudinal study of working-class boys in south London, it was found that by the age of 18, those from poor families were twice as likely to have a criminal record as those whose family income had been assessed as adequate. One in five offenders with two or more convictions came from a low income background compared with one in eighteen among the rest of the cohort (West and Farrington 1973). Boys who became delinquent were significantly more likely to be living in rented rather than owner-occupied homes. Moving out of London also halved the chances that boys would become involved in crime, although it was not apparent how far this related to the change of environment as opposed to change of friends or fewer opportunities to commit crime, or to parental determination to provide a better environment for their children (Farrington 1996).

The combined strength of these 'social disadvantage' factors is considerable, but the mechanism through which they affect children's behaviour must largely be indirect. Part of their influence can, for example, be attributed to the stress that they place on parents, resulting in less effective supervision and more erratic supervision. In the previously mentioned West Midlands study, it not only became apparent that the most socially disadvantaged mothers tended to exert the least supervision, but also that those who lived in the inner city found it harder to monitor their children than those with equally low incomes living on outer estates (Wilson 1980, 1987). The Oregon Social Learning Center's researches, meanwhile, found that statistical associations between children's early delinquency and the socio-economic status of their parents were entirely mediated by differences in family management practices observed in the home (Larzelere and Patterson 1990).

PREVENTING DELINQUENCY

Classifications of the major childhood risk factors for delinquency are an attempt to superimpose order on what is, in reality, a complex situation. The risks are often interrelated and coincide in ways that make it difficult to disentangle their independent significance (Farrington 1996). As they cluster together in a young person's background, so their predictive strength can increase disproportionately (Rutter 1980). Yet the lines of causation are not easily traced. To take one example, it is established fact that adolescents who mix with delinquent friends are at high risk of delinquency themselves. But is the delinquent peer group a cause of juvenile offending, or is it simply a consequence of young criminals choosing each other's company? On a more pragmatic note, would fewer young people be drawn into crime, drugs and other anti-social activities if they were better equipped to resist the pressure from their peers? The last question raises the crucial issue of whether current knowledge about risk factors can, despite caveats about causation, be successfully applied in prevention initiatives. The answer, supplied by a growing fund of outcome studies from pioneering programmes, is positive. For example:

- A family support programme for mothers on low incomes in New York, which began during pregnancy, included home visits by professionals giving advice on health, nutrition, child development and parenting. The children received free day care of a high quality up to the age of five. Ten years later, only 6 per cent of the children who had been part of the project had juvenile court records compared with 22 per cent of a control group from comparable backgrounds (Lally et al. 1988).

- In the High/Scope Perry Preschool programme children from a disadvantaged black community in Michigan attended up to two years of high quality pre-school education, including home visiting and a curriculum designed to encourage reasoning ability and help children to learn from their play. Comparisons with a control group showed that as young adults the participants were better educated, better housed, more likely to be employed and less likely to be involved in drugs or crime. For every $1 invested in the original programme it was estimated that $7 had been saved for taxpayers in real terms by age 27 (Schweinhart et al. 1993).

- Aggressive and hyperactive boys in Montreal were trained, between the ages of 7 and 9, in anger management and other personal and social skills, while their parents pursued a course in family management skills on lines developed by the Oregon Social Learning Center. They reported fewer burglaries and other crimes, compared with a control group, at ages 12 and 15, although there was no significant difference in the proportion of juvenile court cases (Tremblay et al. 1994).[2]

These examples stand out because the evaluations monitored children's progress for long enough to demonstrate reduced levels of delinquency. There is, however, a longer list of programmes with an accredited track record in tackling particular risk factors, even if the outcomes in terms of offending are not known. In America, projects that help parents to communicate with their children, set clear expectations, reinforce positive behaviour and provide consistent sanctions have been used to bring the behaviour of conduct disordered children within a normal range. Social competence curricula that train children in basic interpersonal skills have produced durable improvements in behaviour and problem-solving skills in primary schools. Programmes designed to ease children's transition to large middle or secondary schools have improved academic performance and reduced truancy (Howell et al. 1995). Children have been taught to resist peer influences to smoke, drink alcohol or use cannabis and there is evidence that the training can be delivered more effectively by older peers than by teachers (Farrington 1996). A considerable range of comparable work can be found in the UK, including several adaptations of promising American approaches. There have been few rigorous evaluations of relevant work in Britain, although the case for high quality nursery education (Sylva 1994) and anti-bullying initiatives (Smith and Sharp 1994) are widely understood and accepted. At present, it is rare for agencies delivering family support and other relevant services (for example NEWPIN: see Pound, this volume) to recognise delinquency prevention as an aspect of their work. Even so, many desirable ingredients for a properly co-ordinated youth crime prevention initiative can already be found on the ground (Utting et al. 1993).

The search for an appropriate blueprint returns us to the US, and the strategy devised by David Hawkins and Richard Catalano, two professors at the University of Washington, for planning local programmes and putting them into practice. Known as 'Communities that Care', it gives full weight to the understanding that the multiple problems associated with delinquency can only be addressed through multiple solutions. It recognises that prevention is a matter of enhancing the protective factors in a child's background as well as countering the risks, and it acknowledges that different approaches are going to be appropriate at different stages in a child's development. In terms of practice, it also underlines the pivotal importance of multi-disciplinary working and co-operation between agencies in the field. To achieve this objective, the programme not only insists that the support of 'key leaders' in a community be secured as a prerequisite, but also that they and members of the management board that runs the local programme should undergo training in the principles and methods to be applied. That foundation prepares them to carry out an in-depth assessment of risk factors in their locality and a survey of existing resources. The information collected is then used to determine local priorities and, working from a menu of tried and tested approaches, to apply appropriate remedies (Hawkins and Catalano 1992).

'Communities that Care' achieves the virtuous combination of a rigorous process with a high degree of adaptability to local circumstances. That helps explain why it has been adopted by the federal government as part of its 'comprehensive' strategy for serious, violent and chronic juvenile offenders (Office of Juvenile Justice and Delinquency Prevention 1995). It is also, at the time of writing, being studied by the Joseph Rowntree Foundation for a possible pilot application in Britain (Farrington 1996). The fact that the risk factors on which it focuses apply to drug misuse, school failure and teenage pregnancy as well as property crime and violence clearly enhance its appeal for policy makers.

But for those in search of a theoretical base, Hawkins and Catalano also propose 'The Social Development Strategy', a model in which the quality of attachments formed by children and adolescents is viewed as the key to healthy social behaviour. Babies who have strong, warm, supportive relationships with their mothers are off to an undeniably good start. But the strategy argues that children will also benefit, as they grow, from bonds with other family members, significant adults, teachers and friends who are able to encourage their competence and set clear expectations for their behaviour. Such attachments mean young people are less likely to engage in anti-social behaviour because they are reluctant to threaten the bond by incurring disapproval. They also feel valued as individuals (see Murray, this volume). The bond may, indeed, allow the trusted parent or adult to be psychologically present as an internal guardian when the temptation to commit crime appears (Hirschi 1969). However, 'The Social Development Strategy' extends this concept by seeking to include social institutions, notably schools, and the wider communities in which young people are raised. It anticipates that children who are attached and committed to their schools and neighbourhoods will be more likely to play by the rules. It follows, however, that those institutions have a duty to examine their own prevailing values and 'norms'. A school where drug dealing or bullying is rife, for example, will be part of the problem, not the solution.

To encourage bonding, whether within families, schools or communities, it is argued that children and young people must have opportunities to participate. To do that they must also be invested with the skills that make it possible to contribute. As a third basic requirement it is suggested that they must receive the praise and recognition needed to reinforce their sense of belonging and self-worth (Hawkins and Catalano 1992).

This is a positive note on which to conclude, having dwelt at some length on the negative associations between inadequate child-rearing, education and delinquency. How interesting, though, that having begun with one political soundbite, this chapter should end in close proximity to another: the impressive social benefits that flow when children grow up knowing that they 'belong'. In other words, when they feel that they are 'stakeholders' in their families, their communities and in society as a whole.

NOTES

1. The Home Office statistics relate to England and Wales in 1994 and refer to burglary, theft and other 'indictable offences' that can be heard by a Crown Court jury.
2. The authors suggest that 'booster' training sessions between ages 12 and 15 would have yielded better results.

REFERENCES

Barclay, G.C. with Tavares, C. and Prout, A. (1995) *Digest 3: Information on the Criminal Justice System in England and Wales.* London: Home Office Research and Statistics Department.

Bowlby, J. (1946) *Forty-four Juvenile Thieves: their characters and home life.* London: Baillière Tindall and Cox.

Farrington, D.P. (1996) *Understanding and Preventing Youth Crime.* York: Joseph Rowntree Foundation/York Publishing Services.

Graham, J. and Bowling, B. (1996) *Young People and Crime.* London: Home Office Research Study 145.

Graham, J. and Utting, D. (1996) 'Families, Schools and Criminality Prevention' in T. Bennett (ed.) *Preventing Crime and Disorder: Targeting Strategies and Responsibilities.* University of Cambridge Institute of Criminology, Cambridge Cropwood Series.

Hawkins, J.D. and Catalano, R.F. (1992) *Communities that Care. Action for Drug Abuse Prevention.* San Francisco, CA: Jossey Bass.

Hirschi, T. (1969) *Causes of Delinquency.* Berkeley: University of California Press.

Howell, J.C., Krisberg, B., Hawkins, J.D. and Wilson, J.J. (1995) *A Sourcebook. Serious, Violent and Chronic Juvenile Offenders.* London: Sage.

Lally, J.R., Mangione, P.L. and Honig, A.S. (1988) 'The Syracuse University Family Development Research Project: Long-range impact of an early intervention with low-income children and their families' in D.R. Powell (ed.), *Annual Advances in Applied Developmental Psychology: Vol. 3. Parent Education as Early Childhood Intervention: Emerging directions in theory, research and practice.* New Jersey: Ablex, Norwood, pp.79-104.

Larzelere, R.E. and Patterson, G.R. (1990) 'Parental Management: mediator of the effect of socioeconomic status on early delinquency', *Criminology* 28(2): 301–24.

Learmonth, J. (1995) *More Willingly to School? An Independent Evaluation of the Truancy and Disaffected Pupils GEST Programme*. London: Department for Education and Employment.

Loeber, R. and Stouthamer-Loeber, M. (1986) 'Family Factors as Correlates and Predictors of Juvenile Conduct Problems and Delinquency' in M. Tonry and N. Morris (eds), *Crime and Justice – an annual review of research*. Vol 7. Chicago: University of Chicago Press.

Mayhew, P., Mirlees-Black, C. and Aye Maung, N. (1995) *Trends in Crime: Findings from the 1994 British Crime Survey*. London: Home Office (Research Findings 14).

Mortimore, P., Sammons, P., Stoll, L., Lewis, D. and Ecob, R. (1988) *School Matters. The Junior Years*. London: Open Books.

Office of Juvenile Justice and Delinquency Prevention (1995) *Guide for Implementing the Comprehensive Strategy for Serious, Violent and Chronic Juvenile Offenders*. Washington DC: Office of Juvenile Justice and Delinquency Prevention.

Patterson, G.R. (1994) 'Some Alternatives to Seven Myths about Treating Families of Antisocial Children' in C. Henricson (ed.), *Crime and the Family*. (Conference Report. Proceedings of an international conference held in London, 3 February 1994.) London: Family Policy Studies Centre.

Phillips, A. (1993) *The Trouble with Boys*. London: Pandora.

Renken, B., Egeland, B., Marvinney, D., Manglesdorf, S. and Sroufe, L.A. (1989) 'Early Childhood Antecedents of Aggression and Passive-Withdrawal in Early Elementary School', *Journal of Personality* 57(2): 257–81.

Rutter, M. (1980) *Changing Youth in a Changing Society*. Cambridge, MA: Harvard University Press.

Rutter, M. (1981) *Maternal Deprivation Reassessed*. London: Penguin.

Rutter, M. (1996) 'Concluding Remarks' in G.R. Bock and J.A. Goode (eds), *Genetics of Criminal and Antisocial Behaviour: Ciba Foundation Symposium 194*. Chichester: Wiley.

Rutter, M., Maughan, B., Mortimore, P., and Ouston, J. (1979) *Fifteen Thousand Hours*. London: Open Books.

Schweinhart, L.J., Barnes, H.V. and Weikart, D.P. (1993) *Significant Benefits: The High/Scope Perry Preschool Study Through Age 27*. Ypsilanti, MI: High/Scope Educational Research Foundation.

Smith, P.K. and Sharp, S. (1994) *School Bullying. Insights and Perspectives*. London: Routledge.

Sylva, K. (1994) 'The Impact of Early Learning on Children's Later Development' in Sir C. Ball (ed.), *Start Right: The Importance of Early Learning*. London: Royal Society for the Encouragement of Arts, Manufactures and Commerce (RSA).

Tremblay, R.E., Kurtz, L., Mèsse, L.C., Vitaro, F. and Pihl, R.O. (1994) *A Bimodal Preventive Intervention for Disruptive Kindergarten Boys: its impact through mid-adolescence.* Research Unit on Children's Psycho-Social Maladjustment, University of Montreal.

Utting, D., Bright, J. and Henricson, C. (1993) *Crime and the Family: improving child-rearing and preventing delinquency.* London: Family Policy Studies Centre.

Wadsworth, M. (1979) *Roots of Delinquency.* London: Martin Robertson.

West, D.J. (1982) *Delinquency: Its Roots, Careers and Prospects.* London: Heinemann.

West, D.J. and Farrington, D.P. (1973) *Who Becomes Delinquent?* London: Heinemann.

Wilson, H. (1980) 'Parental Supervision: a neglected aspect of delinquency', *British Journal of Criminology* 20(3): 203–35.

Wilson, H. (1987) 'Parental Supervision Re-examined', *British Journal of Criminology* 27(3): 275–301.

6 Friendly Society

Ray Pahl

Today traditional morality is shaken and no other has been brought forward to replace it. The old duties have lost their power without our being able to see clearly and with assurance where our new duties lie. Different minds hold opposed ideas and we are passing through a period of crisis. It is not then surprising that we do not feel the pressure of moral rules as those felt in the past. They cannot appear to us in their old majesty since they are practically non-existent. (Durkheim 1906)

It is currently fashionable to bemoan the loss of social glue. Amitai Etzioni, author of the widely-noticed book *The Spirit of Community* (1993) sees 'British society slipping in an American direction in terms of its moral infrastructure' (Etzioni 1995). Those who wish to counter this putative tendency by extolling family values have to face the awkwardness of the statistics on divorce, the sexual abuse of children and marital violence. The embarrassment of a divorce-prone Royal family, and the amusement provided by priapic Members of Parliament whose private lives become public are among the many circumstances that prevent the widespread acceptance of the exhortations of those who wish to promote the virtues of the so-called conventional family. Such a family is generally perceived as having a caring and supportive mother figure, and an effective breadwinning and authority providing father. This nice balance of affective and instrumental values was seen by mid-century American sociologists, such as Talcott Parsons, as being appropriately functional for the needs of a modern industrial society which included the creation and socialisation of the next generation of docile and productive workers. Now, 40 years on, a recent cartoon in the *New Yorker* shows two 'middle Americans' sitting morosely at a bar, and one says to the other: 'So how's the family? Still disintegrating?'

Before rushing too readily to blame the self-interest and greed of the more extreme Thatcherite philosophy of the 1980s as the cause of the current crisis and to slide into another moral panic, it is as well to recall that bemoaning the lack of social cohesion of contemporary times in comparison with some putative golden age a couple of generations before, has a history of at least 2000 years. In ancient Rome, Martial complained of the transience or superficiality of certain urban relationships: 'In all the city there is no man so near and yet so far from me', he wrote, referring to his next-door neighbour. Horace deplored the sources of income of the very rich: 'Some men derive their income from Government contracts [and other] people's capital keeps on growing, kept growing by interest – fostered by time, just like a tree.' Many of these jaded Roman satirists believed that the good life could be found in the country (Lowenstein 1965, Williams 1973).

New Labour is searching for the Big Idea, and there is a danger that in an attempt to sail between the Scylla of rampant individualism and the Charybdis of patriarchal and authoritarian familism, some new moral entrepreneurs may be beguiled by the false charms of communitarianism. According to Etzioni: 'Communities provide psychological and pragmatic support for those who stand up to the State. They are required for individual sanity, sustenance and political backing' (Etzioni 1995, p. 24). I find it very difficult to find any empirical substance to justify such a claim.

So, what is community? Superficially most people associate it with a place, a spirit that has been lost or the camaraderie of common interests – the angling community, the business community or the community of scholars. Consider first the idea of community as a place (and see Nicholson, this volume, for a contrary view). Those with nostalgic and romantic notions of a mythical past may imagine some sort of village community. Typically such places were characterised by rigid status hierarchies, where everyone knew his or her place and the power of the squire was potentially enormous. In more seemingly egalitarian contexts based on small-holdings or peasant-type farming, countless anthropological and sociological studies have shown in detail how these social worlds were bound by intense rivalries and conflicts. People are highly sensitive about their social ranking in these societies: caution and cunning are needed if families are to maintain their position and the older generation are to die secure in the knowledge they have maintained or enhanced their status and respectability – if not their wealth. Even today, the unsolved murders in remote French hamlets and in tight-knit urban villages remind us of the intensity of community involvement and the impossibility of outsiders penetrating it.

Few would claim that that kind of 'anthropological' community
is what they had in mind. They might prefer a more sociological
nostalgia, based on 'the working class community' of pub, pigeon
fancying and brass bands. These were occupational communities,
based on the work of men as miners, steelworkers or shipbuilders.
They were rigidly segregated by gender and many of the sociological
studies of the 1950s are now fiercely criticised for their almost
complete neglect of women and any account of their subordinate
position in the home, in the labour market and in the largely
male-dominated world of formal and informal voluntary organisations. These were communities of oppression, and the bonds of
solidarity were the bonds of resistance. Oppression was externally
induced by the technical and managerial constraints of the industry
and internally induced by a conformist male ideology which was
hard for most women and for those few men with the aspirations
and ability to escape (Wight 1993).

These and other types of localised communities of oppression
and resistance have mostly disappeared, although they are being
recreated in declining small market towns and remote rural areas.
With little local employment, declining public transport and with
those services and facilities that remain struggling to survive, common deprivation is returning as a spur to action. In such places
informal systems of co-operative self-help such as LETS (Local
Exchange Trading Scheme) are flourishing. Such initiatives are
frequently initiated by lone parents who have the time, capacity
and need for mutual support. Some of these organised communities
of resistance may not be place-based – the fight against the poll tax
being the obvious example.

There is also, of course, the community of association of comfortable England. Here the affluent arrange local festivals of the arts,
invite speakers to political and other groups, tidy up and cultivate
their local heritage, and keep everything neat and spick and span.
Such activities tend to exclude the majority of the population on
what used to be called the council estates. This is the context for
community as a hobby or leisure interest. For most of such people in
hobby communities, their real involvement is with their families and
kin, their work and their friends, wherever they are.

I have mentioned what may be called communities of control,
communities of common deprivation and hobby communities, but
this is not an exclusive list; it simply indicates something of the
pitfalls associated with the idea of place-based community. The
communitarians would be unlikely to champion these brands of
community: they see themselves in Etzioni's terms as 'an environ-

mental movement dedicated to the betterment of our moral, social and political environment' (Etzioni 1993). But where is this movement going to operate? The answer seems to be to create new communities, that is, non-geographic communities that Etzioni claims 'fulfil many of the social and moral functions of traditional communities'. Notice that Etzioni takes as given that the traditional communities did serve these functions – a highly contentious notion – but he also asserts as given that work-based and professional communities inevitably produce positive and socially beneficial results. A sociological case has to be made, not simply asserted. For many people, the workplace has become intensely more competitive in recent years. Employers' strategies to discipline and control workers have been very effective: downsizing, de-layering, contracting out, hiring on short-term contracts and similar measures create an uneasy and anxious workforce. The 'feel good factor' remains elusive. Those who have become self-employed find little opportunity to have matey solidarity with colleagues. Mostly, as they are well aware, they are on their own. It is tough; it is sometimes lonely, but they have little choice. They long for some respite and envy those with secure pensions to look forward to.

In a less-stressed age it was, indeed, possible that social workers, teachers, advertising executives and publishers met each other at conferences and developed a degree of camaraderie that extended over some years. Now, they either cannot afford to go to conferences or they spend all their time angrily attacking each other or the less than humane society that is cutting their jobs and reducing their security. Etzioni would doubtless prefer the situation to be otherwise, so that these professional groupings could 'have the moral infrastructure we consider essential for a civil and humane society'. However, it is surely naive to imagine that workplace stress and anxiety results simply from turning our back on 'community'.

Curiously, the well established sociological knowledge about what clearly does create a sense of communal solidarity seems to have been overlooked by Etzioni, although the ideas have been around for a long time. The neatest account was provided by Coleman in his pamphlet on *Community Conflict*, published almost 40 years ago. Although very brief, it says more about place-based community than most of what has come after it. The trouble is, that like many of the best sociological insights, once stated, people will say they have known them all along. Community life in the past was imposed on people, being largely based on involuntary relationships. Now, people choose their associates and, perhaps more importantly, choose with whom not to associate.

Coleman rightly predicted, that 'the prospect for the future is toward an increase in the proportion of externally caused community controversies' (Coleman 1957). This is because the local community is very rarely the locus of important social decisions, so community spirit based on conflict is more and more related to national affairs and national decisions. If anyone wants to create community spirit in comfortable, Tory-voting England, then threaten to build a motorway or a high-speed rail link close by. But whether that helps in the creation of a more humane society is highly debatable. The problem with conflict-induced community spirit is that if the community loses – as is increasingly likely – the consequent apathy is that much deeper. If the action leads to success, then the immediate reason for the solidarity collapses and the tendency is for local factions to make local social and political capital out of the part they played in the struggle. This can produce new divisions and much bitterness. It is a rare locale that does not reflect the increasing polarisation and inequality of the past 17 years. Sometimes the emergence of local issue politics highlights divisions and tensions that were concealed or dormant. Not only does the activation of 'community spirit' frequently open up a can of worms, it can also set community against community. In the messy world of issue politics, those who shout loudest, who are the most cunning or the luckiest, win. The rest are disgruntled if resources go elsewhere. There is little discussion of this divisive nature of community life among the communitarians, despite the wealth of anthropological and sociological studies undertaken in the past 50 years that have described it (Bell and Newby 1971, Abrams and McCulloch 1976).

So, if sociologists have exposed the myths and fallacies of the idea of the community, why does a dead idea refuse to lie down? Why are political leaders in America and Europe so keen to adopt communitarian rhetoric without thinking through more carefully the implications of what they assert? Part of the answer is that people are desperately keen to find a middle way between the public and the private. Some of the practical suggestions of the movement, divorced from the rhetoric, sound like good sense to specific groups of the population. Since the movement spatters out various suggestions, it is easy for people to take on board those they would like to believe in and overlook those aspects which might make them feel uneasy if they subjected them to closer scrutiny. The idea that people with rights also have responsibilities carries resonance on left and right: if communitarians are the people who take this notion most seriously, then many are perhaps more prepared to give them the benefit of the doubt, rather than appear to be supporting unhealthy dependencies. Communitarians do not understand the difference between dependency and attachment.

If the communitarian philosophy fails to be sociologically convincing, what is to be put in its place? My own inclination is to start with what is, rather than what ought to be. If the desire is to celebrate and to support those who engage in communal and collective endeavours, then we should see who actually does this, rather than those who ought to do it. In practice, those who are most in need of supportive and communal activity are lone parents. Those in the very category pilloried by communitarians are setting up support groups for themselves, and various other cooperative activities for others in the same place (see Pound, this volume). As Carol Stack has shown in *All our Kin* (1974), lone, black mothers and a deprived urban environment in the US can create valuable and essential solidarities. The same can be shown for many deprived and oppressed minorities.

Such minorities may express their solidarity in opposition to the majority and, as long as they remain conscious of their excluded status, their sense of identity will remain. New forms of exclusion create new potentials for identity. These new solidarities of the oppressed are likely to be in inner-city areas – often the very areas that cause communitarians the most dismay.

Those who are most praised by the new moral entrepreneurs, the doting, caring parents taking their child care responsibilities seriously by devoting considerable time to their children, have little time for much else. Both partners are likely to be in employment – if only on a part-time basis for the woman. They probably have to spend much of their week in tiring travel, commuting to work, collecting children, visiting elderly relatives, driving to out-of-town shopping centres or taking their children swimming or ice-skating. At evenings or weekends they are more likely to be exhausted, rather than active citizens. The harassed, time-challenged middle-class parents are obliged to be highly selective on how they choose their friends and associates.

Hence, those who do have the time, energy and inclination to engage in public-spirited work are more likely to be single. The lone parents are more likely to be younger; however, the widows, widowers, divorcees and pensioners will be older. Some vigorous women in their sixties and seventies can make fine community activists, if not over-committed as grandmothers.

One of the massive fallacies of the current debate is the assumption that because of the decline of 'the traditional community' social and geographical mobility has made social atoms of us all. If the family is seen as the only putative source of social cohesion and control, then higher rates of divorce and the rapid growth of lone-parent families is seen as a dangerous dilution of social glue. One answer, therefore, is to seek to strengthen the male breadwinner role for the sake of his dependants (Dennis and Erdos 1993). However, all the survey material on the younger generation suggests that there can be no return to the patriarchal working-class family (Wilkinson 1994).

The reason most of us are not mere social atoms fighting our corner in competitive markets is that we have our friends, our mates, our support groups. Girlfriends and boyfriends come and go; children grow up and find their own identities elsewhere, partners come and partners go, but friends provide the continuity to our identities. Such is the strength of weak ties. Sometimes, it is true, siblings or cousins can also be friends, but, more often, best friends comfort in times of bereavement or the break-up of a relationship. We need our friends and our friends need us. The idea that fraternity is limited to male-bonded trade unionists is a sexist anachronism.

'Friendship is an Expression of Community'
(Aristotle 1955)

Political scientists and activists have made much of liberty and equality over the past 200 years. Fraternity has been much neglected since Aristotle's classic discussion of friendship in Books Eight and Nine of his *Ethics*. The Ancient Greeks likened sexual attraction and desire as something akin to hunger or thirst, and not, therefore, open to much philosophical moralising. Friendship, on the other hand, Aristotle considered to be fundamental to human happiness and well-being. 'No one would choose a friendless existence on condition of having all the other good things in the world' (1955). Admittedly, the roots of fraternity owe more to the Greek word for a clansman than to simple friendship, but certainly, taken in the spirit of its revolutionary cry, fraternity is about the quality of relationships between people. To fraternise is to come into friendly association with others. A lifelong attachment may be the result.

Friends are those most likely to form 'pure relationships', which Anthony Giddens claims are an essential element in the contemporary restructuring of intimacy (Giddens 1992, p. 58). Aristotle argued that friendship inevitably carries with it moral connotations.

It is only between those who are good, and resemble one another in their goodness, that friendship is perfect. Such friends are both good in themselves, and, so far as they are good, desire the good of one another.

But it is those who desire the good of their friends for their friends' sake who are most completely friends, since each loves the other for what the other is in himself, and not for something he has about him which he need not have. Accordingly the friendship of such men lasts as long as they keep their goodness – and goodness is a lasting quality. And when two such men are friends, each is good not only absolutely but in relation to the other, the good being both good in themselves and profitable to one another. (Aristotle 1955, p. 233)

With true friends we do not immediately calculate what we have to pay back for being comforted or for acting as an unpaid therapist during one of life's crises. A man may have a former spouse or lover as his best friend: she knows him in some ways better than he does himself, and can be relied on to give advice that is honest and not designed defensively to put herself in a good light. Women, perhaps, make better friends and maintain contact with their old work colleagues, with other mothers who were contemporaries, or with near neighbours when they were tied at home with young children. Sociologists have shown how the idea of friendship has suffused kinship, so that we are more likely to choose those relatives to whom we wish to remain close (Finch and Mason 1993).

Friends help each other, support each other and maintain links over long periods of a person's life. They help people to find jobs, they provide somewhere to stay in an emergency and, above all, they provide social support and affirmation of identity in a world that can leave people bereft of a partner, job and family in a short space of time.

One of the few sociologists to have conducted empirical research on friendship has undermined the conventional wisdom that friendship is class-linked, with the working class being more kin-oriented than the middle class. These are contentious labels, but it now seems that friends are more important than relatives or neighbours in providing help with shopping, house maintenance, keeping an eye on the house and similar practical work on a day-to-day basis. Friends are also of crucial importance as confidantes (Willmott 1987). In some research on family and kinship which I carried out on the Isle of Sheppey some years ago, one of my respondents remarked that if she ever had problems in relation to her husband her pride would make her want to keep this from her family. The family in this case is taken to mean the 70 or 80 people living in the area to whom she is related, largely through her siblings (Wilson and Pahl 1988).

Willmott has argued that the 'middle class' styles of friendship are now moving down to the 'working class', that this diffusion is now a main element in sustaining social order. If this is so, then an understanding of people's friendly relationships becomes of central political importance.

Politicians have probably neglected to consider friendship seriously because they cannot see clearly how to fit friends into an institutional context. Sociologists have tended to abstract from relationships and have studied types of social networks and the forms and norms of reciprocity. Such language does not resonate with politicians who may be prepared to learn economists' jargon but have not been persuaded to do the same for anthropology or sociology. However, if politicians recognised the social importance of friendship it would do much to avoid the alienating consequences of much contemporary political rhetoric.

Fearful of overtones of Thatcherite individualism based on competition and greed, Tony Blair wants to substitute social-ism for a selfish and uncaring individualism. In doing this, he is likely to make a very serious blunder by misunderstanding how people are actually behaving in their everyday lives. They are being social as individuals. Their individuality is vitally important to them. The distinction between individualism and individuality is crucial, and is a significant missing element of much discussion in contemporary politics. By focusing on community and communitarianism as alternatives to the discarded individualist ideology of the 1980s, the significance of individuality may be overlooked. People may then fear that their own individuality is less likely to be well nourished and developed under New Labour.

Individuality implies diversity, tolerance, spontaneity and creativity. We flourish with our friends. Instead of a rather pious couple-ism and familism, New Labour could lead and reflect the mood of the 1990s. People are not social atoms, anonymously colliding in a harsh and competitive environment. They are generally warm and friendly people trying to come to terms with themselves and their relationships. They need support, not censure. There is no need to fall for a phoney communitarianism: what is needed is an acceptance that most people are struggling on as best they can with the help of their friends.

The mood of the late 1990s is surely that people are engaged in a struggle to find an identity for themselves which is sensitive to them as the individuals they see themselves to be. They reject the notion that they should subordinate themselves to collective categories. As we know from our own *personal* experience, our attachment to collectives is mediated by our personal experience. It is an obvious, yet crucial, insight that people read collectivities through their experience as individuals. Simply because people may use collective forms to assert their identities it would be a great mistake to assume that this implies uniformities of identity. By being wary of the selfish self of the 1980s, we are in danger of ignoring the *self-conscious* self of the 1990s.

Bringing fraternity on to the political agenda might lead to greater social cohesion but it would surely involve a massive relearning exercise for those wedded to the 'disciplines' of markets, boot camps and similar. Attachment theory is precisely relevant here. If children are anxiously and insecurely attached to their parents, this will have consequences for their capacities to make true friendships, in the Aristotelian sense, when they are adults.

But the conditions of emotional security can be undermined by social insecurity. To the extent that an individual's sense of self is based on the social and economic circumstances of her significant carers during childhood, then present insecurities – journalistically described as the lack of the 'feel good factor' – will have direct consequences for the fraternity factor of the next generation. These are not simply private matters. Building in trust and security to the workplace, making people trust that their lifetime contributions will pay for their security in old age, that promises made by water suppliers that water will be supplied or those who manage the rail service that the trains they ride on are safe and will keep their timetables, and so much else, all require political regulation, which helps to provide the social infrastructure for emotional security.

It may be objected that the world has always been risky and insecure: it is just that more people are now more conscious of the risks of which they were previously unaware and that insecurity has spread to those who have been cocooned by professional protectionist strategies of social closure. The attack on privileged enclaves gets a shrill response in the liberal press, but, some may claim, it is time that such people were kept on their toes. A little anxiety and stress, it is said, helps to keep the adrenalin flowing nicely.

Such arguments are difficult to handle. Complaints about the lack of cohesion are, as we have seen, part of the human condition. So also is a degree of anxiety (Pahl 1995, Chapter 8). The citizens of Athens may have had high-quality relationships, but what about the slaves? Also, what of Philip Slater's discussion about how the low status of women and the male terror of women were mutually reinforcing in Hellenic society. Greek fathers were largely absent, so that the child's world before the age of six or seven was almost entirely female dominated. Homosexuality was widely and acceptably practised (Slater 1968). There are clearly many different contexts in which secure attachments can be made. Research on attachment theory in different social contexts by sociologists has yet to be done. Also more needs to be known about gender differences in patterns of friendship and the significance of sexuality in attachment theory. One fruitful approach was pioneered by Bott 40 years ago. She showed how patterns of social relationships were directly related to the nature of the conjugal role. Thus, partners with segregated conjugal role relationships were more likely to have separate networks of same gender friends (Bott 1957). However, as more joint partner role relationships have spread down the social scale (and, indeed, into the upper class too), so partners are more likely to have joint friends. This may lead to social tension if the partners split up. Some evidence for such difficulties is provided by the British Household Panel Study. Amongst married men, 68 per cent got in touch with a close friend (not a spouse or partner) by writing, visiting or telephoning during the previous week. However, amongst the divorced men the proportion increased to 79 per cent. The comparable figure for women is 80 per cent and 89 per cent, implying that women are more likely to have and to draw upon close friends than are men.[1]

When parents and lovers very often involve us in so much ambivalence and dependency, it is understandable that in a more reflexive or self-conscious age we should turn to friends to affirm and reaffirm our identities. Friends are the guarantors of our identity and whilst they may be, as it were, extensions of family relations in psychoanalytic terms – such as motherly love or fatherly protection – they can be more than that. True, deep friends – what the Russians call *droog* as opposed to acquaintance or *tovarish* – are rare, and people are unlikely to have more than two or three in a lifetime. Such friends exchange self-knowledge and confirm each other's existence. In his interesting account of the importance of friendship in the former Soviet Union, Shlapentokh claims that friendship formed the basis for covert opposition to the state. Many would see a close friend (that is a *droog*) every day and such relationships are qualitatively different from what we in the West would call friendly relations. In one survey 16 per cent of respondents met their friends each day, 10 per cent two or three times a week and a further 22 per cent at least weekly (Kogan 1981 cited in Shlapentokh 1989, p. 171). The essence of these deep, close friendships is the rejection of the idea of intervention or control by any third party.

> Friendship is an obstacle to the absolute dominance of the state over the individual. Moreover, friendship frequently constitutes the basis for the creation of underground organizations and anti-governmental activities. (Shlapentokh 1989, p. 172)

Friends served as a crucial source of trustworthy information, as a source of scarce but necessary goods and as a way of getting access to jobs, better education and better health services. Parents and children sometimes betrayed each other to the Party: friends would never do so. Since deep trust in these select friends is essential, these close friends would have been known since childhood or at least since their college days. By linking these very close friends with other friends, a very efficient social network could be mobilised. It is said that only three links were needed to reach the General Secretary of the Communist Party or the President.[2] Under the old regime people recognised that the bonds of friendship can easily be mobilised to assist a common friend.

Unfortunately, the coming of the market has undermined the importance of friendship since, in a sense, the mafia has taken over. Friendship is, of course, still important but money is now, perhaps, more so. The greater the degree of administrative discretion in a society, the greater the potential for active friendship. As access to resources and facilities becomes more monetised, so a basis for friendship is undermined. Maybe contemporary Russians have substituted serial sexual relationships for the enduring friendships of the old order. One by-product of a totalitarian society is the increased political saliency of intense friendships. More open market societies may encourage more superficial relationships.

Certainly, some people can develop such close friendships with parents, siblings, spouse or partner. I suspect that seeking such closeness is the cause of much divorce. It is because more people are seeking quality relationships that they become dissatisfied with less. Here is a modern dilemma: in the search for a secure adult bond, unhappily married parents who divorce in the hope of finding a better-quality relationship may thus create anxiety and insecurity in their children, making it more difficult for them to develop mature, high-quality relationships when they, in turn, become adults. Divorce and separation severely test the strength and quality of children's attachments to their parents.

Politicians may, understandably, wish to keep away from such complexities. Unhappily for them, they cannot. The social relationships of the contemporary world are now more complex and cannot be encompassed by the clichés and stereotypes once found on the back of cornflake packets. If security and trust have been undermined in the name of efficient downsizing or whatever, the long-term consequences for society could be considerable. There is a deep-seated urge for individuality in our society, and the individuality is created, enhanced and strengthened in a fundamental way by and through our friends.[3] A good society is a friendly society. We still have a long way to go to discover how best to strengthen that. Phoney ideas about community and communitarianism get in the way of such a discovery but, it seems to me, many of the contributors to this book are offering some hopeful ways forward.

NOTES

1. Data from the BHPS relates to Wave 4, 1994. Further work is being done by the author on these data at the ESRC Centre on Micro-Social Change at the University of Essex.
2. In over 25 years of visiting the former Soviet Union I have been consistently assured that this is true. Maybe, as my contacts were all in the intelligentsia, it would be unwise to generalise.
3. Little has claimed, following Kohut, that friendship flourishes 'when over-arching identities are fragmented, as in times of rapid cultural exchange, or in turning points in individual lives' (Little 1989, p. 149).

REFERENCES

Abrams, P. and McCulloch, A. (1976) *Communes, Sociology and Society*. Cambridge: Cambridge University Press.

Aristotle (1955) *The Ethics of Aristotle*, trans. by J.A.K. Thomson. Harmondsworth: Penguin Books.

Bell, C. and Newby, H. (1971) *Community Studies*. London: Allen and Unwin.

Bott, E. (1957) *Family and Social Network*. London: Tavistock.

Coleman, J. (1957) *Community Conflict*. New York: The Free Press.

Dennis, N. and Erdos, G. (1993) (Second edn) *Families without Fatherhood*. London: Institute of Economic Affairs.

Durkheim, E. (1906) *Sociology and Philosophy*, trans. by D.F. Pocock. New York: The Free Press.

Etzioni, A. (1993) *The Spirit of Community*. New York, Crown Publishers.

Etzioni, A. (1995) 'Common Values', *New Statesman and Society*, 12 May, pp. 24–5.

Finch, J. and Mason, J. (1993) *Negotiating Family Responsibilities*. London: Routledge.

Giddens, A. (1992) *The Transformation of Intimacy*. Cambridge and Oxford: Polity Press.

Little, G. (1989) 'Freud, Friendship and Politics' in (eds), R. Porter and S. Tomaselli *The Dialectics of Friendship*. London: Routledge.

Lowenstein, S.F. (1965) 'Urban Images of Roman Authors', *Comparative Studies in Society and History* 8: 110–23.

Pahl, R. (1991) 'The Search for Social Cohesion from Durkheim to the European Community', *European Journal of Sociology* 32: 345–60.

Pahl, R. (1995) *After Success: Fin-de-siècle Anxiety and Identity*. Cambridge and Oxford: Polity Press.

Shlapentokh, V. (1989) *Public and Private Life of the Soviet People*. Oxford: Oxford University Press.

Slater, P. (1968) *The Glory of Hera*. Boston, MA: Beacon Press.

Stack, C. B. (1974) *All Our Kin*. New York: Harper and Row.

Wight, D. (1993) *Workers Not Wasters*. Edinburgh: Edinburgh University Press.

Wilkinson, H. (1994) *No Turning Back*. London: Demos.

Williams, R. (1973) *The Country and the City*. London: Chatto and Windus.

Willmott, P. (1987) *Friendship Networks and Social Support*. London: Policy Studies Institute.

Wilson, P. and Pahl, R. (1988) 'The Changing Sociological Construct of the Family', *Sociological Review* 36(2): 233–72.

7 Gender Crisis and Community

Beatrix Campbell

In a society riven by the rigours of global economic restructuring on the one hand and neo-liberal economics and social authoritarianism on the other, there is a convention in political discourse which avoids the large look and focuses instead on the local. These are discourses of blame, which accuse the poor of producing their poverty, which lament the atomisation of urban networks, the collapse of traditional institutions and workplaces, and above all reproach the manners and morals of modern mothers.

These are familiar laments which have been aired regularly since the 1950s and accompany not only public debates about crime and the changing character of community, particularly the emergence of communities based on identities and interests, but also the emergence of women in the public sphere beyond the confined space of domesticity. These discourses are most clearly expressed in the notion of the underclass, assiduously advocated by the Institute of Economic Affairs and the *Sunday Times*, with its promotion of the ideas of the American Charles Murray (Murray 1990). Murray and his acolytes blame community crime on the purported purge of the fathers by the mothers, and the emergence of 'dangerous' masculinities on the absence of masculine role models for men. Similar sentiments are also found in the very different preoccupations of the communitarians, whose major exponent in Britain is the irascible American sociologist Amitai Etzioni (1993), who has been promoted by the think-tank Demos and apparently endorsed by the New Labour leadership. Etzioni attributes a perceived crisis of community to the purported flight of mothers from the family, creating what he calls a 'parenting deficit'. It is surely significant that Demos' first foray into the politics of parenting is their publication of this excerpt from his rambling text. Clearly Etzioni services a new mode of misogyny which infuses the Demos project.

Where Murray's and Etzioni's hypotheses converge is in their anxiety about the relative autonomy of modern mothers. Murray argues that fathers have been purged from families and communities, leaving boys to grow up in neighbourhoods with no fathers where, not so long ago, children had 'plentiful examples of good fathers around them'. This is causing, he argues, a 'generational catastrophe'; it is creating an 'underclass' with values that are 'contaminating the life of entire neighbourhoods'. It is 'illegitimacy' that is 'the best predictor of an underclass in the making', an underclass that does not share the values of the society that sustains it, an underclass without culture, without class. He assumes, therefore, that communities are bereft of masculinity when, of course, masculinity remains palpable in poor neighbourhoods no less than among social elites. Indeed, far from being bereft of role models, poor boys are saturated by images of the most macho masculinities which dominate much popular culture. The cultures of criminalised coteries of young men and the local itinerancy of many pauperised men, moving between their mothers and other women, is a modern manifestation of an older tradition of both work and play which rendered men visitors to the homes they shared with women and children. Etzioni's 'parenting deficit' hypothesis argues, simply, that there is a 'dearth of parental involvement of both varieties: mothers and fathers' because women have done what men have done: left the home. 'All women did was demand for themselves what men had long possessed, working outside the home not only for their own personal satisfaction, but because of what they often perceived was economic necessity. Whatever the cause, the result is an empty nest.' However, what he misunderstands is the nature of women's movement into the public realm beyond the home and what he ignores is the transformation of relations between children and adults during the three decades in which women have reclaimed freedom of movement across social space. An examination of women's working time, of the different priorities of men and women in workplace politics and the enduring differential between men and women's paid working time and unpaid domestic labour reveals that women have not simply mirrored men's relationship to public and private worlds. Indeed, it is women's participation in the public realm that has unmasked the polarisation between public and private that was produced by the transaction between capital and organised labour, a historic compromise that secured men's flight from the world of women and children in the domestic domain, enshrined in the notion of the male breadwinner which has so potently shaped the life of communities in the modern era. In Britain, women's long march into paid labour has been contingent on their continuing responsibility for the care of men and children. And it is worth reminding ourselves that this long march began after the Second World War, but has not been accompanied by an energetic commitment by the 'men's movement' either to public provision for children or to a reduction in men's waged working time in the name of parenthood. In any case, Etzioni is simply wrong about relations between children and women who work full time, women whose employment is defined by a working day designed for 'absent' fathers. Full-time working women in Britain actually spent more dedicated time with their pre-school children in the 1980s than the full-time home makers of the 1960s, according to Jonathan Gershuny of the Centre for Micro-Social Change (see Gershuny in Hewitt 1993, p. 61).

Women have not abandoned their children. Indeed the dramatic sex differential in paid working time in Britain reveals that women's re-emergence into the labour market (with most mothers working part-time) has been conditional, precisely, on continuing to care for men and children. Furthermore, the changing contract between adults and children, carrying a commitment to more, not less, connection and companionship, is revealed in the growth of dedicated time spent by parents of both genders with their children. When Murray and Etzioni lament the collapse of contemporary parenting they invoke a golden age of resepectable, fathered family life in the 1950s. But during the golden era, according to Gershuny, the average working father spent only 11 minutes a day dedicated to his children. What Murray and Etzioni and their British acolytes erase is the history of fatherhood, a history which is expressed in the campaign to secure men as breadwinners, a project that produced fathers not as parents but as providers. What they may, however, be bemoaning is not so much women's abandonment of their children, but women's growing independence from men. Their complaint about an underclass of unruly children is perhaps a complaint against unruly women who refuse to be policed by men. The rise and rise in British divorce statistics may be seen as an expression of women's disappointment with men, not their flight from their children. Indeed the divorce phenomenon, and the readiness of thousands of women to contemplate lone parenting in poverty in preference to a life with men who give them more pain than pleasure, represents a mass movement within civil society to challenge men's failure to co-operate with women and children.

What the divorce phenomenon has also unmasked is fathers' disconnection from their children, which has been echoed by the only mass movement among fathers in the 1990s – the protest of divorced fathers against the Child Support Agency's albeit crude attempts to make men contribute significantly towards the costs of their children. During the anxious debates about parenthood, community and crime there has been no endorsement from politicians of the continuing commitment of women to their children, nor indeed to the slow but significant shift in fathers' participation in child care. If there is a parenting deficit then it is still defined by what it always was: a deficit in domestic democracy between men and women. If there is a crisis of childhood then it is surely revealed in the poverty of millions of children, in the response to new advocacy agencies for children. Ten thousand calls from children are made to Childline every week to share their pain about brutality and abuse at home, most often at the hands of their fathers, and at school, typically at the hands of their peers. The spatial crisis of childhood is apparent in the conquest of the car which has colonised the social space that was once the domain of childhood – the street.

What we now know about the lives of children represents a formidable accusation against adults. It comes from a new consciousness of children's cultures, their needs, their distress and their rights. Children's assertiveness is not so much an effect of their abandonment by adults, but evidence of new allies for children among a generation of adults sensitised both by the expansion of the caring professions and by feminism. The rediscovery of children's suffering has also produced a new awareness – one that remains buried in populist political discourses – of the difference between what boys and girls do with their pain. Girls' self-destruction has failed to arouse the kind of political angst that is generated by the depressed destructiveness of boys.

What salience does attachment theory have for the perceived crisis of public peace in British society? The challenge to attachment theory is to assimilate the multiple attachments that shape social solidarity across different continents and cultures, as well as the impact of gendered social relations upon the subjectivities of men and women. If masculinity, for example, is always defined as the 'not feminine', if fatherhood is about the transmission of masculinity as difference and dominance, rather than simply the transmission of care, then the template of modern masculinities cannot be understood solely or primarily as an effect of bad or good mothering. The growth of criminalised coteries of young men and boys is habitually ascribed to a crisis of parenting in the post-war period. And yet the correlation between crime and masculinity has been clear since records began. And that correlation is vastly more significant than any other variable, from ethnicity to domestic circumstances. And since 96 per cent of prisoners are men and more than 80 per cent of serious offenders appearing before the courts are male then the tendency to explain their commitment to crime as a failure only of mothering is scarcely sustainable.

Challenging the claims that criminal masculinities can be ascribed to the absence of a male role model, Oliver James, in his scrupulous study of violence in contemporary British culture (1995), argues that it is not the absence of the father that hurts boys but 'the presence of mourning and the preceding acrimony' that accompanies separation, and what boys do with their distress. We cannot talk about crime without talking about the cultures of masculinity that men have bequeathed to boys. But the correlation between masculinity and crime is erased in the public debates. It has become the problem with no name.

Attachment theory may usefully engage with those cultural histories to help theorise young men's and boys' attachment to mainstream popular cultures of masculinity, particularly those that affirm their connection to crime, and the determined disconnection of respectable men from 'dangerous masculinities'. The government's campaign against car crime, for example, bestialises the boys who comprise the overwhelming majority of participants in car crime, particularly the offence of Taking Without the Owner's Consent. TWOCcers are represented as hyenas in the £5 million Home Office publicity campaign against car crime. And yet young TWOCcers share a passion for cars with mainstream man, a passion which is encouraged by an industry which has impregnated fantasies about this quintessentially modern commodity with masculinised notions of power, flight and freedom. Attachment theory could also creatively comment on the different responses to the criminal justice system among males and females which has been confirmed by Home Office research (Home Office 1995). This report argues that parenthood 'constitutes a potent influence on desistance from offending'. But the responsibilities of parenthood are 'much more likely to be accepted by females, leading to an abrupt end to delinquent activities', while for males, fatherhood can provide 'the trigger for moving away from the peer group', or 'it can push some into fleeing from their relationship with their partner and withdrawing further into their peer groups'. The Home Office researchers found that for many young men their attachment to their peer group – other young men – produced the 'stark, if somewhat discouraging finding' that many young male offenders carry on offending well into their mid-twenties.

The strength of young men's attachment to masculinity as difference and dominance becomes more obvious when we explore the cultures associated with crime: authoritarianism, militarism, exclusive assemblies which affirm the most macho modes of masculinity and a commitment to a sexist sexual division of labour within private and public spheres. Criminalised coteries mirror the ethics and structures valorised by mainstream, masculine assemblies ranging from the police to the House of Commons.

Attachment theory does not help explain why neighbourhoods are fissured not only by generation but by gender, why one gender provides the overwhelming majority of participants in the kind of criminal offending that exhausts communities already wearied by the withdrawal of both public and private capital; it does not help us understand why different genders and generations do different things with their distress, with their power and their powerlessness. The lacuna in the debates about community and crime, and in New Labour's appeal to strong communities and civil society as a bulwark against disorder and conflict, is any discussion of the heavy role of masculinity in shaping domestic and community conflicts and solidarities. Indeed, it is commonplace to render masculinity invisible, to assume its absence from the local, the familial and the communal.

The argument here, then, is that masculinities are not absent. It is also that communities are not falling apart because of a failure of mothering. What we see in poor neighbourhoods is a struggle over space: criminalised coteries hijack the public space they share with their community. The geographer Bill Hillier has argued that young men create lacunae, blots of public space appropriated by them which are evacuated by the rest of their community (Hillier and Hanson 1984, Campbell 1993). The conquest of these corners may be no different from the nice tendencies among men to construct their own locales, clubs, pubs, sports, welfares, institutes and lodges which have sometimes dominated a local landscape and which become monuments not to communal congregation, but to masculine exclusivity (see Taylor, this volume). Those cultural histories are now perceived to be in crisis because they reveal masculinity as a problematic: neighbourhoods are menaced not by mothers but by men and boys; and because, as the Australian scholar Bob Connell has argued (1995), patriarchy, 'the main axis of power in the contemporary European/American gender order' is threatened by changes in domestic structures and by feminism. Strategies which have been predicated on power over women no longer enjoy social legitimacy, while mainstream masculinity is unable to offer any other model of gender relations. The palpable differences between the ways men and women deal with their troubles can be interpreted in the context of de Certeau's helpful notion of community as a 'space of enunciation' (de Certeau 1984). The social space of community is the locale of 'encounter, assembly, simultaneity, either through conflict or co-operation' (Lefebvre 1991). This approach erases the problem of power and constitutes community as part of a Holy Trinity – family, community and nation – which is immaculately conceived, small but perfectly formed. This rhetoric, which refuses to assimilate the great discoveries of the last three decades both about children's conditions of existence and the cultural revolution in relations between the genders, is reiterated at the core of New Labour's manifesto: 'When Blair talks about the importance of strong families, it is because he regards them as the foundation of a cohesive society and of strong communities ... He became critical of what he felt was many on the left's uninterest in social order and their confusion of liberation from prejudice with apparent disregard for moral structures' (Mandelson and Liddle 1996).

What has become apparent in the 1990s is that genders inhabit social space in different ways, a fact which is both asserted and erased in the current polemics about community (Frazer and Lacey 1993). The rediscovery of gendered space is an effect of the attack on local collectivity by neo-liberal economic strategies, which is, in turn, shadowed by the assault on community well-being by boys, and by the failure of masculinities – both 'dangerous' and 'respectable' – to match the cultural revolution in women's movements across the public and private landscape. Communities are shaped both by the work of care, largely performed by mothers, and by the spatial strategies of men whose cultural history has valorised conquest and control. Just as there is a formidable correlation between crime and masculinity, so there is a striking correlation between mothers and community action. Despite the rhetorical invocation of community responsibility by New Labour, it extends little endorsement of the efforts of vigorous networks of active citizenship in some of Britain's poorest places, often sustained by the most maligned constituency in Britain – mothers. It is the traditional work of mothering that connects many women, often single parents, with the public sphere. Indeed, they inhabit the interface between public and private. It is primarily mothers, through their responsibility for men and children, who become communities' negotiators with public institutions. It is they who connect with the schools, the local authorities, the police and the courts. Often launched into politics by their campaigns to protect children's free-

dom of movement and to preserve the fabric of their neighbourhoods, they staff redoubts of self-help which may constitute their
communities' only political resource. And yet they enjoy no cham-
pions in the social authoritarianism of *fin de siècle* politics in
Britain. Historically, power and control over space and resources,
either through the institutionalised control over social space or
through control by war and chaos, has been exercised at the expense of women. Indeed, the spatialisation of power, of care and of
crime cannot be understood without reference to a politics of gender. What attachment theory could bring to these debates is an
analysis of care and an analysis of masculinised 'structures of feeling', passed on from fathers to sons, which denigrate femininity
while celebrating coercion and control as ways of doing business.
We need to ask ourselves whether the cultures of attachment given
to their sons by men are more formative and potent than those
bequeathed by their mothers.

REFERENCES

Campbell, B. (1993) *Goliath: Britain's Dangerous Places*. London: Meth-
uen.
Connell, R.W. (1995) *Masculinities*. Cambridge: Polity Press.
de Certeau, M. (1984) *The Practice of Everyday Life*. Berkeley: University
of California Press.
Etzioni, A. (1993) *The Spirit of Community*. New York: Touchstone.
Frazer, E. and Nicola Lacey, N. (1993) *The Politics of Community: A
Feminist Critique of the Liberal-Communitarian Debate*. Hemel
Hempstead: Harvester Wheatsheaf.
Hewitt, P. (1993) *About Time*. London: Rivers Oram Press.
Hillier, B. and Hanson, J. (1984) *The Social Logic of Space*. Cambridge:
Cambridge University Press.
Home Office (1995) *Young People and Crime*. London: HMSO.
James, O. (1995) *Juvenile Violence in a Winner–Loser Culture*. London:
Free Association Books.
Lefebvre, H. (1991) *The Production of Space*. Oxford: Blackwell.
Mandelson, P. and Liddle, R. (1996) *The Blair Revolution*. London: Faber.
Murray, C. (1990) *The Emerging British Underclass*. London: IEA.

8 Place and Local Identity

George Nicholson

INTRODUCTION

The process of life is marked by the continuous creation of wholes from parts. (Alexander 1979)

There has been a revival of interest in community and neighbourhood planning. What is interesting is that this has come about as a reaction both to public policy and the activities of the private property market. People are demanding more say in decisions that affect their lives, disillusioned with the received wisdom of politicians, professionals and academics alike. Who can blame them?

Public planning policy post-war has had two main features. The first was the encouragement of the decentralisation of our cities by the creation of new and expanded towns. The second was related to the development process, which involved a massive programme of slum clearance and the redevelopment of much of the existing housing stock. This was also an era which spawned the concept of comprehensive development. Led and often funded by the public sector, vast areas of our major cities were literally taken apart and put back together again. Coupled with developing ideas of the 'city and the car', with the inevitable inner ring-road, further damage was wreaked, in the process cutting off the centre of the city from its hinterland. London was to escape this fate, but the population of parts of central London dropped by up to 40 per cent, as a result of decentralisation and housing renewal, whilst other major cities such as Birmingham suffered even more. The legacy of this period will take decades to put right.

One of the main casualties of those times was to be the social structure of cities as planners and architects, seduced by utopian visions of cities of the future – a product of the modernist period – promoted change almost as a goal in itself. This was a philosophy which was hostile to notions of space and place. As Foucault has said: 'Space was treated as the dead, the fixed, the undialectical, the immobile. Time on the other hand, was richness, fecundity, life, dialectic. The use of spatial terms seems to have the air of anti-history. If one started to talk in terms of space that meant that one was hostile to time' (Foucault 1980). In effect, as Hillier and Hanson (1984) have pointed out, urban designers conspired to despatialise society and desocialise space. Their main criticism of post-war planning was that it had social objectives but often unsociable results.

If public policy was one side of the equation, the other, represented by the property industry, also left its mark. As public investment was reduced and public policy weakened in the early 1970s, the pace of private sector activity was to quicken, filling the vacuum. The property booms of the 1970s and 1980s saw a dramatic increase in, first, speculative office building and latterly, frantic activity in the housing and retail sectors. Large tracts of land and buildings were acquired by developers, mostly in the poorer central city areas, where the need for new housing and community facilities for existing residents was greatest.

Unsurprisingly, given the scale of change brought about, initially by public policy and then private sector activity, there was bound to be a reaction to both, sooner or later. When it came, it was not, however, as a result of any realisation of the effects of their actions by public authorities or developers, but from people on the ground who had witnessed at first hand the physical and social destruction of their neighbourhoods and cities. One such turning point was the campaign to save Covent Garden in central London from a comprehensive redevelopment scheme proposed by the Greater London Council. Another was the battle by residents of the South Bank, also in central London, to prevent a huge speculative office development on a site next to Waterloo Bridge, which had been previously designated for housing. Both flagged the same problem: the absence of social content in planning policy, and its replacement by a physical focus which was 'people blind'. The basic building block – the residents of a city – was simply not a part of the equation.

THE BASIC BUILDING BLOCK

There are no higher and lower functions in cities, or at least there should not be. (Lynch 1981)

But just how does one build people into the planning process? The impetus behind a project to find some of the answers and indeed the genesis of a later report for the London Planning Advisory Committee

(Nicholson et al. 1994) came at a conference staged in 1990 by Communities and Homes in Central London (CHiCL, an umbrella organisation embracing central London neighbourhood organisations). Intentionally called: 'Vision for London', it was a reaction to what appeared a deliberate attempt by government to reduce planning in London to what could be written on the back of Nicholas Ridley's cigarette packet. The basis of the argument by CHiCL, then as now, was that future plans, whether strategic or local, should embrace the idea of community structure, setting it out in a way that could be identified in human and physical terms. As is so often the case, this was not a new idea. Sir Patrick Abercrombie, in his two plans for London drawn up in the early 1940s, based them on the idea that the existing community structure of London was fundamental to the replanning of the capital. He produced a social and functional analysis map of London, setting out the community structure of London at the time. In his famous diagram in the 1943 plan, the example of Eltham was used to illustrate his concept of a community, a term he used to describe a whole settlement. Having broken London down into its traditional settlement pattern, he then used a theoretical model to break this down further into what he termed neighbourhood units.

Therein lay a contradiction. Something organic like a human settlement does not easily transfer into a theoretical set of standards, which is why Christopher Alexander (1965) was so critical of Abercrombie, seeing the structures which emerged as too rigid, creating an artificial separation between areas. To Alexander, the essence of planning was 'the felt thing', whereas Abercrombie proposed a very mechanistic, top–down form of planning which seemed to Alexander to suffer from a compulsive desire for neatness and order. But at another level, Abercrombie's intention was exactly right – that of linking people to place. Both Lynch (1981) and Castells (1983) later criticised the separation they believed had occurred between the two, something which had precipitated a downgrading in the importance of identity and meaning. They both believed that this process, led by planners and architects, on the one hand, and politicians and property interests, on the other, had effectively alienated people from their surroundings.

The Abercrombie plans also, in part, sowed the seeds of their own destruction. In setting out the social and functional analysis of London, Abercrombie fundamentally weakened his proposals when he overlaid the community structure in central London with broader concepts such as The City and West End. The effect was that rather than the idea of community dominating the aims of development as he suggested it should, in central London exactly the opposite occurred. All subsequent plans for London reinforced rather than questioned what was happening, to the extent that by the time the Greater London Development Plan (GLDP) appeared in 1976, community was not even mentioned. The concept of community as envisaged by Abercrombie's plans had been replaced by the idea of the Londoner as an individual. Part of the reason was undoubtedly that the plans drawn up by Abercrombie were from an architectural tradition which saw cities very much in spatial terms; whereas by the time the GLDP was being produced, a new profession – town and country planning – was in the ascendant. More wedded to an approach which analysed problems from a statistical standpoint, the strategic plan for London (the UK's first) became merely a written statement rather than a vision of the capital. Subjective (and spatial) concepts such as neighbourhood and community, Alexander's 'felt things', were lost as the new science of city management promoted a need to be 'objective'. The problem with this approach, then as now, is that it has a tendency to seek similarities between places. Everywhere becomes relative and nowhere special. Place is lost and the body corporate takes over. The irony is that experience suggests it is a form of decision making which, whilst masquerading as strategic, is in fact fatally flawed, suffering from a seemingly incurable tendency to be inward looking, partial, over-rigid and, worst of all, hostile to anything that might undermine the notion of 'the borough'. That situation has remained up until the recent revival of interest in the concept of neighbourhood planning, led by neighbourhood and community-based organisations reacting against the way city dwellers had been reduced to numbers, or their aspirations to topics.

Interestingly, some sociologists have aided and abetted this growing interest in neighbourhood by insisting that a modern community is no longer a place-bound concept, but one that draws more on a network model of society based on ethnic, gender, work or friendship links. It has been suggested by Pahl (1995), for example, that the concept of a place-bound neighbourhood is hostile to this notion of community. The problem with his analysis is that it ignores three things: first, everyone lives somewhere; second, the land where people live has to be managed and developed; and third, a spatial approach in any case includes notions of community as well as those of neighbourhood. To suggest that sense of place is a nostalgic notion rooted in the past is too exclusive and narrow a view of the world. Agnew and Duncan (1989) pointed to the confusion between place and community in the social sciences. The crux of the confusion lay in the 'ambiguous legacy of the term community'. Rather than distinguishing its two connotations – a morally valued way of life, on the one hand, and the constituting of social relations in a discrete geographical setting, on the other – they felt that the two had been conflated. 'A specific set of social relations, those of a morally valued way of life, had transcended the generic sense of community as place.' In the process place had become devalued.

It was in response to all these different strands of thinking that CHiCL set out to research two different areas of London, North Southwark and North Kensington. Both have been the target of immense change, but with distinct differences. North Southwark has seen tremendous physical change as a result of economic restructuring and land market pressures, while the resident population has remained relatively stable. North Kensington too has been the subject of immense physical change, but as a result of an almost complete renewal of the housing stock, with a consequent upheaval of the resident population. As it turned out, these two areas could not have been better chosen to explore two central questions: first, what sense of place do people have and could it provide a basis for developing concepts of neighbourhood and community? And second, how do people respond to change in an area? But first some theory.

SPACE, PLACE AND THE NEIGHBOURHOOD IDEA

Man does not live by words alone; all 'subjects' are situated in a space in which they must either recognise themselves or lose themselves, a space which they may both enjoy and modify. (Lefebvre 1974)

Numerous writers and academics have given eloquent testament to people's sense of place and its role in underpinning neighbourhood and community. Whether it is Unwin's idea of fostering the feeling of local unity in an area (1921), Perry's notion of transforming the neighbourhood from its spontaneous and instinctual basis through deliberate design, Hillier and Hanson's concept of embodying intelligibility in spatial form (1984), Anderson's territorial specificity (1986), Castells' spatial meaningfulness (1983) or Lynch's sense of connection (1981), all are rooted in Lynch's hypothesis that sense of place is the join between the form of the environment and human perception and cognition, and cannot be analysed except as an interaction between person and place.

But in all the key words to emerge from the literature on space, place and neighbourhood, two stand out – structure and process.

What kind of structure are we aiming for and what kind of process are we going to adopt to achieve it? Perhaps the starting point is Alexander's notion of a 'pattern and a thing'. To Alexander, the key to understanding is recognising that 'a pattern is a "process" and a "thing" – a description of a thing which is alive and a description of the process which will generate the thing' (Alexander 1979). This is very much in keeping with his earlier writing on artificial and real cities. Alexander saw the neighbourhood as a 'living pattern which resolves a system of forces, or allows them to resolve themselves, each pattern creating an organisation which maintains that portion of the world in balance'. From this Alexander developed the notion of a language (something Lefebvre had also done), seeing it as the vehicle for a shared vision. Of course this is the ideal. As he points out, all too often language becomes rigid or specialised, encouraging fragmentation and hence control by professionals. To counter this he qualified the idea by stating: 'a language is a living language only when each person in society, a neighbourhood or town has his own version of this language'. This is why people's perceptions are so important as a starting point. As Alexander put it: 'a language is not an intellectual thing, it is a "felt thing" – a thing lived through, which expresses people's innermost attitudes about their way of life, their hopes and fears about ways in which they live and work together – a communal knowledge of a way of life that will be good for them'. In much the same way that Hillier and Hanson talked about the importance of understanding 'the balance between local to global and global to local' (see box overleaf), Alexander's work points to the importance of developing an urban management system based on 'process not planning' and equally 'getting the balance between order and disorder'. The importance of this approach is that it does not burden the process with fixed notions. On the other hand, the philosophy is tied to a positive vision of the city with people's perception as the starting point. What we are after is the 'felt thing'.

THE DECISIONS PARADOX

Kevin Lynch's notion of a good settlement was one that 'enhances the continuity of culture, increase a sense of connection to one's environment in space and time and permits growth and development within continuity' (Lynch 1981). This sense of continuity and connection are important, because they suggest the need to recognise people's sense of themselves and their surroundings as a

Local to Global = bottom–up	Global to Local = top–down
parts	wholes
the neighbourhood	the borough
spatially based	service based
holistic	partial
complexity	simplicity
overlap	specificity
principles	standards
emphasis on difference	worry over precedent
open	closed
flexible	rigid
content	procedure
meaning	words
vision	regulation
wholes	parts

(Nicholson et al. 1994)

starting point. This develops the continuity of an area or, to use a better word, its meaning. Recognising things as they are, and building on what you have are two important aspects of a neighbourhood approach. Local identity depends on emphasising differences and stressing uniqueness rather than seeking similarities.

This is where the literature on urbanism comes closest to attachment theory. The language of Alexander and Lynch – 'identity', 'sense of connection', 'continuity', 'stability' and 'the need to maintain a secure base', is certainly very similar and, in the last instance, uses precisely the same words. This should not be surprising since the whole thrust of their thinking had been to bring about a reunion of people and place. Another common thread running through the literature is that there is no real conflict between notions of community and those of neighbourhood. If anything, as Davies and Herbert (1993) show in their book *Communities within Cities*, there are more grounds for querying the network approach to community than a neighbourhood based approach to planning. That may be so, but what is undeniable is the importance of being able to distinguish between the two approaches. As a starting point, it is helpful to consider the neighbourhood as a spatial concept and community as a functional/network concept based on interest groupings. What is needed is a model which can accommodate the notions of both neighbourhood and community, rather than seeking to promote one to the exclusion of the other.

The literature also points to what has been called 'the re-enchantment of the built environment'. This is tied up with a rediscovery of the importance of place. However, as recent work for the Department of the Environment points out (DoE 1991), the crux of a sense of identity is just those feelings which will not be represented by any hard data. This should not deter us from seeking to pin it down. In any event, one of the criticisms of planning as currently practised is that many decisions are currently taken in a 'fog. There simply is not the level of detail available to facilitate a sensitive decision. This is often a problem which relates to scale: the finer grained the scale, the more significant the impact. Generalised aims – the hallmark of the current topic-based approach to planning and plan making – become a recipe for uniformity and the production of places in which no one has a stake.

It was in order better to understand these concepts that the areas known as The Borough, part of Cathedral ward in North Southwark, and Kensal Town, part of Golborne ward in North Kensington, were chosen. It was deliberately decided to target areas which had no status other than being names on a map. Neither have boundaries to delineate them as administrative areas. What were the results?

PUTTING NEIGHBOURHOODS BACK ON THE MAP

There is scope for a more focused social dimension to urban policy to capitalise on the place loyalty of local communities. (DoE 1994)

The first conclusion from the surveys conducted in each area, was that people do possess a strong sense of place. When asked to give a name for the area in which they lived, 90 per cent and 81 per cent, respectively, of residents were able to offer one unprompted. A second conclusion was that people's sense of place is more sophisticated than hitherto thought, in that it includes a certain spatial hierarchy. The analysis of responses and the areas people plotted on a base map produced a number of sub-areas, smaller than wards. These constitute what were tentatively designated 'neighbourhoods'.

It was expected that it would be unlikely that everyone would give the same boundary, because of the spread of respondents. But the responses clearly showed some overlap, revealing a common 'core area'. This is interesting because the idea of a core area carries with it the idea of periphery, which in turn lends itself to the notion of fuzzy boundaries. If developed, this approach could avoid the age-old problem of the application of rigid boundaries. In this sense the mechanisms for promoting neighbourhood and community identity are different from those for the delivery of other services such as health and social work, which obviously require precisely defined boundaries for each catchment area. It was also clear that people more readily identified with this more local scale than either the ward or the wider borough. This led to the third conclusion, that people's perception of the space in which they live is multi-layered, something confirmed in the MORI surveys conducted in response to Boundary Commission proposals for Southwark in 1993 and in Lewisham in 1984.

A fourth conclusion from the London studies was that people do indeed have a strong sense of community. However, there was a clear contrast between the survey areas. Kensal Town residents tended to be more aware of and feel part of communities bounded by ethnicity, whereas in The Borough, respondents' descriptions of community had a more geographical focus. In both areas local propinquity was an important factor. A fifth conclusion from the research was that casting the neighbourhood as a spatial model and community as a network model is too simplistic. Perhaps it is more useful to start by viewing the possibilities as lying somewhere on a spectrum stretching from a pure network model at one extreme to a pure neighbourhood model on the other. Both these poles could be said to be artificial. In reality, the situation is likely to be more multi-dimensional.

By leaving the matter of spatial distribution open, it is equally possible to discover an urban village as it is to discover a community without propinquity (Ronayne 1988). Coupled with the notion of multi-layering, this confirms the point made by Davies and Herbert (1993), that through time the number of different elements or features identified as being important has increased substantially. The aim must be to build up a complete picture of the neighbourhood under study and the processes at work within it, with a view to developing a context for policy development that most closely reflects the needs and interests of its residents. This should provide an effective antidote to what Anderson (1986) calls 'the curse of over simplification' which has led to a quest for easy solutions and a parallel reduction in the amount of basic research and survey work which used to underpin planning practice.

A sixth conclusion was that people are highly sensitive to change, both in terms of detailed alterations and more general changes to the character of the area. Interestingly, the sample of respondents took opposing positions. In Kensal, people tended to argue that there had not been enough change, whereas in The Borough respondents felt that there had been too much. In places such as the two study areas, change can reinforce those things which are good about an area or undermine them. Policy makers may agree with residents on the one hand, but, on the other hand, may hold that wider concerns necessitate a course of action which might not be in the residents' interests. Equally, they may disagree with the residents about the nature of their area and develop proposals regardless. This raises the point about inside and outside views of an area.

To complement an understanding of change, the survey explored positive and negative characteristics of the areas as perceived by residents. In both cases, the positive features tended to be more fixed or ingrained in the area – factors such as good transport links, stability or a quiet area. Correspondingly, in both areas, the features regarded as negative tended to be of a more temporary, less integral nature, such as cleanliness or crime. This led to the seventh conclusion – that a decision affecting the positive features about an area could damage it permanently, whereas negative features could be improved by better management.

Thus there is a difference of emphasis at work here which needs to be acknowledged. Without this, when it comes to making a judgement as to what sort of area it is, or what sort of changes are necessary to it, it is very possible that people with an outside view will weigh some negative features about an area more highly than some positive things felt by those holding an inside view. This contrast between inside and outside views is something the European Foundation for the Improvement of Living and Working Conditions (Chanan 1992) looked at in a three-year study of how neighbourhoods cope with change. This concluded that one of the crucial elements of successful intervention is whether there is a correspondence between the way outside actors define the situation and the way local people define it.

During the course of the CHiCL study, contact was also made with Sandwell Metropolitan Borough Council, one of a number of authorities nationwide which have adopted a community development strategy as a council-wide strategic policy. At the same time, the findings of the study were submitted to the public inquiry into the Southwark Unitary Development Plan (UDP). Our impression is that most community development strategies as currently practised are not in fact about community development at all. In the main, they are attempts at a more sensitive delivery of council services. Not that there is anything wrong in essence with that. It is undoubtedly necessary but not sufficient. Community development should lead to community empowerment and the direct involvement of residents in the delivery of certain services and the management of projects designed to improve the economic base of an area, as well as seeking improvements to the local environment. Projects such as the ambitious redevelopment of part of London's South Bank by Coin Street Community Builders and many others under the umbrella of the fast emerging Development Trusts movement, have been shown to take a more holistic view of an area than the traditional site-based approach to land use planning. Yet, flawed as they are, the crop of community development strategies currently on offer do at least hold out the potential for further adaptation. Sandwell currently has a community development strategy adopted at borough level but a unitary development plan which is lacking in neighbourhood or community focus. Southwark, on the other hand, has no community development strategy, but has attempted to introduce notions of community and neighbourhood into its unitary development plan. Both authorities reflect how vertically structured service delivery still is in practice. Departments still do not communicate and separate policy is developed either in spite of a corporate policy framework, or because of the lack of one. The final report of the study recommends that to be successful, a neighbourhood-based planning strategy needs to be linked to a borough-wide community development strategy, and vice versa.

The study for the London Planning Advisory Committee (LPAC) concluded with a series of recommendations, the main ones being:

1. Boroughs should institute a process whereby communities and neighbourhoods may be identified, using the techniques developed during the study and others which have been developed elsewhere.

2. Boroughs should set this process within a policy context combining those mechanisms in (a) neighbourhood-based UDPs and (b) a borough-wide Community Development Strategy.

3. Neighbourhood and community definition should be regularly reviewed to ensure that it remains relevant.

4. Government guidelines concerning UDP preparation should be reviewed to promote a neighbourhood-based approach to planning.

5. The Department of the Environment should be encouraged to issue a Planning Policy Guidance Note on Community Planning and Regeneration.

CONCLUSIONS

No one would claim that the study undertaken by CHiCL for the LPAC provides all the answers. But it does demonstrate the bones of a process which, with further qualitative work, might just lead to the sort of neighbourhood and community-based planning that could be truly empowering. One of the other main aims of the study for LPAC was to start to develop an inter-disciplinary perspective. The project, whilst rooted in practical experience of the planning process at both the strategic and neighbourhood level, drew its inspiration from three quite distinct disciplines: architecture, geography and planning. In addition, academic subjects such as anthropology, sociology and social psychology also provided useful sources.

Concepts such as neighbourhood and community have a long history in the planning arena. Equally, theories on space and place have a long pedigree in several academic disciplines. Recently, there has been a resurgence of interest in many of these ideas, associated with what appears to be a convergence between different schools of thought, which in the past have been kept apart by rigid divisions in both the professional and academic worlds. Indeed, even now there is little evidence of an inter-disciplinary approach, and it is only possible to discern this convergence by reading across disciplines. It is exciting to note that the production of this book shows how psychological disciplines can be included in this assimilation of ideas.

In a critique published in *Le Monde Diplomatique* (July 1995), it was stated that the left had exhausted itself of ideas *'a bout de souffle'*. We may now have powerful new alliances which could be the launch pad for a new agenda.

REFERENCES

Abercrombie, P. (1945) *Greater London Plan: 1944*. London, HMSO.

Agnew, A. and Duncan, J (1989) *The Power of Place*. Boston, MA: Unwin Hyman.

Alexander, C. (1965) 'The City is not a Tree', *Architectural Forum* 122: (1)58–62; (2)58–61.

Alexander, C. (1979) *The Timeless Way of Building*. New York: Oxford University Press.

Anderson, S. (1986) 'Studies Towards an Ecological Model of the Urban Environment' in S. Anderson (ed.), *On Streets*. Cambridge, MA: MIT Press.

Berman, M. (1982) *All That Is Solid Melts Into Air. The Experience of Modernity.* New York: Simon and Schuster.

Castells, M. (1983) *The City and the Grassroots.* London: Edward Arnold.

Chanan, G. (1992) *Out of the Shadows: Local Community Action and the European Community.* Dublin: European Foundation for the Improvement of Living and Working Conditions.

Chanan, G. and Koos, V. (1990) *Social Change and Local Action.* Dublin: European Foundation for the Improvement of Living and Working Conditions.

Davies, K.D. and Herbert, D.T. (1993) *Communities within Cities.* London: Belhaven Press.

Department of the Environment (1991) *Local Government Bill.* London: HMSO.

Department of the Environment Inner Cities Research Programme (1994) *Assessing the Impact of Urban Policy.* London: HMSO.

Evans, B. and Chaker, W. (1992) *A Sense of Place: Place, Space and the Development Process.* London: South Bank University.

Foucault, M. (1980) *Power/knowledge.* Brighton: Harvester.

Hillier, B. and Hanson, J. (1984) *The Social Logic of Space.* Cambridge: Cambridge University Press.

Jacobs, J. (1961) *The Death and Life of Great American Cities.* London: Peregrin Books.

Lefebvre, H. (1974) *The Production of Space.* Oxford: Blackwell.

Ley, D. (1989) 'Modernism, Post Modernism and the Struggle for Place' in A. Agnew and J. Duncan (eds), *The Power of Place.* Boston, MA: Unwin Hyman.

Lynch, K. (1981) *A Theory of Good City Form.* Cambridge, MA: MIT Press.

Nicholson, G.E. (1988) 'City as Commodity or Community, *Architects Journal* 30 (March) 34–52.

Nicholson, G.E. (1992) 'The Rebirth of Community Planning' in A. Thornley (ed.), *The Crisis of London.* London: Routledge.

Nicholson, G.E. and McLean-Thorne, D. (1991) *Your Place Comes First.* London: North Southwark Community Development Group.

Nicholson, G.E. and McLean-Thorne, D. and Pile, S. (1994) *Place and Local Identity.* London: London Planning Advisory Committee.

Nuffield Foundation (1986) *Report of Committee of Inquiry into Town and Country Planning.* London: Nuffield Foundation.

Pahl, R. (1995) 'Friendly Society', *New Statesman and Society,* 10 March, 20–2.

Ronayne, T. (1988) *Coping with Social and Economic Change at Neighbourhood Level: Phase One Report.* Dublin: Work Research Centre.

Scherer, J. (1972) *Contemporary Community.* London: Tavistock Publications.

Tuan, Y.F. (1977) *Space Place; The Perspective of Experience.* London: Edward Arnold.

Unwin, R. (1920-21) *Distribution – papers and discussions*. London: Town Planning Institute.

Walmsley, D.J. (1988) *Urban Living: The Individual in the City*. Harlow: Longman.

9 Is There an Alternative to the Global Society?

Ian Taylor

DEMONISING THE OTHER

At a meeting of a local council in the North of England which I attended in 1995, strategies for crime prevention and community safety were generating agitated discussion. A 'keynote presentation' made by the local Chief Superintendent of Police opened with a video, showing a succession of very young men breaking into cars in a local car park over a 24-hour period. The presentation then moved on to a discussion of the thief-catching potential of a new indelible chemical dye that can be discharged from sprinkler systems built into private and public buildings onto the heads of any intruder – so 'marking' them for months, in ways which would enable their apprehension via infra-red techniques during later investigations. By the end of this presentation, the bulk of the audience (which mainly consisted of good-hearted local Labour and Liberal councillors) had worked themselves up into a frenzy of vengeful and punitive sentiment, and they then spent the rest of the meeting connecting up the behaviours seen on the video to the 'problem families' who, everyone agreed, were making everyone's life a misery on local estates and in other local areas of the city. Active support was given to a proposal currently appearing in an Association of Municipal Authorities policy paper for a new contractually-based 'conditional tenancy' – clearly a potential step towards the exclusion of families identified as socially problematic even from our 'sink' estates.

A couple of weeks later, I was at a dinner party given by neighbours in the South Manchester suburb where I live, in which the round-the-table discussion consisted of a lengthy series of complaints about crime and disorder in the city, and turned to an assessment of the costs and benefits of something like 'the Singapore solution – a return to the physical forms of punishment which, in the late 1970s, following the work of Michel Foucault, we had all assumed to have been replaced by more sophisticated, modernist forms of discipline and punishment. The notion of 'community' or communitarianism being celebrated here was that of a coercive moral code associated with the kinds of societies that would, until very recently, have been thought of by the self-satisfied citizens of England as essentially under-developed – 'pre-modern' or Third World – societies.

I introduce these personal experiences in order to emphasise the urgency of my theme. We are living through a period in which the idea of attachment and identity built around family, neighbourhood, school and work is seriously threatened by the process of 'globalisation' (particularly of economic activity and patterns of consumption and mass culture) and what has been called the 'disembedding' of 'social relations'. The sociologist Tony Giddens speaks of this disembedding as involving 'the "lifting out" of social relations and their rearticulation across indefinite tracts of time-space' (Giddens 1991, p. 18).

But we are also heavily involved in a period in which a radically individualistic culture, on the one hand triumphantly proclaiming its historical victory over collectivist thinking and practices, is, on the other hand, anxiously engaged in the exclusion and demonisation of all kinds of Others (from single mothers, New Age travellers and unskilled young men, to vagrants and the homeless) from public recognition and citizenship. This process of exclusion and demonisation seems intimately to be related to the massive crisis in the manufacturing labour market that characterised most advanced capitalist societies in the 1980s, but which was particularly marked in Britain (cf. Ormerod, this volume). There is a widespread sense, at all levels of this social formation, that the economic future of 'the country' and of most individuals within it is in no sense guaranteed. There is a widespread 'fear of falling' – either in one's own personal fortunes (in respect of individual or household income or joblessness *per se*) or in respect of the prospects faced by the next generation (one's own children). Britain – the first industrial society in the world – is also nonetheless a society which has never experienced a thoroughgoing 'bourgeois revolution': for these reasons, it remains heavily divided by class and also more heavily resistant, throughout this last century, to serious modernisation and change. It is important to investigate how our widely reported sense of fear and insecurity is linked to the understanding, now very widespread throughout society, that Britain is going to find it very difficult to compete with societies in

North America, Europe and the Pacific Rim, which have nearly all been more adaptable and dynamic in their responses to the 'New Times' of global competition. The sad truth about the imposition of a particularly callous form of free market discipline in Britain during the 1980s – 'Thatcherism' – is precisely that it has had so little general effect in terms of modernising the infrastructure – for example, in transport – and practices in respect of consumer or citizen service, both in the public and private sectors. The unmistakable sense of decline of employment prospects and service provision is also underwritten by the wider sense of insecurity born of the marketisation of economic relations as such (as in the insecurity of those still in employment), as well as by an awareness of the range of new 'risks', (for example, to the environment) that are involved in societies of 'High Modernity' (Beck 1992).[1] But the fundamental issue in Britain is the accelerating recognition that the conventions which held together an unequal, more or less developed (though essentially uncompetitive and unmodernised) society through the earlier post-war period are no longer sustainable. The business class which now so assuredly dominates the economy, on the whole is now employing more unskilled young women than men. Unskilled young men are now clearly surplus to the requirements of capital. And it is this residualised rump of manual labourers without employment which is the object of fear and loathing on the part of the rest of civil society, and the target for as much discipline and exclusion as the penal system can be reformed to deliver (cf. Taylor and Jamieson 1996).

GLOBALISATION

The 'demise of mass manufacturing' in the West is one presenting aspect of a much more fundamental transformation in the character of international economic activity – notably, the arrival of a new, highly flexible form of investment, production and profit making, variously described as post-Fordism and/or disorganised capitalism. Transnational corporations – vertically and horizontally linked into quite different areas of productive activity – range across the globe, and a set of entirely new 'circuits' of capitalist production of commodities, investment and exploitation of productive capital and uses of money have come to dominate national economies throughout the world. The domination of these 'global circuits' of capital in most countries of the world is more or less assured, albeit with different levels of penetration (Romania at the one extreme, perhaps; the US at the other). But the restless and competitive nature of 'capital' in general, and the new global consumer capitalism in particular, means that there is no final point of stability or stasis.

One defining feature of this 'global society' is the amount of time which is spent by citizens (who Lash and Urry (1994) retitle the 'mobile subjects' of Post-Fordism) 'tuned in' to television, other visual media and/or the rapidly-changing consumer market-place. The American scholar, Joshua Meyrowitz, argues in a closely related study that the impact of the electronic media in the United States has been to dissolve the consumers' 'sense of place':

Electronic media have combined previously distinct social settings, moved the dividing line between private and public behaviour toward the private, and weakened the relationship between social situations and physical places. The logic underlying situational patterns of behaviour in a print-oriented society, therefore, has been radically subverted. Many Americans no longer seem to 'know their place' because the traditionally interlocking components of 'place' have been split apart by electronic media. Wherever one is now – at home, at work or in the car – one may be in touch and tuned in. (Meyrowitz, 1985, p. 308).

An inescapable consequence of this escalation of the global electronic mediascape, according to Meyrowitz (1985), is the massive loss of knowledge of the 'real world' on the part of the typical American consumer-citizen, who may exhibit an amazing level of detailed knowledge of television and video films, their plots and stars, computer games, and of sports stars who appear on television, but have virtually no sense of the larger global realities 'in the real world' and also very little sense of the history or significance of his or her own locality and city.

This same process – of loss of a sense of place, coupled with immersion in a fast-moving world of television stars and other commodities of the international marketplace – is the object of analysis of the unending series of cultural and media studies that fill the shelves of up-market bookstores in Britain and in many other parts of the world – a particular new instance (a secondary 'circuit' in its own right) of international cultural production, which, conveniently enough for the British academic, has now adopted English as the international language of social commentary, as well as of business and trade. The loss of 'a sense of place'

in international media/international culture is in this sense reproduced in the kind of academic and journalistic writing which is
currently given pride of place as cultural critique.

TRIBES AND NATIONS

Connected to the loss of a popular sense of mastery over one's own
economic destiny (and/or the sense that this was manageable 'nationally'), and running in parallel with the subversion of national or local
identities or histories by transnational consumption industries and
electronic media, is the rebirth of nationalist and other 'particularist'
forms of politics and self-identification. With others, the social
philosopher Michael Walzer refers to this phenomenon as 'the return
of the tribes', and sees this as most marked in Eastern Europe, as a
consequence, precisely, of the kind of market liberalism which has
been unleashed there in place of the Stalinist command economy – a
kind of populist free-for-all, in which people inevitably organise
themselves into inclusionary and exclusionary 'ranks and orders', for
their own kind and against others, in the never-ending Hobbesian
struggle for survival and gain (Walzer 1992). Understandably, along
with many other contemporary social thinkers, reflecting on events
in Bosnia, Chechnya and elsewhere, Walzer is pessimistic about the
consequences of this 'return of the tribes' in Eastern Europe in particular, which he sees to be a product of the insecurities contradicto-
rily produced by the new freedoms in that part of the world and likely
to spread. More complex and defensible forms of social solidarity and
identity, he argues, depend on the existence of conditions of security
which, as Paul Ormerod argues elsewhere in this volume, are difficult
to envisage in places like Eastern Europe. In another, equally cau-
tious, essay, Walzer turns his attention to the presence of 'huge
populations of guest workers and illegal immigrants' in Western societies and ponders the problem of how such peoples (internal tribes in
a host society) might be given some form of participation and social
justice, insisting that the exclusion of such populations from 'the
spheres of justice' would be the end of any claim such societies might
make to be essentially democratic in form (Walzer 1993). What
Walzer does not do, however, is to examine the ways in which the
unreflexive talk of 'tribalism' which has come to be acceptable in
contemporary journalism and conversation (for example, in treat-
ments of subordinated populations – the 'tribal' underclass itself) can
have its own political effects. Not least of these effects is a suppres-
sion of any honest recognition and appraisal of the trend to increas-

ing inequality, both in respect of economic security and in respect of any wider sense of membership of the broad civil society, and the different impacts this drive towards unequal societies might be having both within and across different 'tribal' groups.

The Tribal and the Local in the 1990s

There must be a suspicion that some of the influential arguments about globalisation and the new tribalism may just be overdone, or, perhaps we should say, too one-dimensional. First, some of the specific arguments (for example, about an international 'Americanised' media that will dominate the world and extinguish all traces of local culture) now have a quite extended historical lineage (for example, in the panic over American horror and war comics in the 1950s), well pre-dating the arrival of a specifically post-Fordist international economy.

Second, it is by no means clear – in countries like England – whether recognition of the new 'global realities' of 'post-Fordism' as the source of the present economic difficulties is widespread or universal. It is important to notice the very different, diffuse and often very local folk-wisdoms through which the realities of social and economic decline are popularly understood. These beliefs may range from jingoistic conspiracy theories (especially with respect to 'Brussels') to more specific attributions of 'blame' or incompetence, directed, for example, at individual politicians at national or local level. The irrationality of these beliefs (when seen from the point of critically-minded cultural theorists, on the one hand, or clear-headed economists, on the other) does not detract from the very powerful purchase which such beliefs may have on the social imagination.

Third, a closely connected observation, we should recognise that generalisations about the arrival of a new and 'post-modern' culture as such, composed primarily of the flickering and rapidly changing 'texts' of the mediascape and the consumer marketplace, may work for the 'headquarter cities' of culture and communication, like Los Angeles, without being so comprehensive (descriptively or analytically) in their accounts of other, less prominent or metropolitan cities or, in particular, for societies and locations on the very cutting edge of global change. As commentators like Patrick Wright so often remind us, Britain, in particular, is 'a very old country' (Wright 1985): it may be that the 'resistance to change' and the embrace of the past, and also the power of local identity, is especially influential here. Commentators may deplore the ways in which local identities are now 'inauthentically' reproduced – for example, in local industrial museums or in other heritage events or sites. But it is important to recognise this reinvention of local identity at work, alongside the coverage of 'the local' in local radio, television and newspaper reports, rather than being unwilling, in the manner of some post-modern commentary, to glimpse the reality of these very local processes.

I want to highlight here just three different, ostensibly unconnected, aspects of the local situation in England: football, local and regional difference and the Corporation – three continuing features of what we must always recognise is 'an old country' which define its specificity, in distinction to the American metropole.

Football

It is impossible to ignore the sense in which football, Britain's most popular spectator sport, has itself very suddenly been subject to the kinds of 'globalising' forces of the market to which I have been alluding in this chapter (cf. also Taylor 1995). Football can now be watched on terrestrial or satellite television on nearly every evening of the week, and the schedules of television and radio have quickly been transformed to accommodate this 'wall-to-wall' coverage of football, with unknown consequences on the organisation of divisions of household labour and the social organisation of time. It would be naive to see this as anything other than the wholesale marketisation of football as a new form of consumer industry; it makes no sense to see Manchester United plc (with an annual turnover in 1993–94 of over £44 million) as what we used to call simply 'a football club' (*Guardian*, 25 March 1995).

However, I argue that it is just as important to recognise the more prosaic but organic source of the success of 'market football' in England in the 1990s. The market in home and away strips, minikits (for the car window), T-shirts, scarves, tracksuits and other regalia is nothing if not a statement of affiliation and, very often, of local origin and attachment. This statement of local origins has always been important among what we used to call the 'working class'. But there is no question that the declaration of support for individual football clubs serves other important functions within the business classes (as well as other social classes) of England in the 1990s – not least, in the support it gives to the continuing reproduction of male domination in these circles. In political circles, we know that 'football talk' is intended to display evidence of a common and popular touch, especially when politicians are out in their weekend constituencies. But this does not exhaust the importance of football as some kind of continuing, residual marker of regional or local identity, and also as a container or signifier of messages other than football. It is important to note how the most aggressive and troublesome fans of the English national team, like those who caused the postponement of the Ireland–England game in Dublin in February 1995, are most often from areas of England which political economists would define as 'peripheral' areas (Hartlepool, Port Vale and so on) – regions that have been left to 'sink' in the turmoil of deindustrialisation and the 'freeing of the market forces' – young men 'trying to make a name' for themselves and their forgotten locality. So also is it important to listen to the plaintive, paranoid pleas of the young English men, explaining that their support of the English team is a matter of 'patriotism' and 'defence of one's country' – a desperate desire 'to do service' for the country and be recognised for so doing. On a more regular, week-in and week-out basis, in a variety of local settings, young men (and some young women) will describe their own local sense of place, with levels of commitment that are incomprehensible in many other societies (like the US), in terms of the qualities, and perhaps the detailed histories, of the local football team. They will also develop accounts of the relationship and rivalries of that club to other clubs in other parts of the country, articulated around key games or transfers, which constitute a widely shared sense of local knowledge. This does not take quite the same form as it assumes in Italy, where groups of the so-called ultra supporters actually hold formal meetings during the periods between games, with elections for leadership positions and other responsibilities. But it is intriguing how the 'marketisation' of professional football in England in the late 1980s resulted in the formation of the so-called fanzine (fan magazine) movement, and the 'empowerment' of some sections of the local fans, who have now succeeded in introducing this kind of football knowledge, replete with a mass of local signifiers, into early evening and local television. Something is at work in the imaginations of English football fans about local identity and local character – and the relationship of these local 'particularities' to the larger social configuration that is 'the country'. Amongst followers of major clubs like Manchester United, something else is added to 'the imagination' about the relationship of the local icon – 'the Reds' – to a larger European community (drawing on the fans' personal 'experience' of cities like Barcelona, Budapest or Milan, and their determination to locate Manchester as a member of this new European headquarter group). The 'critical issue', to which I want to return, is how this imaginary attachment to locality can be articulated on other terrains.

Local and Regional Difference

Both on the terraces and on television, football fans, with more or less humour (though usually with rather less toleration), display a rich kind of folk knowledge of what they believe to be the differences between cities, towns and regions of England. In the early 1980s, in the days of the miners' strike, supporters of the clubs of South Yorkshire had to endure many cruel taunts about the fate of the local mining industry from fans of various London clubs. Manchester United, in the mid-1990s, as the main club of a headquarter city, 'the capital of the North', is widely resented, especially elsewhere in the old industrial North, for its ostentatious and apparently limitless wealth. West Ham United has been defined, for many years, as a club that personifies the proud traditions of the labour aristocracy of London's East End, where Chelsea has been associated with the 'fast money' and lifestyles of the commercial middle class doing its business in the West End.

The origin or the 'truth' of these local and urban myths, as circulated around the football clubs of England, need not detain us here. The point is that these myths run in parallel to a much more broadly based, historically well established set of ideas and beliefs about the social and moral character of regions and places. Some of these beliefs are associated, by imputation, with local accent and patterns of speech – which is to say that 'ways of speaking' English are thought to reveal something of the character of place: resilient (the Geordie), stubborn (the Tyke), opportunistic (the Scouser, the Cockney East Ender) or businesslike (the Brummie). They also organise a particular conception of the character of England or, indeed, the Celtic fringe (Wales, Scotland, the North of Ireland and Eire). These themes resonate through local theatre and, sometimes, local newspapers, and also in contemporary representations of region and place in cinema, on prime-time television (*Boys from the Blackstuff, Auf Wiedersehen Pet, Minder, Taggart* and so on), and also in television advertising. They are a form of myth about England as a patchwork of regions (and the UK as a patchwork of connected national segments), each with its own distinctive character, that does not easily go away, and they have certainly not 'disappeared into air' automatically as a result of the fundamental crises of the local labour markets in these regions over the last 20 years.

The intriguing issue, sociologically, is whether these myths of regional difference do speak to some important differences in the 'structures' of social provision and quality of life in particular regions and places – no doubt produced, originally, by the industrial or occupational cultures in their founding years, but now re-articulated in more contemporary forms. Research in which I have recently been engaged in the North of England, for example, suggests that the massive crisis in the steel industry of Sheffield and South Yorkshire did not result in anything like the level of emigration from that region as occurred in Liverpool in the 1970s, subsequent to the crisis of the Mersey shipbuilding industry (cf. Taylor et al. 1996). The same research also confirms that there are some real continuities in the commercial rebirth of Manchester in the 1990s and the earlier history of Manchester as 'England's first industrial city'. This research shows the continuing importance of local specificity and difference, and the continuing powerful hold of 'local culture' (either, as in Manchester's case, as a dynamic locality connected to a wider commercial world or, as in Sheffield, as a kind of enclave city, trying hard to retain its sense of solidarity born, initially, of its dual economy of cutlery and steel, the archetypal places of public resorts, the pub and the chapel). This stubborn sense of local culture also reveals itself in England in the resistance shown to proposals to alter local government boundaries, especially where a change of traditional county boundaries is involved. Discussion of how this particular sense of local identity, with its firm historical resonance, might relate to future political campaigns (for example, in respect of devolution of powers from Strasbourg or Westminster) is clearly important – no matter how 'ill-thought' may be the current thinking of the Labour Party in this respect.

The Corporation

If there is one institution which marked off the English region as having some autonomy of, and local specificity or variation in relation to, the national or international economy, especially in the early post-war period, it was the local authority – referred to in many cities simply as 'the Corporation'. 'The Corporation' never provided more than a small proportion of the local citizenry with paid employment, and in no way could be credited with any significant role in whatever economic advances occurred, at the high point of Britain's 'period of post-war affluence', the late 1950s to early 1960s. What it did do was to provide what initially was thought to be decent housing for many thousands of citizens, and also provided a workable and affordable system of public transport. It also underwrote the provision of free education (and school meals) for the mass of the citizens. In its most developed formulations – for example, in Herbert Morrison's London County Council in the 1950s – 'the Corporation' (County Hall) was a major force in the civilising of public spaces, including the public parks, sports and leisure facilities, street lighting and other forms of what is now called 'street furniture'.

Each of these achievements of 'the Corporation', 'Town Hall bureaucracy' or 'municipal socialism' has been subject to various kinds of criticism, with increasing stridency, since the 1970s, not least by proponents of 'individual choice', though it is worth pausing in 1996 to reflect on the quality of the alternatives now provided (in the sphere of housing and transport, for example) by 'the market'. Dick Atkinson is surely right to argue against this tradition of top–down urban provision as a viable form of 'civics' in the 1990s, and to argue for new forms of collaborative relationship between urban professionals, volunteers and electors in different local communities (Atkinson 1994). But my main concern here is to venture the thought that this tradition of local action and practice (allocating responsibilities for civic action to the Town Hall) is another, long-established feature of English life which simply has not 'vanished into air'. It is quite clear that local authorities no longer have the resources they could command in the late 1970s, and it is also clear that local authority culture remains in need of radical re-appraisal and reorganisation in face of the particular challenges posed locally by the global economy. There is no question that local authorities will have to conduct their activities, on very many fronts, 'in partnership' with many other local institutions (for example, in the spheres of education, policing and urban development) – in ways that will result in constant changes of local authority form and function. A particularly promising line of action here must lie in the development of new relationships between local government and the different kinds of 'secondary associations' through which social life is organised (from tenants' associations to local Crime Watch organisations) (see Benington, this volume). It is also clear that the local authority in England in the 1990s never achieved the form and significance of other, even longer-established, local representative bodies (like the *contradas* – or neighbourhood associations – of Siena, Italy, or the cantons of Switzerland) and that it would be idle to think that they could do this in the future – though it is precisely in these places, with their strong sense of local government, connecting to local sense of place and attachment, that recorded crime rates are lowest. It would be equally idle, however, to think that the local authorities, working hard alongside other leaders of the local 'growth coalition' in the search for national or international investment and for the refurbishment of their cities in what they see to be the public interest, can be inattentive to the voices of local populations, or that there are no ways of rethinking the relationship of 'the Corporation' to the broad range of local citizens, including the problematic and excluded populations. In the context of old England, where things do not universally melt into air, it may be that 'there is no alternative' (to coin a well known phrase) to the local authority as the link between 'the global' and 'the local' and nowhere else to which a local population (for all that it will be linked in one part of its imagination into a global marketplace) can turn for the representation of the practical and utopian local interest (the local 'parliament') or, even, source of social support. Nor can the new breed of urban professionals involved in redevelopment programmes or the voluntary organisations standing in for the national state in various spheres ignore the local authority – the Corporation – as a site of struggle and political and social intervention. It is surely not beyond the scope of our own imaginations, in the late-1990s, to think of ways in which the local authority can be reconstituted as a different symbol of local attachment and value.

CONCLUSION

References to 'football', to the folkloric idea of local or regional identity and to the achievements and continuing significance of local councils can very easily be dismissed as an exercise of resignation or nostalgia – or, even worse, as an active attempt to recreate such 'traditional institutions' (with all of their unfortunate, gendered and/or inefficient and other problematic qualities) in the present, rapidly changing circumstances. This has not been my intention. What has been my concern is to explore some aspects of the ways in which citizens of this society do still seem to create, or reference, their local feeling and attachment, and to take seriously the possibility that they could continue to do so. However effective the reach of global media, there must be some sense in which people will organise their lives and identities in terms of structures and systems of local governance and local identification. But we also want to recognise the truth about this unreformed, unequal and troubled, very old society – that it has often managed, even in very difficult times (the inter-war Depression, or the early post-war period of social reconstruction), to evoke 'attachment' (both to 'place' and also to 'a way of life'). The fearful and antagonistic experience of every-day life in Britain in the late 1990s suggests that the England of this period will not be one that encourages a similar attachment amongst large proportions of its citizens, unless the familiar icons of the local landscape can once again be accorded signifi-cance and allegiance, albeit in new and imaginative ways.

NOTE

1. Ulrich Beck's concern in *Risk Society* to highlight the extensive and unpredictable range of new risks associated with High Modern Socie-ties, was dramatically underlined in Britain during 1996 by the mas-sive scare surrounding the safety of British beef (threatened by 'mad cow disease') and, in particular, the challenge this posed to nationalist sentiment in Britain with respect to the inherent superiority of 'the British way'.

REFERENCES

Atkinson, D. (1994) *The Common Sense of Community.* London: Demos (Paper No.11).

Beck, U. (1992) *Risk Society.* London: Sage.

Giddens, T. (1991) *Modernity and Self-Identity.* Cambridge: Polity Press.

Lash, S. and Urry, J. (1994) *Economies of Signs and Space.* London: Sage.

Meyrowitz, J. (1985) *No Sense of Place: the Impact of Electronic Media on Social Behaviour.* New York: Oxford University Press.

Taylor, I. (1995) 'It's a Whole New Ball Game', *Salford Papers in Sociology* 17.

Taylor, I., Evans, K. and Fraser, P. (1996) *A Tale of Two Cities: Global Change, Local Feeling and Everyday Life in the North of England: A Study in Manchester and Sheffield.* London: Routledge.

Taylor, I. and Jamieson, R. (1996) '"Little Mesters": Nostalgia and Protest: Masculinity in the North of England' in S. Westwood and J. Williams (eds), *Imagining Cities.* London: Routledge.

Walzer, M. (1992) 'The New Tribalism; Notes on a Difficult Problem', *Dissent* (Spring) 164–71.

Walzer, M. (1993) 'Exclusion, Inclusion and the Democratic State', *Dissent* (Winter) 55–64.

Wright, P. (1985) *On Living in an Old Country*. London: Verso.

10 The Business of 'Community'

Jonathan Gosling

INTRODUCTION

The terms 'community' and 'organisation' are often taken to refer to quite different aspects of social life. Organisations have goals, tasks, formal structures and overtly sanctioned authority. 'Community', on the other hand, refers to a more general sort of belonging, often associated with a place, and characterised by informal relationships. Private organisations are owned, and can be bought and sold; communities cannot be owned by outsiders, and do not 'employ' their members.

There is also a tendency to idealise community life in opposition to life within formal organisations (see Pahl, this volume, for a critique of this view). In such comparisons, organisations – especially those in which we find employment – are identified, rightly or wrongly, as sites of alienation and of inauthentic relations. The reasons for this are fairly straightforward: companies and public services want us to work for them in roles requiring aspects of, but not the whole, self. In the old days they wanted 'hands'; these days it is our knowledge and intelligence. Neither then, nor now, were they interested in our personal lives and our attachments. Commercial organisations make profits by extracting from labour a 'surplus value' over and above what it costs to employ and reproduce that labour: that is how capitalism – including post-industrial varieties – works. Community, on the other hand, is remembered as a place of belonging, but not, significantly, of ownership.

However the distinction is becoming less clear. Several influential writers argue either that organisations should be more like communities (Handy 1994), or that communities should be more organised (for example, Etzioni 1993). This chapter will show that contemporary concepts of community are becoming closer to those of organisations, stressing elective membership, social contract, effectiveness and even efficiency. But these new notions of community create a lacuna around belonging, motivation and commitment. This occluded area of experience is associated with nostalgic images of authentic relationships, self-evidently meaningful activities, permanent containing social structures, and continuities – in short, with attachment. When referred to in organisational contexts under the banner of community these images engender a sense of belonging to a transcendent unity: an anthropomorphic pan-humanity. On one hand this raises ethical questions about the adequacy of such images to serve as vehicles for spirituality, for transcendent belonging; on the other hand it points to some practical steps for leaders wishing to make use of these processes.

ORGANISATIONS AS COMMUNITIES

Maybe organisations are becoming more like communities; and maybe they should become so. This section will examine such propositions by considering significant trends in contemporary organisation.

Localisation and Federation

Charles Handy suggests that federal political structures emerging in Europe will tend to emphasise allegiances to localities, specifically cities, which will have increased powers over their affairs under the principle of subsidiarity. The same process is taking place in large companies and public sector organisations, many of which are experimenting with federal structures – Cable and Wireless has an explicit federation of its 69 companies, and Unilever describes itself a 'multi-local' multinational corporation (Unilever 1996). One purpose is to be closer, more in touch and responsive to local product and labour markets; another is to foster a local sense of ownership and commitment amongst employees, and the 'empowerment' of managers. The idea is that a business should be associated with locality, and be of a small enough scale to be comprehended in its entirety – more or less – by its members. This might be summed up, ironically, in Schumacher's phrase, 'Small is Beautiful' (1974).

But there is another rather different logic to the localisation of business, exemplified in the demergers of ICI/Zeneca and more recently the Hanson Trust. In the business strategy literature this trend has been promoted most vigorously as the concept of 'core competence' (Prahalad and Hamel 1990) – the idea that a business (or, for that matter an NHS Trust) should identify the one or two things it can do much better than its rivals, and concentrate on those. This may result in employees feeling a greater sense of immediate connection to the fortunes of the business, but it most decidedly does not produce a catholic, inclusive sense of belonging or ownership. Indeed quite the opposite may be the case: peripheral processes are often 'outsourced' (contracted out) in the attempt to focus on core competence, the clear message being that any interests other than those directly contributing to unique competitive advantage should be excluded from the business. This is surely the other side of localisation and federation. It may permit greater diversity between provinces or business units, but within each of these entities there is less space for peripheral, experimental, or other 'non-core' activities – and perhaps also less tolerance of counter-cultural sympathies and 'deviant' behaviour. Ironically, therefore, localisation may effect a deterioration in the kind of generous inclusive qualities that it is supposed to enhance. Alternatively, of course, there may be nothing ironic about it: the purpose may not be so much inclusion as control – from the point of view of federal politicians and senior managers of businesses, localisation may be valuable not because people feel more involved, but because they exercise more effective self-control (and control of colleagues) on behalf of the corporation. This is certainly the tenor of some of the more critical contemporary literature on, for example, self-managed teams (Turnbull 1996).

Simulated Communities

As knowledge and intelligence become the key sources of value, it will be people rather than tangible assets that are traded on the stock market. But while this would imply placing greater value on retaining people, countervailing pressures are pushing companies to reduce their core employee numbers and to make more use of temporary and part-time staff. The result will be a far higher interest in the competence of those that do the work, whether employed or hired for a particular task – a portfolio. The ability to get value from such workers will to a large extent depend on companies' ability to make them feel a part of the enterprise. Charles Handy (1994) argues that this will be easier if they can become members of it in the same sense in which one 'joins' a community, and this will only be possible if companies, like communities, are not subject to being auctioned continuously on the stock market.[1] As there are few signs of such a radical restructuring of ownership, the practical problem remains one of making people feel a part of the organisation. Hence the immensely energetic and expensive 'culture change' programmes with which so many are enthused. The very fact of the attention and labour required to generate and maintain such enthusiasm exposes the simulation of community: in fact such initiatives are often rather more reminiscent of the holiday camp (without the holiday).

Virtual Organisations and the Problem of Trust

The ubiquity of the internet introduces a spatial distancing in organisations, alongside the temporal limitations referred to above. Combined, these produce what has become known as the 'virtual organisation'. Colleagues may seldom meet face-to-face, so communication is conducted through email, video- and voice telephone, and various symbolic forms representing the organisation in its (physical) absence, such as TV advertisements aimed at employees as much as at customers (see, for example, British Airways' transmissions on TV networks around the world as part of its employee empowerment campaign entitled 'the world favours the brave', BA News, November 1995). In virtual organisations many people who represent the organisation and deliver its services are distributed around the world, and many are on short-term or part-time contracts. They have to be trusted to act in the best interests of the firm, and this has obviously led to speculation about the conditions for engendering trust. Handy (1995) has outlined some implications for organisations, based on the assertion that 'you can't trust someone you do not know, you can't trust someone who is not committed to the goals of the organisation, and you can't trust someone who lets you down' (p. 213). So those leaders wishing to foster a sense of 'community' in their organisations should:

- choose the right people – so make use of probationary contracts;

- keep units small enough for people to know each other;

- promote talk – and get people to meet whenever possible (hi-touch as well as hi-tech);

- reinforce common goals, vision, mission;

- reward loyalty and performance – and be tough on those who let the organisation down.

These may be wise prescriptions, but they also tell us something about the social construct of trust. Handy takes it to be an aspect of a relationship between individuals, secure only in a network of people known to and answerable to each other. Larry Ray (1996) argues that the need for this arrangement is typical of the contemporary condition of 'hyper-differentiation', in which the collectivities to which each of us belong are now categorised in minute classes: instead of referring to mass class-culture groupings, modern market taxonomies, for example, identify individuals in very small groupings of like-minded consumers. Niche marketeers aim at ever smaller populations – and are able to do so because of better information about individuals, and hence more accurate targeting. This process of breaking down membership boundaries to more detailed levels becomes 'hyper-differentiation' when the defining terms of such membership are constantly changed and hence reconfigured. In effect, the boundaries multiply to the extent that they explode and dissolve, leaving individuals to form their own networks of contacts with whom they have enough in common to share some degree of trust.

In more traditional modern societies, institutional regulations provide the conditions for trust and confidence – but these depend on confidence in, and deference towards, professional and juridical procedures, and in the state to manage them. If such confidence prevails, trust amongst strangers is unproblematic at the personal level because it is looked after by the state and by the professional establishment. Alternatively, a more generalised morality may characterise social relations, in which there is shared confidence in good will, that agreements will be kept. This is the traditional notion of community, defined by shared values and expectations. However, Ray also posits a situation of generalised distrust with little confidence in systems and institutions. He argues that individualised market relations generate such mistrust, because each actor is seeking his or her own advantage (but see Ormerod, this volume). The response to such conditions is generally to form and maintain networks of contacts which act as havens of comparative trust in the midst of a multitude of anonymous market relationships (cf. 'kereitsu', as described by Fukuyama 1995).[2] This latter seems to be the kind of solution Handy is proposing, pointing once more to the emergence of small, defended, in-groups; and especially to the manager's crucial task of defining and maintaining a sense of boundedness for those on the inside – of being contained psychologically, of being able to trust one another commercially and professionally, and of being allied to something greater than themselves that justifies self-control.

Marketing Networks

The individualisation and de-massification (the break-up of mass production, mass servicing and so on) of industrial and social institutions produces new organisational forms, with new kinds of belonging. A prime example is the telecommunications industry – now better referred to as 'infocoms' because of the integration of information technology (both software and hardware) and the telephone networks. Any major infocoms project involves knitting together products and services from several providers, and tenders are therefore submitted by competing consortia or alliances. Because telephone networks are (to all intents and purposes) almost invariably either state or public monopolies, the telephone companies are required to provide access to all bidding consortia, including those that may include direct competitors. In a recent government agency contract for an information management system (to be the largest in Europe) the state telecommunications company was servicing all the bidding consortia as well as leading its own consortium. Within the sales department responsible for this project were staff working on competing bids, required to exercise allegiance both to their employer (the telephone company), and to the consortium to which they were temporarily assigned. This situation is of course the result of the telephone company being a near monopoly provider of parts of the system, but it amplifies the prevailing conditions, in which sales and marketing operations act independently of the rest of the corporation. Opportunities arise for sales people to put together bids in which their employing company has only a very small stake – possibly much smaller than a direct competitor who is providing services at the other end of a network. On the one hand this is a failure to sell the company's products; on the other it is an opportunity for the sales department to earn revenues and, crucially, to maintain contacts in the industry with customers, suppliers and current and potential partners. It is, incidentally, also an opportunity to meet potential employees and employers: in other words, to maintain a network within the industry that may be useful given the temporary and unreliable nature of employment contracts generally.

We are used to seeing companies making products and sales departments selling them to customers. Here, however, the crucial function is the creation of networks of actors, in effect creating a new venture in the space between a number of suppliers and customers. Such new ventures are inherently temporary and not owned by anyone in particular. They do, however, have leaders, and are enacted by project teams. These teams function as market intermediators, creating deals establishing networks that may in due course be more influential but less visible or regulated than formally constituted firms.

Paternalistic Local Links

There are also, contrary to much of the above, some companies expressing paternalistic intentions, and many large industrial complexes encourage formal and informal links with their locality. British Nuclear Fuels Ltd (BNFL), through its site at Sellafield, for example, is still the main employer in West Cumbria, and senior managers are active on local charitable and statutory bodies. The site trades unions – especially the GMB (General and Municipal Boilermakers Union) – are significant forces in local politics. Nevertheless, BNFL has shifted half the Sellafield site workforce on to 'outsourced' contracts, and there is no longer a sense that the company will look after all its current and past employees. This can be seen as a logical conclusion of the externalisation of the reproductive costs of labour. Until very recently isolated parts of the country have been more or less self-sufficient providers of labour, and so companies have invested in the long-term reproduction of their 'human resources'. With more mobility and a general loosening of emotional as well as contractual ties to places and employers, these costs need no longer be borne by companies. In fact, globalisation acts against this: Reebok's UK headquarters and distribution centre are in Lancaster, a small town with very little industrial activity. The main labour requirement is for warehouse personnel, but there are not enough other firms in the area to sustain a supply of these skills, nor to make training cost effective. There is thus an incentive to the company to move to the main conurbations, and to abandon its paternalistic links to the local community (although it may of course maintain a high level of care for its employees).

Collegial Values

There are some organisations that, nominally at least, think of themselves as communities: universities are a prime example, often defined as 'a community of scholars'. Managers, in this scheme, administer mundane resources on behalf of the scholars in such a manner as to preserve opportunities for scholarship. But this is by and large now a nostalgic fantasy. The production of academic goods is as regimented and managed as any other intellectual knowledge production process, and one can observe the same tendency to form tight personal networks, organise in small groupings, move frequently between institutions, and pay more attention to the terms of individual employment contracts than to collegial values. It may be, of course, that the knowledge creation process requires a form of collaborative work that could be seen as a form of community – there are certainly language communities defined by those who speak a particular jargon. It might even be that, taking an ecological view, academics as a whole, or some local populations of the species, are endangered communities. But this is taking us into the next section, in which I will discuss the ways which communities can be conceived in terms of organisation.

COMMUNITIES AS ORGANISATIONS

Images of community are necessarily diffuse and ambiguous. Sometimes these images are crystallised into ideals, and act as ideological touchstones for political programmes. 'Community' is, in reality, too complex, idiosyncratic and laden with unconscious meanings to be captured in any single theoretical or descriptive frame. Nevertheless, it is possible to identify several ways in which the term is interpreted; following Jacobs (1995), I list these as six:

1. *Communities of ascription.* Local neighbourhoods and their social structures, focusing especially on people's shared experiences and outlooks, and on how social networks operate. It is often this image of community that is referred to as 'traditional'. A salient feature of such social networks, however, is that membership of them, and of sub-groups within them, is generally by ascription rather than choice.

2. *Elective communities of interest and commitment,* defined by

shared characteristics other than locality. Although these shared characteristics may be more or less freely chosen (for example, being a vegetarian), defining oneself as a member of such a community is an existential choice. The proliferation of communities of interest can be taken as a sign of increasing value pluralism and of de-traditionalisation. They are often seen as emancipatory in comparison with traditional local communities, which tended to be oppressive towards some sub-groups – particularly women, incomers and so on.

3. *Communitarianism* (especially Etzioni's (1993) version), which returns the focus to the 'social contract' in local communities, emphasising reciprocal responsibilities and duties. Individuals cannot be allowed to do whatever they want (in opposition to libertarianism), while communities can do things for themselves (in opposition to statism).

4. *Social-ism*. Another version of communitarianism arises from the argument that people can only be conceived of and understood in a social context. Societies have to flourish in order for individuals to do so; attention must therefore be given to the development of society as a whole, as well as to choices for individuals (Mulhall and Swift 1992, Bell 1993, Avineri and de-Shalit 1992).

5. *Common sympathy*. Beneath much of the above (and closely allied with 4) lies the desire to see community as a distinct means of describing social relations. Such relations are based on common sympathy, voluntary reciprocity and mutual respect, precisely the qualities emphasised by attachment theory as promoting secure and trusting relationships. These are rather different categories from those used to describe social relations as markets (with a focus on exchange) or as fixed by hierarchies of state and employing organisations (focusing on authority and force).

6. *Community development and self-management*, voiced mainly by practitioners (Atkinson 1994) in opposition to market forces and state bureaucracies. In practical terms it has given rise to co-ops, credit unions, development trusts and numerous self-help and voluntary sector organisations. This is the stuff of civil society, in the defence of which campaigning groups such as the 'Citizens Organising Foundation' are mobilised (MacLeod 1995).

In each of these definitions, communities are arenas for organisation – of social networks, of social identity, of interest groups, of a social contract of rights and obligations. Calls for communities to be revitalised and for organisations to become more like communities share this perspective: a notion of membership experienced via organisational roles; of communities constructed by organisation (see Nicholson, Kennedy, this volume). In this view community members not only share a dependency on pre-organised organisations such as shops, schools, utilities and so on, they also construct a network of organisations in which the community is enacted – from babysitting circles, dinner parties and self-help groups to churches, clubs, political parties, credit unions and so forth.

The community is thus seen as a summation of conscious goals, a multitude of small organisations expressing both the particular interests and the empowerment of its members. A 'healthy' community is one replete with organisations. It is a place in which people recognise 'a community of interest' as a basis for organising. When they do so as consumers of goods or services, or as residents, they identify themselves as stakeholders in specific enterprises. The ability of people living in an area to identify a common interest and to organise around it can have important consequences for more formal organisations – as demonstrated by the Kentish revolt against the Channel tunnel rail link, and many other 'NIMBY' (Not In My Back Yard) pressure groups.

More traditionally, communities are often thought of as places of shared values (See Pahl, Nicholson, this volume). But both the notions of 'place' and of 'shared values' may be becoming problematic. Many 'places' which might once have been described as communities now experience rapid changes in population, often associated with immigrant and refugee populations who may not, initially at least, appear to have much in common in terms of 'shared values'. The expression of common values and assumptions is in any case the more or less conscious organisation of activities whereby, for example, disputes are mediated by commonly recognised authorities, or sanctions are enforced for anti-social behaviour. It is precisely these kinds of activities that break down in areas affected by large-scale changes. Although a frequent response is to call on professionals to take over responsibility for these matters, an alternative is to organise a new, indigenous way of dealing with them. Thus organisation becomes an explicit means for rebuilding a sense of community. There is, however, always a risk that the organisation may be defined and driven more by who it wants to keep out than by those it wishes to include within its boundaries.

MEMBERSHIP AND BELONGING

Membership as hitherto conceived is a status that is desired, consciously chosen or at least acquiesced to. Such a relationship is a form of commitment. In contrast, membership is also derived from attributes that others ascribe to us, and these ascriptions might have the effect of including or excluding us from particular groupings or communities. Other people's assumptions about our motivations, political beliefs and other characteristics effectively classify our membership of – or exclusion from – communities of various sorts. Thus as well as belonging to communities of interest and of organisation, we belong to communities defined by individual prejudice and shared social constructs. These are the communities to which we have 'been committed' in the more pejorative, passive, sense of the word. The 'security' engendered by this process has little to do with attachment and cohesion: quite the reverse, as security is undermined by shortage of homes and involuntary migration. These kinds of groupings are formed at least partially out of unconscious desires to hive off and distinguish parts of the 'whole' of society or of organisation. Communities thus come to represent split-off parts of society into which we project the more undesirable and frightening aspects of humanity that we would rather disown (see Rustin, this volume). These excluded groups then become objects of guilt and aggression (and even envy of the dependent positions afforded them). In this state – or rather, in this kind of relatedness to other social groupings – communities find it difficult to be empowered, or to speak with their own voice, or to alter their behaviour and experience, because their definition and characterisation is not in their own hands. An example is the 'community' of the 'underclass'.

Furthermore, this kind of belonging may be more secure and long-lasting than that derived from 'communities of interest', which can be sporadic and intermittent. Those needing security of membership as well as a clear definition of its boundaries and conditions may be finding fewer and fewer vehicles. Total institutions such as prisons, asylums, religious communities, the Army and Navy are all either in decline or being 'opened up' to more flexible, and less secure, forms of membership. The privatisation of prisons means prisoners are members of a market rather than the state; 'Care in the Community' enables dependent patients (with a distinct community role) to become customers; the abandonment of habit and house by religious orders locates membership in individual vocation; short commissions allow for contingent commit-ment in the services.

In conclusion one might elaborate a clear distinction between being included and 'belonging', on the one hand, and excluded and alienated, on the other. However, every exclusion is by implication an inclusion of an 'out-group', even if one has not selected it as such; and inclusion in even formal institutions is insecure. It is as if one of the criteria for membership of a (post)modern organisation is the constant anticipation of withdrawal, an abiding ambivalence about belonging; an overt, heroic, tragic autonomy.

CONCLUSION

Managers of organisations are increasingly using a rhetoric of com-munity in an attempt to hold them together and to extract a level of commitment beyond simple contractual exchange. However, the dynamics of labour markets, changes in technology and in the social relations of production undermine the 'soft' image of com-munity and constantly threaten any sense of collective responsibil-ity or common sympathy.

On the other hand, communities are almost universally defined in terms of organisation, and often by the number, types and relationships of formal organisations. Members of both ascribed and elective communities seem to have a lot to gain by becoming organised, but it is unlikely that they will do so on a mass scale because meaningful relationships are found in small groupings rather than through membership of a region or of a corporate identity. It will become increasingly complex for people to hold a notion of the system as a whole – that is, to have a sense of citizenship in the widest sense. It may be that, in keeping with the origins of the theory, truly secure attachments are only possible on a small scale, and that it is in the nature of large groups to engender the processes of exclusion and division (Main 1985).

If that is the case, the individualisation and personalisation of employment relationships, and membership of numerous interest or 'lifestyle' groups may allow more intimate and selective memberships – genuine attachments. The tendency of enterprises to work through self-managed teams may have the same effect. However, there are also significant threats to such intimate groupings, apart from the temporary and sporadic nature of many of them. Communications via electronic networks are intrinsically 'remote', and personal only in a very stylised manner (but see Liber, this volume). Employment relationships may indeed be meaningful, but are increasingly unreliable – and the same may be said of domestic and marital relationships. Indeed, people who opt out of the web of contract relationships may have something to teach us: many form small closed communities, reminiscent of the monasteries of the Dark Ages. It is possible that a rather different notion of community may be preserved in such enclaves in times of dissipation and anomie.

To return to the lacuna referred to in the Introduction: organisations use 'community' to refer to authentic, friendly, caring, inclusive relationships, while communities express their potency, effectiveness and identity in terms of organisation. This cross-referencing may be a sort of cross-dressing, an expression of post-modern gender ambivalence or confusion of genres. Communities as organisations and organisations as communities are simulacra, each a pastiche of the other, reflecting the architectural turn that has produced simulated 'olde worlde' style with all mod cons (hence the Wiltshire building firm specialising in new Tudor mansions).

Equally, though, I think the lacuna refers to the loss of intimate personal relationships, of friendship and a sense of authenticity. Neither the language of organisation nor of community allows an exploration of such intimacies, so one must wonder what is the voice that has been excluded (Gilligan 1982).

It seems to me that there are several possible answers. One is that an ethic of care – as distinct from one of justice – is struggling for a voice in this particular discourse. Conjuring with 'community' may be an attempt to voice a concern for people's needs (as well as their rights and duties). Even the most successful have needs for attachment, but are often unable to acknowledge them (Tronto 1993).[3] In spite of the apparent autonomy and independence of the contract culture, it certainly brings home the insecurity of attachments. Talk about community in organisations, and about organisation in a community context, may in fact allude to the desire to talk about relationships in a way which is not possible in the dominant discourse of either.

NOTES

1. Handy goes on to argue that stock markets should be used to raise finance in the form of mortgages on future earnings rather than equity ownership; this would explicitly institute the markets as betting rings, and acknowledge the fact that the ownership of the means of production is in the hands – or rather the minds – of those who work in enterprises.
2. 'Kereitsu' – 'the sharing of capital, technology and personnel in ways not open to firms outside the network' (Fukuyama 1995, p. 162). For

example, Toyota has one-tenth the number of workers as General Motors but reaps the same economies of scale as GM. Small firms are linked with larger firms in the kereitsu relationship which 'imposes reciprocal moral obligations to deal with one another'. They are therefore not able to trade freely elsewhere.

3. 'Those who are powerful are unwilling to admit their dependence upon those who care for them' (Tronto 1993, p. 174).

REFERENCES

Atkinson, R. (1994) The Common Sense of Community. London: Demos.

Avineri, S. and de-Shalit, A. (eds) (1992) Communitarianism and Individualism. Oxford: Oxford University Press.

Bell, D. (1993) Communitarianism and its Critics. Oxford: Clarendon.

Etzioni, A. (1993) The Spirit of Community. New York: Crown.

Fukuyama, F. (1995) Trust: The Social Virtues and the Creation of Prosperity. London: Hamish Hamilton.

Gilligan, C. (1982) In A Different Voice. Cambridge.: Harvard University Press.

Handy, C. (1994) The Empty Raincoat. London: Hutchinson.

Handy, C. (1995) Beyond Certainty. London: Random House.

Jacobs, M. (1995) 'Thoughts on Community'. Paper to the MPhil in Critical Management, Lancaster University, UK.

MacLeod, J. (1995) Community Organising: A practical and theological appraisal. London: Christian Action.

Main, T. (1985) 'Some psychodynamics of large groups' in A. Colman and M. Geller (eds), Group Relations Reader 2. Washington, DC: A.K. Rice Institute.

Mulhall, S. and Swift, A. (1992) Liberals and Communitarians. Oxford: Blackwell.

Prahalad, C.K. and Hamel, G. (1990) 'The Core Competence of the Organisation', Harvard Business Review (May/June) 79–91..

Ray, L. (1996) 'The Economisation of Culture and the Culturalisaton of Economy'. Paper to the Centre for the Study of Cultural Values, May 22, Lancaster University, UK.

Schumacher, E.F. (1974) Small is Beautiful: A Study of Economics as if People Mattered. London: Abacus.

Tronto, J. C. (1993) Moral Boundaries: a Political Argument for an Ethics of Care. New York: Routledge.

Turnbull, S. (1996) 'Self Managed Teams: filling the empty shrine? Meaning and control in a telephone bank'. MPhil in Critical Management, Lancaster University, UK.

Unilever (1996) Annual Report to Shareholders. London: Unilever.

11 New Paradigms and Practices for Local Government: Capacity Building Within Civil Society

John Benington

INTRODUCTION

For too many people local government is now more part of the problem than part of the solution. Local authorities are often experienced as oppressive, unresponsive and inefficient bureaucracies, rather than as the protectors of the local community, the promoters of lively local democracy and the providers of high-quality public services. The local state is always a battleground of competing interests and ideologies, in which the balance of power in the struggle sometimes falls in favour of democratic and progressive practices, but at other moments its effects are clearly divisive and regressive.

In this chapter I will argue that in the current culture of *fin de siècle* angst and societal PMT (pre-millennial tension), and in spite of the damage caused by the government's deeply divisive and demoralising ideology over the past 15 years, local government still has the potential to act as a very positive force: to challenge and to overcome some of the forces of fragmentation and atomisation within society; to rebuild a sense of individual attachment, social meaning and communal belonging to a wider whole; to regenerate a fresh political vision and direction, based upon communal rather than individualistic values, economic justice rather than social exclusion, and new forms of public service that are dependent upon the caring capacities latent within civil society, rather than the competitive forces fostered by the private market. If local government is to remain relevant during this period of profound political, economic and social change, there is little choice but to change in this direction. The ageing of the population, the rise in poverty and social exclusion, the run down of the urban fabric (private affluence amid public squalor), the risk of growing polarisation between classes, races, religions, and genders within our cities – these are key policy issues to which the private competitive market and the centralised bureaucratic state have not only proved to have no solutions, but have also compounded the problems. In the face of such challenges, local government is increasingly required to find new paradigms and new practices as a developmental, capacity building state, supporting and resourcing caring networks within the community.

Public policy in the UK over the past 15 years has been dominated by the private market. This has been a diversion from a much more important axis of relationships between the local state and civil society, together with its network of voluntary activities, informal associations and community organisations. One of the main challenges facing local government now is to rediscover its role as a champion of the local community, helping its many diverse groups and interests to articulate their needs, to find their voice and author-ity (authorship), and to participate actively and democratically in the development of their localities and networks as caring communities.

GETTING ON THE WRONG SIDE OF PEOPLE

In at least two previous historical periods, local government has been seen to be part of wider progressive movements for societal change. In the Victorian period, local authorities were a central part of the crusade, linking reforming politicians, popular movements, and passionate public servants, to improve public health and to promote literacy. In the late 1940s and early 1950s, local authorities were a crucial part of the broad-based movement to establish a comprehensive welfare state, with a mandate to provide a sound foundation of good basic housing, free education, and family support services. In many cities the Council was the spearhead for the post-war regeneration of the physical, social and economic environment, and responsible (as in Coventry after the blitz) for mobilising the vision and the plans for reconstruction, not just of the buildings, but also of the sense of attachment and social meaning that comes from belonging to a distinctive local community.

This vision of a local government rooted in its community is clearly expressed in Winifred Holtby's preface to her semi-autobiographical novel, *South Riding*, first published in 1936 :

But when I came to consider local government, I began to see how it was in essence the first-line defence thrown up by the community against our common enemies – poverty, sickness, ignorance, isolation, mental derangement and social maladjustment. The battle is not faultlessly conducted, nor are the motives of those who take part in it all righteous or disinterested. But the war is, I believe, worth fighting, and this corporate action is at least based upon recognition of one fundamental truth about human nature – we are not only single individuals, each face to face with eternity and our separate spirits; we are members one of another. (Holtby 1936)

However, somewhere along the line, councils and local authorities began to get on the wrong side of the people and of the communities which they were elected to serve. The first warning signals came perhaps with the comprehensive clearance and redevelopment schemes in the 1960s, in inner-city areas of cities like Manchester, Liverpool, Leeds and Glasgow. Residents came to feel with some justification that these schemes were driven more by the logic and the interests of the planners, the development companies and the building contractors, than by their needs either as individuals or as neighbourhoods (see also Nicholson, this volume). There was a great deal of popular protest and resentment not only about the break-up of long-standing communities, but also about the lack of communal facilities and support systems in the new out-of-town estates to which they were rehoused. Community activists in Notting Hill, Moss Side, Hillfields and many other areas mobilised people's associations and neighbourhood committees to agitate and organise against the Council, and to argue for more humanitarian community development (Benington 1975).

It gradually became clear that the problems did not lie simply in particular schemes, but in the whole ethos, labour process and organisation of local authorities. The Fordist system of mass production of standardised public services and the Weberian system of rule-based bureaucratic organisation may have been appropriate for the challenges of the immediate post-war period when it was necessary to rapidly produce thousands of homes fit for heroes – built to Parker Morris standards – and hundreds of school and nursery places to match the baby boom. However, the concern with quantity of output (how many council houses built, how many nursery places provided) was diverting attention from quality of outcomes for the users. Universality, which had been such an important concept in the setting up of the welfare state, was in danger of degenerating into uniformity, and standards into standardisation. There was too much concern with council houses and free school dinners (for example) as public goods, and too little concern with the social relations surrounding them as public services. I will return later in this chapter to the concept of public service as a relationship between people rather than as an exchange of commodities.

Meanwhile, public services were being overtaken by higher levels of responsiveness to customers within the private sector. New technologies made it possible, in the late 1970s and 1980s, in some industries and sectors, to replace assembly-line mass production of standardised products for undifferentiated mass markets with new, more flexible systems of small batch production of tailor-made products for much smaller, differentiated niche markets. It was now possible in some sectors to achieve profitability through economies of scope rather than of scale. Producers could now offer a much wider range of variation in their products and services, and although this was often limited to rather superficial differences in the colour, design and packaging of the product, it could be presented to the customer as a greater range of choice. The new computerised technologies also allowed producers to change product lines much more rapidly, and to respond much more quickly to shifts in patterns of consumer preferences (symbolised by the rapid turnover times in fashion and design in firms like Benetton and Marks and Spencer). Japanese firms such as Nissan, Toyota and Honda also introduced new concepts and systems of quality management, in which the producers no longer relied for their quality control upon rectification at the end of the assembly line, or upon after-sales complaints from customers, but designed quality into every stage of the production, and into aftersales service. Firms began to compete on the basis of quality as much as of price.

All this represented a sharp challenge for the Fordist systems and producer driven culture of much of the public sector, and highlighted the extent to which public services were lagging behind many private firms in their relationships with their users and 'customers'. The new Thatcher government was able to play upon people's growing dissatisfaction with the impolite, inefficient and disempowering ways in which they were often treated by public bureaucracies and public officials, to present a radical alternative model of provision. This challenged and undermined the post-war consensus in favour of a public welfare state designed to meet basic human needs through communal provision of public services, financed by social insurances and redistributive taxes, and designed, debated and allocated by democratically elected representatives in national and local 'parleyments'.

THE NEW RIGHT PARADIGM:
TESCO *ERGO SUM* (I SHOP, THEREFORE I AM)

The new right alternative was based upon a fundamentally different paradigm – that the individual is the basic unit of identity rather than society; that competition rather than co-operation is the basic drive in human beings; that the nuclear family is the only source of attachment, meaning and belonging rather than any wider community; that needs are best met through private purchasing of commodities within the commercial market rather than by communal provision through the state; that the public sector is parasitic upon the monetary wealth supposedly created by the private sector; that choice for consumers and quality of service are best achieved through price competition within a private market, rather than by planning and co-ordination through democratically elected public authorities.

This new right philosophy has been imposed on local government over the past 15 years through the introduction of nearly 150 acts, bills and regulations designed to privatise, marketise, or commercialise all the main spheres of local authority activity, and to shift the balance of power away from elected politicians and public servants towards consumers and private providers. Examples are: compulsory competitive tendering for many services; the shift of many responsibilities towards non-elected quangos and appointed bodies, the introduction of purchaser/provider splits and consumer/client trading relationships within public authorities.

Few would deny that this right-wing revolution has helped to transform the language, thinking and practice of many local authorities. There is now a much greater recognition within local government of business concepts like competition, price, contract, customers, and so on. However, the extent to which these concepts are adequate or appropriate to the primary tasks facing local government in this important period of changing needs is also now increasingly being questioned. Compulsory competitive tendering (CCT) may be a useful device for finding the cheapest way to collect refuse or sweep the streets (although the lowest tender may still not be the best long-term investment of taxpayers' money and may not provide the most cost-effective service). However, CCT is clearly a very crude and inappropriate instrument for deciding how best to mobilise a network of caring support for elderly mentally infirm people in their own homes and neighbourhoods, for example. Complex decisions of this kind, which are becoming increasingly important in local government (especially with the ageing of the population structure and with the steep increase in the proportion of pensioners to people of working age) clearly need a more subtle and sophisticated calculus than that provided by reducing everything to questions of cost in money terms. Judgements about actions and priorities for the care of human beings need to be rooted in deeper moral and social values than those which inform the capitalist market.

It is notable that the Thatcherite model for marketising public services is now being discredited even in terms of commercial business practice. Few modern firms would now favour the setting up of internal markets based upon price competition between separate internal businesses (along the lines of the purchaser/provider splits so favoured by the Conservative government). And few would argue that arm's-length relationships with their sub-contractors, based upon price-competitive tendering, is the best way to achieve quality of product or reliability of service. Increasingly, modern firms are basing their contracts upon close, collaborative, long-term relationships with their (external and internal) suppliers, where the aim is to develop a joint commitment to a common vision and a shared commitment to quality. Similarly, it is increasingly recognised that public services need to build close collaborative, long-term relationships not only with their sub-contractors, suppliers and other public and private sector partners, but also with the voluntary sector and the informal grassroots community.

The new right private market paradigm, which has continued to inform the government's approach to public services, is now seen to be based upon an impoverished philosophy. Its model of society as a supermarket ('Tesco *Ergo Sum*': 'I shop, therefore I am') is as inadequate a response to the diverse, complex and changing needs of the UK population at the end of the twentieth century as the centralised bureaucratic Keynesian welfare state before it. The ideological battle between market and state, between private and public, which has dominated political discourse for the past 50 years, is now being superseded by the recognition of a third sector, civil society, which has been neglected and marginalised in this bi-polar split between two polarised opposites.

NEW PARADIGMS FOR THE PUBLIC SECTOR: ROOTED IN CIVIL SOCIETY, NOT JUST IN THE STATE AND THE MARKET

It is important to start by remembering that the distinctions between state and market, and public and private sectors, are social constructions, and fairly recent ones at that. Raymond Williams points out, for example, that the original meaning of the word 'private' has a very different connotation from its current usage. It came into English from the Latin *privatus*, meaning withdrawn from public life, and from the verb *privare*, to bereave or deprive (for example, as in withdrawn religious orders, and referring to people not holding public or official rank). It was between the sixteenth and the nineteenth centuries that private came to be associated with privilege rather than deprivation (with the implication of exclusivity). The origin of the word 'public' is in the Latin *pubes*, meaning all people of pubic age (except women and slaves, notoriously!) entitled to take part in democratic arenas and processes. Public thus originally meant the whole adult community, conceived of as a democracy; and private implied deprivation of access to this public community.

Habermas, in his book *The Structural Transformation of the Public Sphere* (1962), and in later writings, developed the notion of the public sphere as the central focus within society for democratic debate and deliberation. However, in his terms the democratic public sphere is distinct both from the state and the market. 'The public sphere in Habermas's sense is conceptually distinct from the official economy; it is not an arena of market relations but rather one of discursive relations, a theatre for debating and deliberating rather than for buying and selling. Thus this concept of the public sphere permits us to keep in view the distinction between state apparatuses, economic markets, and democratic associations; distinctions that are essential to democratic theory' (Fraser 1992). Habermas sees this democratic public sphere as being gained by the liberal bourgeoisie of the nineteenth century, and then lost in the twentieth through the growth of consumerism, mass media, and the erosion of 'the public' by concepts like publicity and public relations.

Nancy Fraser and other critical social theorists argue that Habermas idealises the liberal public sphere as a democratic space, and ignores the extent to which it reflected economic and social divisions and inequalities in the wider society (for example, reinforcing the hegemony of white middle-class men, and marginalising the voice of women and the working class in democratic discourse). She concludes that 'any conception of the public sphere that requires a sharp separation between (associational) civil society and the state will be unable to imagine the forms of self-management, inter-public coordination, and political accountability that are essential to a democratic and egalitarian society' (Fraser 1992). Magnusson and Walker talk of the need to 'de-centre' the state as the focus for political activity, and instead to focus the struggle for local democracy on critical social movements within civil society.

> In terms of political spaces, we find critical movements rejecting the state (and its attendant parties and pressure groups) as the natural container for politics. As a result, we find them rejecting state power as the primary object of their activity ... It also involves a stress on non-statist political spaces in which to act: the 'local' and the 'personal' spaces within civil society. Instead of construing these spaces as parochial and non-political – as bourgeois categories demand – critical social movements have begun to recognise global structures in the daily activities of ordinary people. In confronting these structures, some of them have invented new political spaces: ecological regions, cultural networks, zones of liberation ... The exclusions of the state are then challenged by new connections, new solidarities, new ways of expressing community and shared identities. (Magnusson and Walker 1988)

What would such theoretical ideas mean in practice? In the next section I will begin to develop a fresh conception of the role and practice of local government in relation not only to the private market and the central state, but also to civil society.

NEW PRACTICES FOR LOCAL GOVERNMENT: BUILDING THE CAPACITY OF THE COMMUNITY

There is growing evidence and examples of local governments beginning to reinterpret and reorient their role towards civil society and the informal community.

As one response to this, a growing number of local councils are redefining their role in terms of governing the local community, not just administering the local authority, or distributing and delivering services to individuals. This wider 'community governance' role means that in addition to managing the local authority's departments and services through its committees, elected members also try to develop a strategic vision for the economic, social and political development of their locality, and to orchestrate the contributions from a wide range of other public, private, voluntary and community agencies and actors. Many of the ideas about community governance have been influenced by the writings of John Stewart. The philosophical basis for much of what follows in this section is brilliantly discussed in his book with Stewart Ranson (Ranson and Stewart 1994).

One form of community governance is short-term advocacy action to defend constituents' interests in relation to other agencies – for example, the scrutiny committee set up by Kirklees Council to investigate residents' complaints about water disconnections, which led to the local authority making representations on their behalf to the water authority, and negotiating changes in policy and procedure. This committee, which involved local residents as well as backbench councillors, sat like a House of Commons select committee and reported the results of its findings and actions directly back to the full Council meeting. Similarly, Southampton City Council took action with and on behalf of local women to improve the safety of the city by night, through practical improvements in street lighting, foot police patrols, more regular night buses, and so on.

A second form of community governance is the development of strategies to plan ahead for the needs of a particular group or area, often in partnership with other agencies. For example, Leicester, Southwark and Wolverhampton Councils are all developing inter-departmental and inter-agency strategies to prepare for the ageing of their populations. This involves not only co-ordinating the policies and work of all the local authority departments, but also mobilising other agencies and services like police, transport, health, social security, the churches, the universities, local employers, trades unions, and so on, in a concerted plan of action. Focusing on the needs of a particular group within the population, like older people, helps to reorient public services away from the specialism of their particular profession or department, and towards the holistic needs of a group of people in their setting within the community.

A third form of community governance is the local authority taking the initiative to act as the voice of its local people, protecting the interests of the local economy and local community against external threats, and promoting the representation and identity of the area in wider national and international arenas. Examples of this role are Nottinghamshire County Council organising an official public inquiry into the planned closure of the coal mines in its area, chaired by Lord Justice Scrivener, and taking evidence from many different organisations in open session, and publishing a report in which the economic and the social costs and benefits of the closure for different groups within the community were assessed. Another example is the way in which local authorities like Coventry, Luton, Sheffield, Stoke on Trent and many others, which have faced the run down of their traditional industries (auto, steel, potteries) have tried to develop a positive, forward-looking regeneration strategy for their local economy, building on the knowledge, skills and technologies which have been built up in their areas, in order to provide a bridgehead for new industries and employment (for example, potteries as a springboard for advanced ceramics).

All these forms of community governance depend for their potency upon a recognition by the Council and others in the community of the unique role which the local authority is able to play, by virtue of its status as the only body democratically elected to represent the interests of the whole local community, not just its separate factions. The local authority is obliged by its democratic mandate to find ways of representing, reconciling and balancing the diverse needs and often conflicting interests of young people as well as old people, black people as well as white people, women as well as men, unemployed as well as employed, poor as well as rich. The local authority is also required to plan ahead and to take into account the needs and interests of future generations, not just its current citizens and users (another of the limitations of the private market model, with its main focus on current customers).

The role of the local authority is not simply that of referee between different interest groups, because the Council is expected to move beyond these expressions of diversity and criss-crossing identities (along lines of gender, race, class, religion, nationality and so on) to try to find or to create some sense of unity, communal interest and common purpose. Great political skill, social insight and moral judgement is required to build these coalitions of common interest out of the differences and diversities of interest within most multi-cultural areas – especially after a period of 15 years when individualism and competition have been emphasised and encouraged, rather than community and collaboration.

The latent power of this unique mandate to develop and to represent the community (the whole rather than the parts) is evident in many areas at times of crisis and of celebration. It was found at the time of the Lockerbie air disaster, and the Hillsborough football disaster in Sheffield, that people turned to the local authority not only to co-ordinate the emergency services, and to

restore safety and order, but also to help embody the community's
sense of grief. The local authority as much as the Church appears
to carry the latent yearnings of local people for a sense of belonging
and of caring. On the positive side, when Coventry won the FA
cup at Wembley almost the whole local population came down to
the Town Hall to welcome the team home and to celebrate the
city's victory. Many organisations reported a noticeable rise in
people's sense of pride in belonging to the city, and of positive
community spirit in the subsequent weeks. And after the war-time
blitz it was undoubtedly the City Council which became the focus
of the city's hopes and vision for the rebuilding of a new city and a
new cathedral and a new community, symbolised by the logo of a
phoenix rising from the ashes, and embodied in the City Council's
investment in well-planned community and leisure facilities in its
neighbourhood estates.

A local authority which recognises the positive attachment
which many people have to their local community area, and the
latent hopes which they focus on the elected Council as the channel for many of their desires for belonging, will be able to foster a
new kind of relationship to its people. This will be a development
relationship in which the local authority sees part of its job as to
cultivate the capacity and the 'author-ity' of its community – its
capacity to find its voice and to be the author of its own scripts for
the development of the area and of its local economy and community.

How might ideas like this translate into the policies and practices
of local councillors and officers? What would it mean for a local
authority consciously to cultivate developmental relationships with
civil society and the voluntary and informal community sectors?

First, it will be a *listening local authority*. Ward councillors and
front-line staff will be seen as the local authority's eyes and ears in
the grassroots community. They will represent the people to the
authority, not just the authority to the people. Part of their job is
to listen carefully to local people, both as individuals and as
groups, to try to understand as fully as possible what they are
saying (directly and indirectly) about their needs and problems, and
to assure them that their voice has been heard, and will be
responded to with respect by the local authority. This is very different from the stance taken either by a centralised statist bureaucracy (where local needs and problems are seen at best as complaints to be rectified, or at worst as interferences with the grand
long-term plan for the city as a whole), or by a commercialised,
market-like authority (in which people with problems are seen

narrowly as customers to be sold services rather than as citizens with a right to help shape their own solutions). The authority will want to listen not just to individuals but also to groups. Neighbourhood forums may be set up to allow local councillors and field officers to consult with local groups and individuals on a regular basis. Open days for clients and users of departments, and public forums on particular issues which cut across departments (for example, crime and community security) will be organised to encourage people to come and define the problems and to discuss solutions. The Leader of the Council, Chairs of committees, and other senior members and officers will personally attend neighbourhood forums, public forums and open days regularly to listen to what the world looks and feels like from the point of view of those on the receiving end of the authority's policies and programmes. They will come as 'guest listeners' rather than 'guest speakers', and will treat what they hear as very important knowledge in their planning of strategic policies and services. A listening local authority will want to ensure that its citizens are frequently consulted, carefully listened to and honestly responded to.

Second, it will be a *responsive local authority*. The local authority will design systems in which the information and ideas generated by local people and transmitted by ward councillors and front-line staff is received, analysed, discussed and responded to rapidly by people in the strategic decision-making centre of the local authority. Traditionally, ward councillors and front-line staff are seen as being at the very bottom of the organisational hierarchy, the lowest of the low, with all the important strategic decisions seen as being taken at the apex of the pyramid by the Leader and Chief Executive, and the chairs of committees and chief officers. There may be as many as eight or more intermediate tiers in the structure between these two levels in the traditional local government organogram. It has been said that there is a quicker communication channel from parish priest to Pope in the Roman Catholic hierarchy, than there is from fieldworker to chief officer in local government! If real and respectful two-way dialogue is to be developed between the local Council and its people, new, more direct and open patterns of communication will be established within the organisation. The hierarchy will be short-circuited, so that information and ideas received at the front-line of the organisation will be seen as crucial intelligence in the authority's planning and decision-making processes. The model of the decision-making process will change from a vertical hierarchical pyramid to a hub and a rim linked directly to the centre by many spokes, or a latticed network in which there are many neural pathways. This may be more messy for many inside the organisation, but it is likely to be more responsive for those on the outside of the organisation.

Third, it will be a *developmental, capacity building, catalysing local authority*. The Council will judge it prudent to 'invest' time, money and other resources in the development of the human and social capital within its communities. This may mean carrying out cost–benefit comparisons, for example, of the costs to the authority and the local economy, of dealing with the consequences of crime and vandalism, as against investment in preventive schemes like concierge staffing for high-rise flats, local youth centres and programmes, centres for the unemployed, training workshops, community arts festivals, and other forms of community development.

This may include programmes of economic, social, technological and political development. Community economic development might start by surveying unmet social needs within the local neighbourhoods and communities, and will plan programmes of job creation linked to tailor-made training and retraining for unemployed people to meet these needs and to generate socially useful employment. Social development may include practical schemes of local authority support to mobilise and sustain informal networks of carers for older people and the mentally ill within the community. Technological development could include the creation of a network of neighbourhood based information centres linked up to the Town Hall and to other databases, through email and the internet (see Liber, this volume). Political development has to start from a recognition of the extent to which many young people and working-class people have disengaged from formal political processes, and no longer see involvement in political parties or even in voting as relevant channels for expressing their needs or aspirations. Programmes of civic education, voter registration and community action might be designed to try to attract local people back into political interest and involvement, as well as holding Council meetings and committee meetings, in neighbourhood centres rather than in the Town Hall. In addition, new democratic initiatives like public hearings, citizens juries and panels of inquiry and scrutiny provide opportunities to engage with people who have disengaged from, or never been involved with, formal political activities. Community-based political development will not move towards easy consensus, but will struggle to listen to the voices of as many diverse interests and sub-groups within the community as possible, before trying to search and give voice to the common and public interests which may lie beyond this difference and diversity. This will involve acting as a catalyst for new coalitions.

Fourth, it will be a *leading and governing local authority*. A local authority has a responsibility to provide leadership and governing for and with its people. This may involve articulating the values and the vision which will guide the direction and the development of the area. It may involve debating and deciding the fairest balance to be struck between the needs and interests of different groups within the community. It may require courageous action to stand up for minority groups or interests, and to endorse their right to a share of the air-time and of the cake, or to challenge and refute divisive forces (for example, racism and fascism) which may undermine the development of a caring and multi-cultural community. Civic leadership of this kind is no easy option. It runs counter to the current tides of fashion in the UK. It requires the Council to see its role not just as administering the local authority's bureaucracy, or establishing partnerships with the private sector, but also leading and governing the local community. In a fragmented world this implies an attempt to offer people a sense of identity, belonging and meaning within their area or neighbourhood.

Fifth, it will be a *learning local authority*. The models of local governance described above are very different from earlier traditions of command and control. They imply instead a form of governing the community which takes place in a reciprocal and interactive relationship between the people and its elected representatives and public servants (see Figures 11.1 and 11.2). Policies will need to be generated not only in the smoke-filled cabals and committee rooms of the Council, but also in task groups involving many stakeholders (for example, councillors, community organisations, voluntary associations, officers, trade unions, frontline fieldworkers and so on). In dynamic relationships of this kind, great creativity can be released, but mistakes will also be made, and policies and programmes will often need to be modified in the light of experience, and to take account of changes in the external environment. The media make it difficult for politicians to apologise for having made mistakes, or to own up to changing their minds in the light of new circumstances. However, a learning local authority, rooted in civil society, in a new kind of relationship of trust and reciprocity with its people, will require regular course-correction of this kind, as new things are learned in the light of practice and experience.

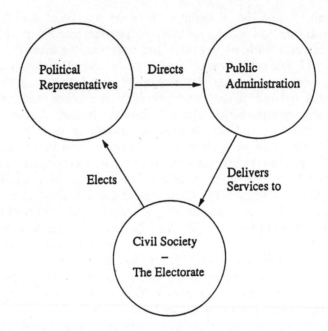

Figure 11.1 A conventional model of the relationship between politics, administration and the electorate.

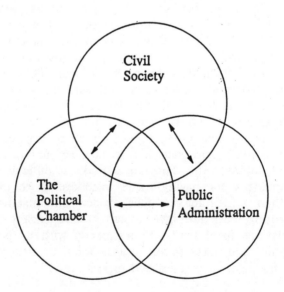

Figure 11.2 A closer more interactive relationship between civil society, politics and public administration.

CONCLUSION

I have argued in this chapter that local authorities have the potential to combat and overcome some of the forces for atomisation and alienation in this society, and to help regenerate a sense of belonging, identity and meaning for individuals and groups within wider communities of interest and of locality. Local Councils gain their mandate for performing this role from their unique position as the only body democratically elected to represent the interests of the whole local community rather than any one of its sub-parts, and future generations, not just current customers. They therefore face the challenge both of responding to the full range and diversity of needs and interests within the sub-groups of their populations, and of searching for the values, the vision and the programmes which can build coalitions of interests between individuals and sub-groups, and which express people's desire to belong to something more meaningful than a private competitive market or a public corporation.

In order to realise this potential, however, local authorities will have to reorient themselves away from their current dominant preoccupation with the relationships between the local state and the private market, and move towards the cultivation of new kinds of relationships within civil society. I have illustrated what this might mean in practice in terms of new roles and relationships for the authority which go beyond administering the bureaucracy and building partnerships with the private sector (both of which are necessary but not sufficient): listening, responding, capacity building, catalysing, leading, governing and learning, in dialogue with local people, voluntary associations and community organisations.

I am under no illusion that civil society is an unproblematic concept or a utopian life-space. Voluntary and community sectors and informal networks and associations are as riven with contradictions and conflicts as are the state and the market. Civil society contains within it a capacity for exploitation, scapegoating, racism, violence, and so on, just as it also contains within it a potential for co-operation, care and communal solidarity. Local authorities face the challenge of how to limit and contain the former, and how to foster and cultivate the latter.

Western societies face awesome choices as we move into the next millennium. At least three different scenarios are possible. The first would be continued risk and uncertainty and a lack of any sense of common vision, purpose or direction. The second would be degeneration into even deeper polarisation and division between the rich and the poor, the powerful and the excluded – a society of barbarism and violence, where the underdogs become underwolves and bite back. The third possible scenario is progression towards a more 'civil'-ised, co-operative and caring society, based upon a recognition of our interdependence as human beings and with our environment. Local authorities have a key role to play in determining which of the three scenarios will prevail.

REFERENCES

Benington, J. (1975) *Local Government Becomes Big Business*. London: CDP Publications.

Fraser, N. (1992) 'Rethinking the Public Sphere' in C. Calhoun (ed.), *Habermas and the Public Sphere*. Cambridge, MA: MIT Press.

Habermas, J. (1962) *The Structural Transformation of the Public Sphere*. Cambridge: Polity Press, 1989.

Holtby, W. (1936) *South Riding*. London: Virago, 1988.

Magnusson, W. and Walker, R. (1988) *Studies in Political Economy* 26 (Summer) 37–71.

Ranson, S. and Stewart, J. (1994) *Management for the Public Domain: Enabling the Learning Society*. Basingstoke: Macmillan.

12 The Life of a Legislator: Can Politicians be Normal People?

Tessa Jowell

INTRODUCTION

This book offers an opportunity to interpret and adapt attachment theory to a multitude of different circumstances and relationships in our contemporary society. Psychological theory of this sort has rarely been applied to understand politics and its players. The resistance to doing so is well illustrated by the lack of a common language to bridge the two worlds of psychology and politics. The ideas contained in the theory of attachment offer ways of building that bridge. They also provide a fascinating new dimension for understanding the nature of the relationships that politicians create within the political process and the beliefs that define party loyalty.

'I can't imagine anyone wanting to do your job', one of my constituents said to me recently. It is a common reaction. Except, that is, among the band of MPs, councillors, activists and aspirant politicians who share infection by the political virus. It is quite extraordinary how, once a person has had a brush with the possibility of elected office, but is not elected, it becomes so hard to admit to having given up the ambition altogether. It can be destructive too. There are people who have blighted the best years of their lives by trying for seat after seat and never making it. They were aspiring MPs, and the aspiration has stopped them from becoming anything else. At the other end, for those who do succeed, there is the prospect of rejection, defeat at the General Election and the return, usually, to obscurity. As Enoch Powell observed, 'all political careers end in disappointment'. Being a politician is much more a way of life than a profession or occupation in any of the senses that we normally recognise. What is it, therefore, that evokes such horror at the way of life among the detached onlooker but produces such insatiable appetite for the thrill, excitement and pursuit of the ambition among those so devoted to it? When I decided to try for the nomination as Labour candidate for Dulwich, a friend, also a politician, said: 'If you try for it, you will get it only if you want it more than you want anything else.' I was appalled. More than *anything* else? More than my family, more than my friends and all the things about my life that I hold really dear? During the selection, however, I did feel that I had left home. The preoccupation is total. The will to win is vital with at least a hundred contenders for any winnable seat. You push yourself forward, toes curled inside your shoes at the sheer embarrassment of being so bold and pushy.

Being a candidate is the hardest time. It is often lonely and the demands, and indeed one's own compulsion, are unremitting. I remember one friend who had just lost a hotly contested selection, confessing her relief at having lost, saying that she had felt as if she belonged only to other people during the selection and that any free time she had, had only been there because someone else had not booked it.

The endless demands on your time after election continue. It is a battle to safeguard any private or family time. Even worse, in the popular mind it is not even considered important, since politicians, if they are to escape the denigration of being lazy, are expected to devote themselves tirelessly and endlessly to living the political life thought to be so intolerable by their electors. Making time for your family in politics is seen as an admission of political failure. How often is a sacking pre-empted by a Minister announcing that he is standing down to spend more time with his family? After my election I was bombarded with kind advice about how to survive the endless demands. 'Never carry a diary', 'Put things in so that if they are looking over your shoulder there are no blanks or they will fill them.' Being elected makes a difference, though. Instead of pursuing only your own ambition and that of your party, you are suddenly entrusted with the duty to represent the constitutional hopes and fears of at least 55,000 people. Then you must be fearless on their behalf.

Politicians have a range of sources of attachments, which may fluctuate in intensity at different times. There is, first of all, the philosophical, moral and intellectual attachment to a set of beliefs that shapes the decision first to join, and then to represent, a particular political party. Then there is the attachment to constituency and the local leadership and to the representative responsibility that it bestows; one may call that a geographical attachment. There is also the tribal attachment of the Westminster relationships. Becoming an MP is a means of achieving ends for the public good. Even now, with all the doubt that the behaviour of a few MPs has cast on the motives of the rest, I believe that the vast majority of MPs are motivated principally by public service. Being an MP is a means of achieving change for the common good, which is an expression of personal and political values. Being elected to do that is not an end in itself and does not in any way guarantee that these intentions will be achieved in practice. The principles need to be kept distinct from the process of politics which can otherwise become an end in itself. It is this responsibility as a representative that for many politicians provides the most powerful attachment. It is attachment to a place, to the constituency in the case of an MP or to the ward in the case of a local councillor. To become either, you have to have been chosen, usually from many others. A friend on her election to Parliament, was reminded that 'she had been anointed by the power of the popular mandate'. Flowery though the expression was, she felt it marked her out and defined her relationships with those who had elected her and that she now represented.

Many MPs are selected and elected to represent the constituencies in which they live, where they have long-established roots. MPs are usually celebrated and respected in their constituencies. Constituents are grateful for the hard work at surgeries, for the pursuit of local issues and advocacy of local causes. The responsibility and privilege of being an elected representative creates in the MP a powerful attachment to the constituency and to its institutions and communities. For most MPs their work on behalf of constituents is not just a contact with reality but, through surgeries, it is the sustained exposure to the raw pain of people who have seen everyone else, and for whom seeking the help of their MP is the last resort. And for the most desperate the attachment to us as their representative is often most powerful. Some surgery visits are made by constituents as much to make sure that we are still there as to pursue progress with their particular case. Constituents want many different things from their MP, as advocate, as social worker, as representative. As a constituent put it to me: 'We want someone that we can look up to but who does not look down on us.' Powerful currents of attachment flow in each direction in such relationships.

But it is by no means all about being a celebrity. There is a lot of ritual humiliation in being an MP. Politicians as a class are reviled. The media's contempt for those who stumble or fall is uncontained. The Speaker will reprimand the recalcitrant, the TV cameras will switch off as 'the big boy' sits down. Being a back-bencher at a certain stage in your career is a very public statement about not being a frontbencher or a Minister. You will know if you do are doing well because you will read about it in the newspapers. You will learn that you are doing badly in the same way. For all but a very few there is no security.

Much of politics is theatre. A good speech badly delivered will be lost. The performance is almost all. The baying and heckling can be terrifying or exhilarating. To begin with it is terrifying. I am lastingly grateful to the colleague who, before my maiden speech, said: 'Just keep looking at the Tories and remember that they all once wore nappies.'

But it is, for nearly all MPs, a way of life detached from the normal domestic routine – the Monday arrival and the Thursday-night exodus, lived between the Westminster campus and the London flat. Most MPs have to get used to living away from home. They have to get used to missing much of their children's lives, to spending much of each year without the intimacy of family life, missing family celebrations because the obligation to a three-line whip is unremitting. But the observance of the rules and culture of Westminster provides a vital other source of attachment. Being attached politically is belonging and being part of that way of life. That sense of belonging is essential because politics and politicians 'live out of other people's time', as was so well observed in *Primary Colors*, the gossip novel about life on the road to the White House.

> Politicians work – they do their public work that is – when civilians don't: mealtimes, evenings, weekends ... . Sometimes at the oddest hours you may break free: an afternoon movie or a midnight dinner. And there are those other fleeting moments when your mind drifts from him (the Presidential candidate) and you fix on the father and son tossing a ball ... or you glance out of a hotel window and spot and elderly couple walking hand in hand ... and you remember: Other people just have lives. Their normality can seem a reproach. It hurts your eyes, like walking out of a matinee into the bright sunlight. Then it passes and ... it is time to move on. (Anonymous 1996)

Keeping in touch with normal life when the daily routine is so unusual creates potential traps for politicians. A leader who does not, for instance, know which record is number one in the Top Twenty will be seen as out of touch, and not just by 15-year-olds. People want political leaders who are in touch with the concerns of the rest of the population and who lead lives that they can recognise. But politicians need that private world too, where relationships are unconditional, which offers connection with a normal world that is not permanently preoccupied by the process of politics. It was Denis Healey who first described the personal and private hinterland, the source of personal enrichment that lies behind politics, as his 'secret planet' (Healey 1994). So much energy goes into nurturing the attachments that are essential to, and which define, political identity that this is often achieved, over time, at the expense of the intimate attachments.

It is particularly hard for politicians to keep the two sets of attachments in some kind of harmony. Unlike most other public figures, politicians claim to stand for something; they claim to set standards, and when they fail to meet them they are pilloried. Nothing brought more ridicule to the Conservative government than to set itself up as the guardian of nuclear family values and then see one after another of its leading figures showing only too obvious human weaknesses. Politicians strive to persuade the public that not everything that is interesting to the public is necessarily in the public interest to know; but try telling that to the *News of the World*. The public is a fickle master: it likes its politicians to be exceptional people but expects them to be normal. But whereas most people live their lives without ever being commented on by a newspaper, politicians live in the media, and when they fail in some quite ordinary way, it is not an ordinary failure. In many successful politicians this conflict sets up an equal and opposite reaction: they know they are different because their business is ultimately the exercise of power over their fellow citizens; but they want space to be normal people, and to be free to suffer from ordinary human weakness. It is a conflict that often cannot be resolved. If you want to be recognised, you cannot always choose when you will be, and when you won't.

It is the connection to these personal and intimate attachments that is ultimately so essential to political effectiveness. This is how the public are able to see politicians as people that they can identify with, and with whom they can share political convictions. It is above all the attachment to these particular beliefs that defines us as being of one party rather than another. For New Labour it is the belief in the central role of community, which recognises our interdependence as human beings, in inclusion of all citizens in the mainstream of society, in reciprocity and responsibility: that we can achieve more together than we can alone. These are founding values of the Labour Party but redefined by New Labour in its new constitution. But as we have seen, redefining and modernising beliefs is a painful and a controversial process, which has also involved the important realigning of established attachments – redefining relationships between the Trade Unions and broadening the balance of accountability in local parties, from the activists to the membership as a whole.

Between them these wide-ranging attachments create powerful bonds, and no doubt go in part to explain why it is so difficult for politicians, once infected by the political bug, to be rid of it. On the whole, politicians leave the stage only when they are pushed off by their electors or when old age or infirmity demands it. A few enjoy the House of Lords when their elective political life is over.

Belonging has its antithesis; and the fear of being in the out-group is a powerful driving force for political unity. But, nonetheless, political parties are always vulnerable to internal dissent. Indeed, political squabbles within political parties are often, indeed usually, more bitter by far than arguments between parties. Despite the compulsion to be part of a wider community of beliefs, there are still forces that produce fragmentation. One can assail the opponents in the other party without any anxiety; it is more tricky when one falls out with, or feels out of sympathy with, one's own party.

Different forms of attachment can be used for a number of purposes, scrupulous and otherwise, by political practitioners. The idea of party loyalty, particularly, appeals to attachments which verge on the intimate and personal by virtue of friendships and shared beliefs and experience. This is a tremendously powerful force, perhaps the most powerful one in party politics. Nothing hurts more than a charge of disloyalty. Moreover, there will be competing claims for one's loyalty, since political parties are aggregations of groups of people, none of whom will agree completely and all the time. There will be a loyalty to other like-minded people in the party, as well as to the party itself; or to the constituency which may be damaged by a policy which the party has adopted because it is in the interests of the majority of the country.

The remarkable thing about these conflicts is that they seldom result in a politician actually resigning, still less changing parties. The ability of politicians to live with their differences is not just a sign of a mature democracy, of give and take: it is overwhelming evidence of the importance of belonging, and of not casting oneself adrift. Just as in a family, so in politics: it is better to have a good row and sleep in one's own bed than to move out in a huff. That is, no doubt, why it is so extremely rare for a politician actually to change party. Even for someone with a massive ego like Winston Churchill (who actually crossed the floor twice) it involves a complete sundering of deeply rooted and personally defining attachments. The intensity of intra-party attachments to shared beliefs and views about party political conduct provide powerful analogies with the behaviour of families.

There is, however, profound resistance to the application of psychological insights to politics. The lack of a common language between psychology and politics underlines this. Many years ago, when I was a councillor in the London Borough of Camden, I was dispatched to defend the Tavistock Clinic in the middle of a ferocious spending round. I remember explaining the importance of psychotherapy in the treatment of disturbed children. The Chair of the Works Committee scratched his head and demanded, 'psycho what?' Everyone else tittered in agreement.

The contemplation of psychological motivation makes people who are leaders, and are expected to be invincible and certain, very nervous indeed. Perhaps it is just too painful to contemplate the private attachments that have been lost or diminished while securing the public ones. The press fuels this anxiety by ridicule. For example, when Antidote, an organisation whose bold aim is to promote 'emotional literacy' in politics, announced its launch, the newspapers were full of mocking copy and Tory politicians dismissing the ideas as 'pure tripe'. The idea that psychological insights might enrich political understanding was caricatured as 'therapists standing behind ministers at the dispatch box whispering dark advice' (Guardian 21 May 1996). The problem that this creates is a resistance to applying valuable psychological research in practice to advance public policy. For example, Lynne Murray (this volume) has done important work on the impact of maternal depression on young children's behaviour. She has described a link between maternal depression, disturbance to early childhood development and subsequent conduct disorder in young boys. Why has this research so far had such little impact on public policy in the context of a government which proclaims its concern about disruptive behaviour in the classroom? Perhaps because effective use of this evidence would require us as politicians to confront the destructive power of depression.

A further obstacle is that politicians tend to be more interested in belief than evidence, perhaps because they can exercise more control over belief. But political decisions that deny the important evidence are not intellectually sound. Often, however, the evidence is inconclusive. Contemporary politics is increasingly intolerant of uncertainty. Partly because the relationship between politics and the media is so interdependent, there is a very short journey between the question being asked and the solution offered. This produces an oversimplification of many issues that fails to convince the public and reinforces the distrust of politicians. Perception in modern politics is often more powerful and persuasive than fact. The popular perception will frequently sideline fact. The beef crisis of 1996 might not have been so damaging for the Conservative government had the legacy of public distrust not built up to such a degree that the early reassurances of the safety of beef, which were based on evidence, were simply not believed by the public. It is not just politicians who have attachment to the process of politics, so too do the electors. They reaffirm this at each General Election. Each General Election is a reaffirmation of attachment (but see Liber, this volume, for a challenge to this view).

Labour identified that it had lost the electors' trust during the 1980s and early 1990s. Rebuilding this bond of trust has been the overriding task for New Labour. Modernisation has been about much more than just putting together a series of policies that will attract popular support while at the same time waiting for the Government to lose. It has been about understanding the nature of the Labour Party that the electors could not trust with their aspirations. The next step has been to embed Labour's traditional values of co-operation and social cohesion in a practical and efficient programme which addresses the problems of the past, which enables us as a nation to respond to the challenges of the approaching millennium and invites the electorate to re-affirm its attachment to these values and beliefs. But a hard part of modernisation has been, after 17 years in opposition, for Labour itself to believe that it will win popular support and become the government. The psychology of opposition is destructive. For opposition creates its own forms of security, but it is an obstacle to effective government. It must be modified and developed in the transition. It is essential that we act on this understanding as we move towards government. Ronald Dworkin provides a test of good government as 'government that treats those that it governs with respect, that is as human beings capable of acting on an intelligent conception of how their lives should be lived' (1977). The ideas generated by a politics of attachment provide skilful guidance as to how that delicate partnership between the government and its citizens can be reached.

REFERENCES

Anonymous (1996) *Primary Colors: A Novel of Politics*. London: Chatto and Windus.
Dworkin, R. (1977) *Taking Rights Seriously*. London: Duckworth.
Healey, D. (1994) *My Secret Planet*. London: Penguin.

13 You Pays Your Money: Models of Capitalism

Paul Ormerod

Extending concepts in the social sciences from one discipline to another is never easy. It is particularly challenging in this context, for the distance between developmental psychology and economics is considerable. Yet there is a clear parallel, set out in the first part of this chapter, between the secure individual of attachment theory, ready and able to explore the world, and the general framework which is required for capitalist economic development. But once beyond this initial stage, the implications of attachment theory are much less obvious. The more market-oriented Anglo-Saxon economies of Britain and America have on many criteria performed well, and serious problems have emerged in the ostensibly gentler European economies, not least of which is a cripplingly high and rising rate of unemployment. After contrasting the experiences of these two models of capitalism, the chapter goes on to examine potential solutions to Europe's predicament. Co-operative behaviour, requiring a marked shift in the attitudes of electorates, is essential. But the political will required to argue for such changes is weak, and in these circumstances the Anglo-Saxon model will appear increasingly attractive to policy makers.

CAPITALISM AND ATTACHMENT THEORY

Capitalism is by far the most successful form of economic organisation invented. Yet it only exists by virtue of what might be thought of as qualities of attachment. As an economic system, it is distinguished from all others primarily because of its capacity to innovate. And innovation, if it is to flourish, requires both a stable and secure overall framework in which the innovators can realise the private gains of their activities, and a willingness and confidence amongst the population to explore, to try new techniques and new methods of working. An important postulate of attachment theory is that security facilitates the development of qualities such as initiative, self-restraint and trust, which are exactly those required for the operation of a capitalist economy.

Adam Smith is regarded as the founding father of free market economic theory, for his insight that the pursuit of enlightened self-interest by individuals and companies can benefit society as a whole. But he believed very firmly that the pursuit of self-interest could only succeed for society as a whole if it took place in the context of a shared view of what constituted reasonable behaviour. Smith recognised that pure self-interest might promote concepts such as trust and a propensity not to steal or murder. Life would rapidly become unworkable if such qualities were not spread widely throughout the population. But he argued that social behaviour such as this was not dependent upon this kind of self-seeking calculation, but was a natural, integral part of human nature. Much of the day-to-day substance of economic behaviour is only rendered practicable precisely because of the existence of such general social virtues. The problems encountered by countries of the former Soviet Union give a dramatic illustration of what can happen when the mere formal trappings of a free market economy are imposed on a society where the informal structure of social values necessary for capitalist success have never existed. A crucial reason why countries such as the Czech Republic and Hungary have managed the transition much more effectively is that such societies have deep roots in the West, located in centuries of the Austro-Hungarian Empire.

But, once we move beyond the deep-seated necessity for most individuals to conduct themselves on the basis of internalised self-restraint if a successful market economy is to operate, the economic implications of attachment theory are by no means obvious. An analogy with individual behaviour may illustrate the point. From the point of view of individual contentment it seems desirable to have a secure family background, but it does not seem necessary for individual success. Many of the great names in world history seem to have been psychopaths, people who cared nothing for the effect of their actions on the lives of others, a perfect opposite to the securely attached. On a more mundane level, Keynes believed that financial markets performed a valuable service to society quite separate from any overt economic function. He regarded many of the individuals attracted to such markets as unbalanced, but it was better to have them employed on Wall Street or in the City rather than pursuing careers of torture or organised crime.

Similarly, in terms of performance, the most powerful and successful economy continues to be the US, which can hardly be thought of by a European as a secure and contented society. But over the past 25 years, for example, manufacturing output in the US has risen more than it has in Japan. In contrast, an economy such as the former DDR offered in many ways a secure society. For the vast majority of its inhabitants, it seemed to give a tolerable standard of living with little stress. But it failed to provide a framework in which initiative and innovation were encouraged.

It is the combination of security and innovation which is the distinguishing feature of capitalist society. Security is provided by the rule of law, the protection of private property rights,[1] and the custom and practice which gives rise to the 'social virtues' of Adam Smith. And it is precisely these same qualities which encourage initiative and innovation.

It is tempting to extend the list of features which characterise a dynamic and innovative society, much in the same way as Mr Prendergast, the prison chaplain in Evelyn Waugh's *Decline and Fall*. Provided he was able to overcome his doubt as to why God had made the world at all, he could see that 'everything else follows – Tower of Babel, Babylonian captivity, Incarnation, Church, bishops, incense, everything'. Many on the European centre-left, once capable of putting aside their instinctive doubts and distaste for the process of capitalism, recite a similar catechism – 'stakeholders, workers' representatives on the board, employment protection rights, paid paternity leave, everything'. Regardless of the intrinsic desirability of any or all of these demands, it cannot be argued that their adoption will automatically lead to a more efficient economy.

AMERICA AND EUROPE: THE RECORD

The overall choice of criteria with which to compare overall economic performance of countries is not completely straightforward, but three factors suggest themselves in a fairly obvious manner. First, the level of income per head; second, its rate of growth; and third, the rate of unemployment. The well-being of the citizens of any country is for the most part closely related to the level of income per head. This is not just a matter of the personal spending power which income confers, but studies across countries show a strong correlation between per capita income and desirable social outcomes such as low child mortality, literacy, and the general provision of education and health services. This result holds most strongly, however, when countries at quite different levels of income per head are compared, and it is less obviously valid when the comparison group is restricted to the wealthiest capitalist economies. Indeed, the use of income per head, and its growth, carries an implicit assumption that only those activities which take place in the marketplace, and hence can be valued, are of relevance. This is a point addressed in more detail below. Our third criterion, the rate of unemployment, is rather more unequivocally an important indicator of social well-being but, as we shall see, there is no necessary correlation between this and the rate of economic growth in the medium term.

A striking feature of twentieth-century capitalism is the dominance of the American economy, not simply in terms of its sheer size but, more importantly, in terms of income per head. The comparison of income per head both across countries at a point in time and within a country over long periods of time is a complicated business. The most scholarly and authoritative estimates are available in Maddison (1995). In the first decade of this century, the US overtook the UK in terms of average national income per head and it remains the richest capitalist economy of the world. Maddison estimates its 1994 per capita GDP (gross domestic product) at almost $23,000, ahead of Switzerland at $21,000, Japan at $19,500 and (West) Germany at $19,000.

Yet the US hardly corresponds to the concept of a secure society. This is not simply a matter of the social divisions which opened up dramatically during the Reagan era. The raw brutality of American capitalism pulsates throughout its history. In the past 20 years Britain, too, has become increasingly divided and unequal, yet, whilst there are many problems with British capitalism, it continues to deliver unparalleled prosperity to the vast majority of citizens. Maddison estimates per capita national income in 1994 at $16,400, a figure almost identical to the average for the European Union (EU) as a whole and one which has doubled in the space of a generation since the early 1960s.

What might be termed the European model of capitalism continues to exercise a hold on the imagination of the liberal left in Britain. Of course, each country on the Continent differs, but it is widely believed in the UK that in some way the general qualities of the European model offer a more desirable outcome, in which there is less social exclusion.

But an initial word of caution is appropriate concerning the relative desirability of the outcomes in European economies. Regional inequalities of income, for example, are typically noticeably more marked elsewhere in Western Europe than they are in the UK, a fact which is rarely appreciated. And a visit, say, to the vast municipal dwelling blocks which surround many of the major cities in France soon dispels any illusions that problems of urban poverty and alienation are confined to Britain.

The golden era of European capitalism was the three decades from 1950, when rapid growth was combined with unprecedented low rates of unemployment. But since then the apparent superiority of the European model is by no means clear. On international definitions, the rate of unemployment in the UK, at 8.5 per cent, is below that of West Germany, and much lower than the 12 per cent of both France and Italy, and the 22 per cent of Spain.

It is an article of faith amongst commentators that the British economy is in relative decline. Even the normally austere pages of the *Economic Journal* carried short articles on this theme in the January 1996 edition. Certainly, for over a century from 1870 to 1979 this was true. Britain was not only the slowest growing European economy over the entire period, but during almost any reasonably defined sub-period as well. Yet since 1979 this relative decline has been halted. This is due more to the marked deterioration in performance in the European exemplars, which liberals urge us to follow, than it is to a resurgence of British capitalism, but it is nevertheless a dramatic turn-round in relative performance.

THE POLITICAL ECONOMY OF THE EUROPEAN CRISIS

A crucial reason for the slowdown in European growth is the sharp rise which took place in the late 1960s and early 1970s in the share of national income going to the labour force (see Ormerod 1996). This was made up of a combination of rapid increases in real wages and of rises in the cost of employing labour. The increase in the proportion of total income going to the labour force meant a reduction in that available for profits. And, as a result, the sustainable medium-term growth rate was reduced. Indeed, the true impact of Europe's high payroll taxes is not seen in terms of low employment growth but in a low rate of output growth.

The connection between the general erosion of corporate profitability in the West, of which the burden on companies of high

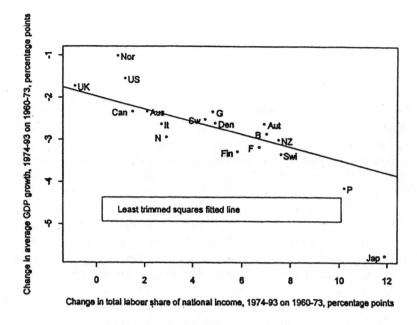

Figure 13.1 Change in annual average GDP growth and labour share 1974–93 on 1960–73, 18 OECD countries.
Source: OECD National Accounts

payroll taxes is one example, and reductions in the rate of growth can be seen in Figure 13.1. This plots for 18 Organisation for Economic Co-operation and Development (OECD) countries the change in the average annual rate of economic growth over the 1974–93 period compared to the 1960–73 period against the change in the share of labour in total national income. Clearly, there is a strong negative relationship between the two.[2] Apart from the special case of Norway, where oil is a very large part of the economy, the slowdown in growth has been least in the US and the UK, the countries in which the increase in labour's share of total national income was the lowest.

Compared to a decade ago, there has in recent years been some recovery of profitability in Europe, but one which is far from sufficient to underpin a sustainable rate of growth of more than 2 per cent a year. And here is an immediate dilemma for the European model, not just of the economy but of social democracy. As a political and economic system it was hugely successful from 1950 to around 1980, thanks to the creation of a virtuous circle. The immediate post-war period offered a great deal of potential for entrepreneurs to reap the rewards of investment. But this opportunity was not destroyed by debilitating struggles over the distribution of national income. By and large, the workers showed restraint, and capital made sufficient profit to generate high growth rates. This latter in turn created buoyant long-term expectations, which further sustained the growth rate. A necessary condition for high growth was restraint by the workers, but the existence of such growth made it easier for restraint to continue. The claims of all – skilled, unskilled, public welfare provision, health, education – could be met from economic growth.

But the erosion of profitability which took place from the late 1960s to the end of the 1970s has set Europe on a lower growth path. Expectations of rising living standards cannot be met so readily, leading in turn to the increasing reluctance of individuals to meet the rising cost of public provision through taxation. France, for example, could easily satisfy the Maastricht convergence criteria on public sector debt by a further round of tax increases. But this is not regarded as politically feasible, even when the alternative is to confront public sector workers in the streets, as happened early in 1996. At the time of writing, in the early summer of the same year, similar altercations are beginning in Germany.

An increase in the rate of economic growth in Europe which is sustainable in the medium to longer term requires, as a necessary condition, a sharp shift of the distribution of national income away from labour and into profits. The intrinsic importance of profits to encourage innovation and investment is enhanced by the increased international mobility of capital as the countries of East Asia and Eastern Europe offer new opportunities.

In the Anglo-Saxon economies, the defence of profits has been achieved by the brutal application of market forces. And it is these same forces which have led to the dramatic widening of the distribution of income in these countries in the past 15 or so years. One option for Europe is therefore the Anglo-Saxon model of capitalism. By reducing the rights of workers, cutting the cost to companies of employing labour, and by making inroads into the welfare state, a climate could undoubtedly be created in which growth could be increased, not exactly to flourish at the rates of the 1950s and 1960s, but nevertheless to register a marked improvement on the performance since the 1970s. And unemployment would fall, although substantial reductions may not emerge for a decade or more, judging from the experience of the UK.

Analytically, this argument, offered by most of the British Conservative Party, is valid. But the costs associated with it are not reflected in standard economic data, such as gross domestic product or unemployment. Rather, they are manifested in a widening of the distribution income, a reduction in social cohesion and an increase in crime.

CO-OPERATIVE SOLUTIONS

It is perhaps appropriate at this stage to reflect upon just how much Europe needs ever higher levels of real per capita income. In the 1930s, in dollar terms, average annual real national income in the countries of Western Europe was between $3000 and $6000. In historical terms, they were already immensely wealthy. But these levels are somewhat below those which obtain today in, say, most of the countries of South America. Apart from a relatively small minority, life was still pretty hard. By the 1960s, the average had increased to $8000 to $10,000, and the benefits of such a rise were obvious in terms of the well-being of the general population.

In the mid-1990s, in most countries of the European Union real national income per head is between $16,000 and $19,000, a doubling since the 1960s, and a level beyond the dreams of the 1930s. The difference even between the 1960s and 1990s is shown very clearly in patterns of personal consumption, with massive household penetration of consumer durables of all kinds, exotic foreign holidays and even dry white wine for the British working classes.

Such prosperity, however, does not seem to have been accompanied by a similar increase in the overall level of contentment. Eurostat have carried out a survey in each EU country since 1973 with the simple aim of finding out how happy people feel. Overall, there is a small increase in the level of happiness between the early 1970s and mid-1990s, but it is very small compared to the increases which have taken place in standard measurements of real income per head. Money does matter, despite the proclamations of the four *nouveaux riches* Yorkshiremen in the Monty Python sketch: 'Ah were 'appier then, though we were poor – *because* we were poor!' But after a certain point, more money seems to make less and less difference to overall happiness.

One important reflection of this is the marked falls over time in the number of annual hours which are worked on average. The benefits of economic growth can be taken either in the form of increases in income, or in the form of an increase in leisure with the level of income remaining the same – in other words, the same pay for fewer hours. In practice, of course, we see a combination of the two. The total number of hours worked each year in the EU is now almost identical to those worked in 1870. Whilst the number of people employed has doubled, this has been offset by a reduction in average annual hours worked by each worker to one-half the levels of 1870. And the tendency for hours to fall has been far more marked in the second half of the 1870–1995 period than in the first half.

In short, money isn't everything, and people have a distinct appetite for more leisure and less work as they become better off. One way in which this could be exploited is to encourage the sharing of work as a method of preserving and creating employment. This need not be taken in the literal sense of two people sharing one full-time job, but could be thought of more imaginatively in terms, say, of shorter working hours either during the working year or redistributed over a lifetime.

Some, but not all, readers may be reassured by the knowledge that Keynes contemplated with equanimity the idea of worksharing as a solution to unemployment. He discussed the concept in a little-remembered passage in his *General Theory of Employment* (1936), and his only objection was that the overall level of real income was still too low for it to be widely applicable. But since the days of Keynes, real incomes in Europe have risen five-fold.

Of course, the basis of Keynes' hesitation for recommending worksharing in the 1930s is that for any individual a reduction in hours would have to be accompanied by a pro rata cut in pay in order for the approach to succeed in its aim. An objection to the idea which is still made is that it would not be applicable, even now, to those on below-average incomes, since they need all the money they can get. But if the choice of hours open to all workers became more flexible, people could make their own decisions.

The costs involved in worksharing are transparent. Those who agree to reduce their annual hours of work get less money. But any potential solution, in whole or in part, to the problem of European unemployment involves costs. The Anglo-Saxon model of capitalism could reduce unemployment substantially, and the costs would fall on the relatively unskilled as the distribution of income widened. Their real wages would be lower than they would otherwise have been, but more of them would be in employment. There is a kind of rough justice in this approach, for at present the costs of high unemployment in the EU are borne mainly by the unemployed themselves, whilst those who remain in work continue to prosper.

Despite the sharp slowdown in growth since the 1970s, there

are several examples of countries in which unemployment has risen by only a small amount. Although the practical ways of containing the rise in unemployment vary amongst these countries, analytically they have a great deal in common. Essentially, their traditions and institutions have enabled them to co-ordinate a sharing of the costs of slower growth to ensure that these do not fall for the most part on the unemployed and unskilled.

An alternative approach was offered for many years by the Scandinavian economies which, until very recently, were successful in keeping unemployment low. In Sweden, for example, between 1950 and 1979 unemployment averaged 1.8 per cent, but only 2.4 per cent between 1980 and 1991, despite a fall in the average annual growth rate from 3.4 to 1.6 per cent. Whenever these economies received adverse shocks, unemployment was absorbed not by Keynesian demand management policies but by long-term increases in the rate of taxation. In other words, unemployment was kept low by the state intervening to alter the distribution of income through taxation. Tax revenues were used to allow the public sector not only to function as an employer of last resort following crises such as the 1973/74 oil price shock, but also to absorb the enormous increase in the number of women in the labour force which took place in those countries.

A combination of a gradual increase in taxpayer resistance and very serious specific shocks led to a temporary breakdown of the Scandinavian approach in the early 1990s. In both Sweden and Finland, the banks effectively bankrupted themselves as a result of their irresponsible speculations in the European property market. The financial crisis resulted in output falling in these economies in a way similar to the Great Depression in the 1930s. Indeed, in Finland, where the problem was aggravated by the collapse of the Soviet Union, real output between 1989 and 1993 fell by 13 per cent, compared to only 4 per cent between 1929 and 1932. Taxation was already very high in these countries at the end of the 1980s, and the electorates were not willing to pay the further substantial increase which would have been necessary to preserve low unemployment.

There are strong signs, however, that the traditional attitudes in these economies still survive, albeit in modified form, and these differences are reflected in the tensions between the Scandinavians and the rest of the EU on employment policies. Unemployment is still high, but it is falling, and in Sweden its present rate of just under 9 per cent is already below the average for the EU as a whole.

A different practical solution is seen in the case of Japan, where unemployment averaged 1.7 per cent between 1950 and 1979, and just 2.4 per cent between 1980 and 1995. And despite Japan having endured a very deep recession for the past four years, it is still only around 3 per cent. Essentially, low unemployment is preserved by the very low levels of productivity in the Japanese domestic private service sector. In the Scandinavian model, the public service sector acts as the employer of last resort, and in Japan it is the private service sector. The costs of the high level of employment relative to output are paid for by the high prices of these services, which can be thought of as a tax on the income of the personal sector as a whole.

Japanese society differs from other Western countries in many aspects, but this is the single most striking difference in terms of the outcome for the overall level of unemployment. The pervading business culture which frowns upon the dismissal of workers during times of recession has undoubtedly curbed the amplitude of the fluctuations in Japanese unemployment arising from the traded sector of the economy during the course of the cycle. But, at least until very recently, the belief that demand would soon resume and validate the decision to retain rather than sack workers has proved correct. So the cultural attitude towards dismissal does not by itself seem to be a major factor accounting for low unemployment. Rather, it is the effective tax on personal incomes levied through high prices of services.

In policy terms, it is difficult to see how such a solution could be co-ordinated in the private sector of the European economy. But in many parts of the trading public sector – including here privatised industries such as those in the UK which are subject to heavy regulation on pricing – it would be possible to carry out such a policy. In other words, to increase prices with the explicit aim of using the resulting revenue to create jobs. It is a matter of political judgement as to whether support could be gathered for an extension of such a policy. The economic argument that this would raise the costs of European industry and hence reduce competitiveness is not a strong one. The resulting increase in costs would only be a matter of a few per cent at most, which could easily be offset by a fall in the effective exchange rate.[3]

The Swiss and Austrian experiences have a number of similarities to that of Japan, and unemployment averaged under 4 per cent in both countries over the 1980–95 period. Although Switzerland, for example, has a highly open and efficient traded sector, the rest of the economy is highly protected and, where necessary, subsidised explicitly. Agriculture is very inefficient by standards in other countries, but it is regarded as an important feature of the Swiss way of life. Both countries absorbed in part the impact of the oil price shock in 1973/74 by expelling foreigners, though this is only a partial explanation of their low unemployment figures. The domestic sector of both economies is highly regulated and, in contradiction to the precepts of orthodox economic theory, per capita income is high, at over $17,000 in Austria and almost $21,000 in Switzerland.

A wide variety of societies – Austria, Japan, Sweden and Switzerland – have preserved low unemployment for the past 20 years despite the marked slowdown in economic growth which they, in common with the rest of the West, have experienced during that time. The precise way in which this has been achieved differs from country to country. But, analytically, the solutions are identical. Each rests on the willingness to finance, at the general expense of society at large, a sector of the economy which acts as an employer of last resort.

The activities of such a sector are regarded as valuable in each of these countries, even though they are inefficient by the standards of free market economics. They are not perceived as sectors which exist purely for the purpose of making work, as would be the case in the classic, though fictional, example of hiring the unemployed to dig holes and promptly fill them in again.

CONCLUSION

The general European problem is two-fold. First, a crisis in profitability. Profits as a share of national income have been too low for at least 20 years, the importance of which is enhanced by the growing potential of investing abroad. The consequence of this has been to reduce the rate of growth which is sustainable in the medium term, perhaps by as much as one percentage point a year.

Second, a weakening of the attitudes of solidarity which are needed to make social democracy work. Transfers of income *within* the personal sector are required, whether to cope with the specific transitional impacts of free trade with the emerging markets of the world or, more generally, to finance non-trading sectors of the economy which will create permanent, meaningful jobs for the unemployed. It is here that the real crisis of European social democracy exists, through factors which in the main have purely internal causes rather than being forced on reluctant governments by rampant forces of free market capitalism. Despite so-called globalisation, despite increasing capital mobility and despite increased free trade, most economic activity in developed countries takes place in sectors which are not exposed to international competition (see Hirst and Thompson 1996 for a detailed empirical critique of the concept of globalisation). By implication, the remedy for unemployment remains within the control of national governments, but only if they are willing to mobilise support to pay for the costs associated with any sustainable solution to this problem.

In essence, Europe is now faced with a clear trade-off between social cohesion and economic performance as conventionally defined. The European welfare state remains viable, provided that a conscious decision is made to accept the costs. And the true costs are not so much the money required each year to finance it, but the slower rate of economic growth which follows as a consequence of the costs imposed on companies and the associated squeeze on profitability. It is a political rather than economic choice as to whether, at current levels of per capita income, a lower rate of economic growth is acceptable.

But a deliberate choice in favour of the welfare state option would need to be accompanied by important changes in the outlook of electorates. When growth was high in the 1950s and 1960s, all claims on national income from different groups could be met to everyone's satisfaction. But lower growth has put enormous strain on the attitudes required to sustain traditional European social democracy. Strong support still exists for the European welfare state, but this quality of social solidarity does not extend to the surrendering of real wages by those in employment in order to support activities which would reabsorb the unemployed.

In this situation, the Anglo-Saxon model of capitalism looks increasingly attractive to more and more European politicians, whatever their public rhetoric may proclaim. It *can* deliver on the conventional criteria such as growth and unemployment, and it is a mistake to belittle the achievements of this model. It does, of course, involve serious indirect costs of the kind with which we in Britain are all too familiar. The political class in Europe at present sit bemused, stunned by the problems which confront them, seeking comfort through communal chanting of the mantra of monetary union. But unless they are able to focus explicitly on the compromises which exist between social cohesion and economic performance, circumstances will compel them to move more and more towards the system and practices of Anglo-Saxon capitalism.

NOTES

1. Using this term widely, to encompass not just literally physical property in the everyday sense of the word, but intellectual property, the right to draw a profit stream from innovative ideas and organisation, and so on.
2. This is easily confirmed by least squares regression. This widely used technique does lack robustness in the sense that the results are sensitive to outliers in the data. But the negative relationship still holds even when least trimmed squares regression is used. This technique is highly robust, having a breakdown point of approximately 0.5, the breakdown point being the largest fraction of the data which may be replaced with arbitrarily large values without making the Euclidean norm of the vector of coefficient estimates tend to infinity.
3. The American economist Paul Krugman (1994) first pointed out with the example of the US dollar that, contrary to the beliefs of many economists, the correlation between real and nominal movements in the effective dollar rate is very high, so that changes in the nominal rate are reflected only very slowly in the domestic price level, if they are reflected at all. A similar result holds for the European currencies, and in particular for the German mark.

REFERENCES

Hirst, P. and Thompson, G. (1996) *Globalisation in Question*. Oxford: Polity Press.

Keynes, J.M. (1936) *The General Theory of Employment*. London: Macmillan.

Krugman, P. (1994) *Peddling Prosperity*. New York: Norton.

Maddison, A. (1995) *Monitoring the World Economy 1820–1992*. Paris: OECD.

Ormerod, P. (1996) '*Growth, Profitability and Unemployment*'. European University Institute Discussion Paper.

14 The Management of Uncertainty

Peter Marris

I want to talk about attachment theory in the context of the social construction of control – especially control over uncertainty. Our attachment to our parenting figures is the first and probably most crucial relationship in which we try to understand relationships in general, control them and make a predictable world. As John Bowlby wrote, the strategies that a child develops in his or her relationship with attachment figures become the basis of the strategies that he or she will follow throughout life. The attachment relationship is so crucial to us in the early years of our life, that even in our relationship to the natural world, our instinct is to understand it in the way in which we understand the social world. Before the advent of modern science, human societies peopled the natural world with gods and goddesses, who determined how it behaved, and had to be appeased, threatened and dealt with, just as we deal with parents.

Attachment theory is not only a theory of emotional development, therefore, but a theory of cognitive development. It is a theory of how we create meaning; how we make a world which is sufficiently predictable for us to be able to handle it and act purposefully. But clearly, if our experience of attachment leads us to adopt strategies for creating a predictable and controllable world, equally the quality of that attachment experience is itself going to be powerfully influenced by social circumstances. It will be influenced by the child-rearing practices of society and the ideologies that inspire them. It will also be profoundly influenced by economic circumstances.

I see the politics of attachment as a circular relationship, where social circumstances partly determine the quality of attachment, and the strategies derived from the experience of attachment in turn determine how people will make the choices that they are able to make later in life, in terms of politics, their own child-rearing, their own careers. That circularity is very well illustrated by Lynne Murray's research (see Murray, this volume). It shows how the social circumstances which influenced whether the parents were economically secure and confident enough themselves to enjoy the attachment relationship, affected the quality of the child's experience.

This brings me to the central dilemma underlying the theme of this book. There is a profound contrast between what most of us – whether we are to the right or left of the political spectrum – believe to be the way in which we should nurture a secure attachment, and what many believe to be the way in which we should nurture a prosperous economy. I think most people would agree that, ideally, every child should have a mother and a father who loyally and devotedly take care of her or him from birth until adulthood: and the mother and father should remain loyal to each other in their child-rearing relationship. In other words, attachment ideally depends upon relationships which remain secure and stable for at least 20 years.

By contrast, many believe the right way to handle economic relationships is precisely the opposite. The successful management of the economy depends increasingly on lack of commitment, constant change and instability. These are the qualities that are believed to create a competitive economy. In the US this strategy is often described admiringly as 'lean and mean'. The goal for the successful firm is to make the fewest possible commitments, particularly the fewest possible commitments to its workers: that's the 'meanness' part. The 'lean' part is to shrink the size of its core to the smallest possible number of relationships.

In the US, perhaps here in Britain too, a similar philosophy is inspiring the management of public services. For instance, in the welfare reforms that are now being proposed in Congress, a block grant to states would replace the present Aid to Families with Dependent Children, which is partly federally funded, and to which eligible poor families are entitled. States, with some restrictions intended to discourage child-bearing by unmarried teenagers, would be free to use these grants as they choose to provide welfare, without being required to make any commitment to anyone for any particular level of benefit. It would undo the structure of welfare that has existed for the past 60 years, applying much the same principles as those which underlie corporate reorganisation: maximise flexibility and minimise commitments. Reducing these commitments – and so the taxes needed to support them – is explicitly defended as a necessary strategy to sustain economic competitiveness.

What lies behind that strategy? Why should economic competitiveness have come to be so emphatically associated with these 'lean and mean' strategies? A few years ago, Western commentators were attributing the outstanding success of the Japanese economy to just the opposite strategies – the lifetime commitment of Japanese firms to their employees, and the quality of performance that this mutual loyalty encouraged. I want to suggest that this shift reflects not only an intensifying of global competition, but a shift from more co-operative to more competitive ways of managing uncertainty, which is socially destructive, undermining the conditions in which secure attachments can easily flourish, and even economically destructive in the long run.

There is a logic to the management of uncertainty. My sense of this logic derives initially from a study that John Benington made of Coventry (Benington et al. 1975) when he and his colleagues were trying to understand the forces, both economic and governmental, which had concentrated poverty and deprivation in a particular area of the city. Their analysis reveals a logic which is quite fundamental to the way uncertainty is managed. It can be seen working itself out in all sorts of different situations and relationships, from the way in which governments handle uncertainty, to family interactions.

The logic goes like this in its simplest form: if you live in an uncertain world, where you do not know for sure what is going to happen, your chances of realising your purposes are greater the more options you have open to you. To take a very simple example, if you want to have a picnic, the chances of being able to hold the picnic without its being rained out are greater if you have a choice of dates on which to hold it. Similarly, if you are trying to put together a business, you need to find a site, employees and financing, but you do not want any one of these unless you can have all the others. As you juggle the way to do this, you try to get options: an option to buy a piece of land, that does not commit you but makes that piece of land available if you need it; a commitment from somebody to come and work for you, if you can get the business started, and so on. You maximise your chances of achieving your purposes by having the greatest freedom to choose amongst a range of actions, depending upon how circumstances develop. But to choose well, you need to know what will happen if you select any one of your options. So other people have to be committed in advance to behaving in ways that are predictable to you as you make your choice. I want to be able to buy your property or not buy it, depending on how things work out. But if I choose to buy your property, I need to know that you are now committed to selling it to me at the price that we agreed. In some circumstances, those who are constrained by their commitment to you can charge you for the privilege. But in a great many relationships, this lack of reciprocity is a privilege of power. We use power, essentially, to protect ourselves against uncertainty; and in doing so, I would argue, we often thrust a greater burden of uncertainty on to those who are weaker than ourselves. To be in command of the situation, I want everybody around me, on whom I might depend for the achievement of my purposes, to be committed to do whatever I may need them to do, without making any reciprocal commitment that would constrain my own freedom. So they have less freedom of action, and may in turn adopt the same strategy towards those subordinate to themselves. At each step down the hierarchy, people are being more and more narrowly constrained in their freedom of action. During my National Service, as a low-ranking airman, I learnt very quickly that it made no sense to have ambitions and purposes, because you never knew what was going to happen. At the bottom of the hierarchy you could be trained as an interpreter of Japanese and then be sent to Poland. In those circumstances, the right response was to be as passive and indifferent as possible.

In an organisation, people resist that kind of subordination if they can. In many mature institutions people use the power of collective bargaining, or control of information, in order to insist upon reciprocity. But that makes the organisation as a whole less adaptable. The organisation may then try to restore its adaptability by putting buffer organisations between itself and the uncertainties of its environment. For instance, large firms will use sub-contractors, who bear the immediate burden of adapting production to market demand. Hence workers in these subordinate firms are particularly vulnerable. They are at the mercy of their own employer's hiring and firing decisions; their employer is in turn at the mercy of the corporations whom he contracts to supply; and the uncertainty of employment is an intimidating sanction against workers' attempts to protect themselves.

In Coventry, at the time of John Benington's study, the concentration of deprivation came about because the people in the area tended to work in the lowest ranks of the marginal firms, so that they were at the bottom of the hierarchy. They were also the victims of the way in which government manipulated housing policy to deal with its own uncertainties. They lived in an area which had been scheduled for redevelopment and represented a classic example of planning blight. Because the area had been scheduled for redevelopment, nothing much could be done to restore the existing properties. At the same time, the funds to finance that redevelopment were constantly being taken back or put forward again, depending upon the fiscal uncertainties that the government was trying to manipulate.

Thus the hierarchical management of uncertainty can be reflected in the marginalisation of neighbourhoods, as well as the exploitation of workers, compounding the loss of secure employment with the loss of a secure home. For instance, General Motors wished to close a plant in Detroit. The city of Detroit was very concerned about the loss of jobs that would result. General Motors claimed the existing site was too small, and preferred to build a new factory on a green field site out in the suburbs. The city of Detroit offered in return to enlarge the site to meet General Motors' needs. It undertook to clear a stable community of about 15,000 people adjoining the site and relocate them, despite intense local protests. But at no point in this negotiation did General Motors ever make a commitment to the city of Detroit that it would actually build on that site or provide jobs. Nor was the city of Detroit in a position to demand that kind of commitment. In the event, the community was destroyed, the site enlarged, but General Motors chose to locate their new facility elsewhere.

The practice of worldwide sub-contracting sets up a race to find the cheapest and least demanding labour, putting pressure to lower wages and working conditions on more prosperous countries. Nike, who build athletic shoes, or Benetton, who make clothes, are the prototype of the successful modern firm. Nike has its headquarters in Oregon, where it designs but does not make shoes. It contracts out to manufacturers, primarily in Taiwan, Korea and the Philippines. But it also has contractors which it is developing in China, Malaysia and other parts of the Far East. It uses new sub-contractors all the time to put pressure on the first-level sub-contractors to maintain the lowest possible price. Through these contractual relationships the headquarters firm can move very rapidly to adapt to the market, without having any real commitments of its own. The person who is actually making the shoe may be working in a sweat shop for very pitiful wages somewhere in Malaysia or China. Benetton organises production in a hierarchy of firms from Northern Italy to sweat shops and home workers in Southern Italy and Turkey. Many leading American clothing companies sub-contract production to firms in Mexico or Central America, where wages and conditions of work have been reported comparable to the worst abuses of the factory system over a century ago.

The strategies which firms adopt to manage the uncertainties of a competitive world economy tend, therefore, to displace the burden of adjustment on to weaker and weaker subordinate actors, leaving those at the bottom with few choices and no economic security. Governments are increasingly turning to similar strategies to decrease deficits and taxes, privatising public services and withdrawing entitlements. Here, too, the poorest suffer most, as they struggle with the consequences of unstable and conflicting policies. At the same time, they are likely to have the fewest psychological resources to withstand this abuse. They are more likely to have suffered early loss of a primary attachment figure, to have experienced attachment as insecure, and to lack supportive relationships. Evidence from studies of bereavement and depression suggest that all these factors, together with vulnerability to sudden and traumatic losses, make recovery from loss more difficult, and predispose people to chronic grief and depression. In these circumstances, the only escape from the crushing anxieties of constant insecurity and fragile self-esteem may lie in moments of spontaneous pleasure and acts of emotional release, regardless of a future you cannot control, in drugs which numb the distress of life, or in withdrawal into another world of spiritual consolation. All these reactions will tend to reinforce the insecurity of their circumstances, or at least do nothing to combat them. The competitive management of uncertainty, as it thrusts the burden of adjusting to uncertainties on to the weakest, impoverishes the emotional quality of their lives and provokes responses which only reinforce their insecurity and deprivation.

How can we try to create a world which is less destructive? First of all, we need to distinguish between economic competition and competition in the management of uncertainty. The prevailing assumption, at least in the US, is that economic competitiveness implies competitiveness in the management of uncertainty. But that is surely too simple. Any economic system depends on creating relationships of trust, on predictability, on a consensus of mutual support, at least amongst the business class itself. These reciprocal commitments create the framework of predictability within which economic competition takes place. Nor can most economic activities be carried out without at least some trust between employer and employee. The loyalty of workers is itself a valuable asset. There is an enormous value to collaboration. Despite the logic of the competitive management of uncertainty that I have tried to lay out, uncertainty is not a zero sum. Making less uncertainty for myself does not necessarily have to mean making more uncertainty for you. It only does so if I adopt a competitive strategy. If instead I try to create collaborative relationships, together we reduce the amount of uncertainty which everyone has to face, because most of our uncertainties arise from the unpredictability of other people's behaviour. The less we are preoccupied with defending ourselves against each other, the more energy we release, and the more we expand the field of reliable relationships in which we can dare to frame our hopes and ambitions. A culture with a relentlessly competitive ethos undermines trust and maximises insecurity, and it is hard to believe that this can be healthy for any society, even in its economic relationships, in the long run.

But collaboration is a favourable strategy only so long as one can trust that other people will indeed collaborate in return. For those with considerable power, it is always tempting to revert to competitive strategies which impose control without reciprocity, because collaborating involves patience, understanding, and selfrestraint, and there is always some risk that you or your collaborators may prove unable or unwilling to honour their undertaking. At the same time, when people are feeling most insecure, they are often least ready to trust in collaboration. Arguments of self-interest cannot by themselves promote strategies of collaboration, because they assume that the conditions of mutual trust are already present. As Emile Durkheim argued in his classic study, the complex interactions of modern industrial societies depend upon an underlying moral consensus. This brings me back to attachment. Where do we find the moral consensus to validate collaborative strategies for managing the uncertainties that we always face?

It seems to me that we do, in fact, share a common moral intuition. We share that moral intuition out of our experience of attachment. Whether or not we have had a happy attachment experience ourselves, we understand those qualities which make for good parenting. I call this the 'morality of children' – the child's ideal of how parents should behave. Parents should be brave, strong, protective, respectful of your autonomy, intelligent, and generally provide all those qualities that will ensure your own safe growing-up. And those, I believe, are the qualities we expect of society. A fundamental moral intuition grows out of the attachment experience, which helps to guide all of us, and which we can use to describe the ideal qualities of a mutually protective society.

But to describe a good society in these terms leaves open the question of its boundaries. There is a risk that, in the face of all the uncertainties of our contemporary world, people will retreat into small communities, which may indeed be very nurturing and protective of each other, but withdraw defensively from any wider collaboration. In the US particularly, the more prosperous suburban towns often idealise themselves as enclaves in which they seek to provide all those Norman Rockwell-like qualities of a happy and mutually supportive community, but they do so by cutting themselves off socially and fiscally from the inner city where all the problems are dumped. This is yet another example of the way in which we are displacing the burden of uncertainty on to those who are weaker than ourselves.

I would argue, then, that the moral community of which we are part has to be as large as the range of relationships whose uncertainties crucially affect our lives, which nowadays covers the entire globe. The quality of a mother's attachment to her child, in Britain or the US, will be influenced by the hours she has to be away from home earning money, by the security or insecurity of her own and her husband's job, by the family tensions that these anxieties provoke. On the other side of the world, another mother is making the shoes she buys to put on her child's feet and the teddy bear she buys for Christmas. Unless these two mothers can find a way to collaborate against the insecurities which threaten both of them, they will both, in the long run, become the victims of the competitive management of uncertainty, divided by their fear and their impotence. And the same is true for all of us. I suggest, then, that the quality of attachment that our children and grandchildren will enjoy – and hence the hope or cynicism, trust or suspicion with which they confront the world – will be determined by our ability to sustain collaborative relationships on a worldwide scale to manage the profound economic and environmental uncertainties they will face.

The framework for such collaboration is beginning to emerge, for instance, from the recent conferences on women's reproductive and social rights and development in Cairo and Beijing. The success of these events depends in turn on the network of local, national and international organisations which determine the agendas, help to negotiate the resolutions, and press for the implementation of these commitments. I believe this kind of network, as much or more than conventional politics, will articulate the politics of attachment in the twenty-first century: and that politics is, above all, a politics of reciprocal commitment.

REFERENCE

Benington, J., Bond N. and Skelton, P. (1975) *Prosperity and the Persistence of Inequality: Coventry CPD Final Report*, London: CPD Publications.

15 Digital Community: 'Only Connect'

Oleg Liber

INTRODUCTION

The last two decades have seen an exponential growth in electronic communications and, in the last few years, media interest has become intense. There is no doubt that new information technologies are having a profound impact on many aspects of life, affecting economic, civic and social domains. Yet media focus has been concerned primarily with the potential threat of these developments to society. Stories abound about the supposed activities of archetypal hackers and 'nerds', who spend countless hours hunched in front of computers connected to the internet, looking at dirty pictures, hacking into government and corporate systems, playing fantasy games and communicating with each other in jargon-laden computer-speak.

This attention on the supposed dangers of unregulated communication obscures the enormous potential information technologies have for enabling widespread participation in the political process. Meanwhile the finance and business worlds quietly colonise information networks, transforming economies and reducing the ability of governments to manage their economies.

I want to argue that new information technologies, rather than just creating a playground for lost adolescents, can be harnessed as a powerful social medium in the modern world. They enable new forms of communication between people that were hitherto unimaginable, and with at least the same potential impact as the telephone and television. New relationships become possible, and through them the expression of new attachments. The origins of social life are, after all, to be found in the exquisitely balanced communications that operate between infant and parent as attachment unfolds (Holmes, Murray, this volume). So it is appropriate to approach new technologies through the study of communication and relationship; through cybernetics. Communities based on shared interest are emerging, freed from geographical constraint, and where no one is in authority. But opportunities exist to be an authority where people can participate in understanding and developing answers to shared concerns.

People express their relationships to each other through the many systems of which they are part. These may be family systems, social networks, places of employment, regional communities, trade unions, political parties and so on, some of which may intersect and some may not. All of these are maintained by the 'conversations' of their members. They are constructed from relationships between their members, which are maintained through communication. While patterns of communication are constrained by organisational structure, they may be enabled by communication technologies.

There has been much written about the influence of communication technologies on the structure of commerce and industry, and the nature of employment. In the past, industrial management has been characterised by layers of management, each reporting up and commanding down a pyramidal structure. New technologies have led to radical new management ideas, leading to massive restructuring. We have seen the emergence of flatter management involving layers of management being stripped out; organisations have been downsized, rightsized; departmental functions have been outsourced, and business processes have been re-engineered. All of this has been made possible by new communications. These changes have in some cases led to greater flexibility and responsiveness; in others to more efficiency. In some they have led to more respect and responsibility for employees; in others to more insecurity and reduction in working conditions. The point is not that communication technologies make things better, but that they offer choices. Enlightened organisations use technology to liberate their employees from unnecessary constraints, and to free the creative potential that emerges from rich interaction between secure individuals, in exactly the same way as particular patterns of communication in families lead to securely attached and independent children. Oppressive organisations use technology to terrorise their employees in order to maximise their productivity. Lean and mean organisations lead to lean and mean people, just as insecurely attached children become socially dysfunctional.

An example of the choice technology offers is the idea of teleworking, where clerical, administrative and managerial work can take place away from the office – at the worker's home, for instance, using electronic communications to transmit and receive the products of this work. On the one hand, teleworking can remove the inconvenience and expense of travel; on the other, it can lead to the loss of important social interactions that are made possible by gathering together in one location. Which of these prevails is determined by the ethos of the organisation. If the purpose is only to reduce cost and increase productivity, then it is likely that social costs will be ignored. On the other hand, if teleworking is driven by concern for the employee, then it will be organised differently, and social issues will be addressed.

Everything I have observed about communications and industry applies to political organisations, including all levels of government, trade unions, political parties and single issue groups. Before I discuss the new possibilities offered by new technologies, it is worth examining how the emergence of older ones, most notably the invention of printing, affected political processes.

Printing led to the growth of literacy. It made possible the creation, publication and dissemination of ideas that would previously have been restricted to oral communication, and thereby allowed national and international political ideas to spread. In turn this led to the widespread struggle for human rights – for universal suffrage and for literacy. No longer could politicians deliberate in private on the actions of government; newspapers and journals were able to communicate their speeches to the people along with the critiques of their opponents. For the first time, nations became integrated; all subjects were able at the very least to know what the state was up to, if not influence it. Inevitably there was a demand for participation; if people were part of the nation, they needed to act as such – they insisted on democratic involvement. The eventual outcome was universal suffrage. Where dictatorship exists, it can no longer be excused by the fact that the processes of representation are too unwieldy. The technology that allows the printing of newspapers also permits the printing of ballot papers.

Since then, mass communication technology has remained structurally similar; it provides a rich communication channel from the few to the many. The primary concern of those at the source of information may be no more than the viability of their enterprise, rather than the system it should serve. Their success would then be judged by numbers of sales or viewers rather than by the breadth and accuracy of their reporting. Despite current print technology becoming much more sophisticated, newspapers still play essentially the same role they always have, but have been joined by radio and television news and current affairs programmes. Government speaks to the people, and its message is amplified, examined, has 'spin' put on it, and travels at lightning speed. In contrast, the people's ability to respond is tiny. All we can do, that must be taken notice of, is put a cross on a ballot paper once every five years. It is hard to imagine a more minimal or less articulate form of democracy without it disappearing altogether. So, although this technology allowed people to participate in selecting their government, it has not helped us to get involved in shaping the policies that govern our communities and nations.

Participative democracy, where people can be involved in making specific policy decisions, would be the next step in extending democracy. Despite all major political parties claiming to listen to the electorate, there are few proposals as to how this might be done. It is as if only the well-informed (that is, politicians) were able to make decisions that concern the well-being of the nation, except for the odd occasion when referenda are called for, more for political expediency than for any principled reason. Of course, it is true that the whole population could not act as a parliament, yet it could be argued that the more powerful they become, the more estranged local and national politicians will be from 'normal' life (see Jowell, this volume) in which case they are less able to ground their decision making in the needs and aspirations of their electors. This paradox can only be resolved by giving recognition to the domains where people can and should be able to engage in decision making, and by designing new channels to allow these networks or communities to maintain a dynamic relationship with government; to inform and be informed by these different levels of concern.

Another mass communication technology, the telephone, has made direct communication between people possible, but it only allows one-to-one discussion, and for this reason has not been exploited as a means of extending democracy. Democracy presumes group activity – telephones only permit dialogue, and so far there has been no way of capturing the essence of millions of conversations to influence political decisions.

Recent developments in computer and communications technologies can change all this. Computers and digital technologies are integrating communications. Now television can travel down telephone wires, and telephone discussions through the airwaves – and both take place via satellite. Local radio stations from the US can be received via the internet in Europe; and international telephone conversations can take place via the internet for a local call charge. Information restricted in one country can be accessed from systems running in another. Opinions of all sorts and on all issues can be found, considered and discussed on the internet. The integration of communications technologies is producing a new, hybrid system, one that can be one-to-one and one-to-many, distributed yet coherent. This emergent communication technology can provide the tool for a new form of connection – at precisely the moment in history when representative democracy appears to be facing a crisis of disillusionment.

So, as in the case of industrial organisation, technology offers choices to the political system. It can be used to monitor and manipulate public opinion, or it can be used to foster richer communication and interaction in the political process – one of the principal themes of this book. It depends on whether those active in government see themselves as our political masters or our political servants. If it is to be the former, then the relationship between government and governed will tend to be abusive, and will promote abusive patterns in society; the latter, on the other hand, by offering responsible participation, would promote responsible attitudes and behaviour.

THE INTERNET AND THE MEDIA

It is important to recognise that the capabilities offered by the international network of networks known as the internet are structurally different from existing mass communication technologies, and so cannot be judged from the same standpoint. The internet provides a medium for publishing, for one-to-one interaction, and for group discussion. It allows multimedia communications – text, sound, still and moving images. However, each of these is different in important respects from its antecedents.

Existing publishing systems tend to be tightly controlled. Academic publication is subject to peer review and editorial selection processes; journalistic publication likewise undergoes editorial control, and very few prospective writers ever get their creations to print. This filtering process, it is argued, provides a quality control, but also gives a few people the power to promote their own preferences and prejudices to the reading audience, whether consciously or unconsciously. It also balances the cost of publications with income, and tends to favour texts that are likely to lead to high-volume sales.

Publishing on the internet is very different. There are no filters to prevent anyone from publishing whatever they want. For a small charge, anyone can rent a small space on a 'server' and publish whatever they want on the internet. However, they also need to publicise their creation. This they do by contacting other sites that they have visited and requesting an index entry, or a hypertext 'link'. These may or may not be created, and even when they are, there is no guarantee that anyone will visit and read the document, and there will certainly be no financial reward. So, publishing on the internet is different in almost every respect from traditional publishing, and complements rather than competes with it; which it why it cannot be judged by the same yardstick. What it does provide is the possibility of universal publishing, and therefore access to many viewpoints. If you want to find out about the experience of living in one of the world's hotspots, you can read what local people say, as well as listening to the BBC's correspondent. Before this is dismissed as unrealistic, and that ordinary people will never want to write and publish their experiences, it is worth noting that it was originally thought that ordinary people would find no use for the telephone, and that it would always be a tool for specialised communication.

This raises difficult questions – How does one sort through millions of texts to find those that matter? How can we assess the truth of what we read? The answer is not to think of this in the same terms as other publications but more in terms of personal conversations. When people 'surf' the internet, they often start by visiting a site that has been recommended – by a friend, in a magazine, on the radio, or by some other means. This site will have links to others that are connected in some way – by content, or style, or world view. Over time, readers will find sites they like to visit often, that they trust to provide interesting links – to whose outlook they subscribe. So finding information on the internet is more like conversations between friends than the authoritative utterances of traditional publications. This is one of the ways in which the internet is perceived by many of its users as being more egalitarian; the power ascribed to author and reader is more balanced.

Perhaps the most mature aspect of the internet is its discussion groups, known as newsgroups. Originally established as a means for discussion between academics, this service has grown to cover many thousands of topics. Anyone can browse through the list of these, join those they are interested in, and participate in the discussions. These take the form of texts beginning a discussion topic, to which responses can be made. Further responses can be made to the original topic statement, or to other responses, resulting in a tree structure of statements. This is different in several ways from face-to-face discussions. The pace of the discussion is much slower; whereas in normal conversations our mouths often start to work before our minds, in electronic discussions one can take time to consider and edit one's response; and the conversation can continue for days and weeks. Secondly, although the loss of non-verbal signals may remove opportunities for irony and humour, it also means that interrupting and shouting cannot happen, nor is shyness and self-consciousness an issue. The loss in external signs that denote authority means that people are more likely to be critical of each other's views. So, there are discussions that involve a wide range of participants, from professors to school children, arguing about issues of mutual interest without any of the inhibitions that may arise in formal settings.

Another electronic communciation tool is email (electronic mail). This is the system that allows people to exchange private correspondence through the internet. As long as you have someone's address, you can type a letter and send it to them, whether it is a friend living abroad or the President of the United States. Its ease of use and immediacy is leading to the rebirth of letter writing – I have always been terrible at writing letters, but use email daily. It is leading to an increase in the communications received by newspapers, TV and radio programmes, and politicians.

These three aspects of the internet provide a new means by which people can connect with each other, and can begin to develop a new literacy; where writing is as important as reading, thereby opening new pathways and challenging the stranglehold that 'official' channels have had on the provision of information. By using this new facility, people will become better informed, will encounter a wider range of viewpoints, and will become more able to participate in making decisions about their social space, local or global. In the process new and strange phenomena will emerge; for example, some people adopt different identities when on the internet, changing their names and gender, and expressing themselves in ways they find difficult or impossible in 'real' life. And, there is evidence that internet users are not the stereotype 'nerd', but come from diverse backgrounds and age groups. Perhaps the internet lifts constraints on the way people feel able to form relationships; on the other hand, the relationships they form may be less rich. Whatever the case, new possibilities are opened up by the internet, and these can be shaped to enable or to restrict its users. What is certain is that it can lead to changes as profound as those triggered by the invention of printing.

CYBERNETICS

The previous section has outlined the way in which the internet is currently being used, but this is embryonic as compared to the possibilities opened up by advances in global communications technology. Although the internet allows the transmission of all forms of data, including text, sound, images and movies, it does so rather slowly. However, the networking of society by the creation of data superhighways (high-capacity fibre optic cabling) is transforming this, and will allow new forms of interaction that need to be explored.

Inevitably, media companies see new data superhighways as a means for getting more entertainment into homes, and more money into their pockets. They see this new channel simply as a bigger and better way of transmitting information from the few to the many. But it can do much more: it also creates the possibility of getting information back from the many to those with the job of integrating society – whether they be politicians, civil servants, commercial service providers, or managers. It also opens the completely new possibility of many-to-many communication, a basic condition for connection and participation.

I do not suggest that designing a system that supports rich feedback and interaction between different organisational levels is simple and straightforward, but I do argue that these communications create the possibility for investigating new ways of organising ourselves, ways that are not possible without fast communications. If these can allow for greater interaction and participation, and enable a transformation in the privilege and authority that political and managerial power has given, then every effort must be made to explore them. To do so will require the development and examination of models of communication and organisation; the science that is concerned with this is cybernetics.

In recent years, the word cybernetics has re-entered common parlance. We now hear of cyberspace, cybercafés, cybervillage and so on. In fact, it is the name given to a transdisciplinary science that came to prominence in the late 1940s – defined as the 'science of control and communication' (Wiener 1948) or the 'science of organisation' (Beer 1959). It comes from the Greek *kybernetes*, meaning 'steersman'. Cybernetics concerns itself with communication, and its relation to organisation. In complex systems, communications flow down richly interconnected networks, some of which are hierarchical in structure, others lateral. These structures determine the range of possibilities for the system in question. For example, systems where communications only flow up and down hierarchical channels tend to be rigid and exhibit poor adaptability; those with additional rich lateral communications are more flexible and adaptable.

The world view offered by cybernetics has led to new insights and perspectives in many areas of investigation, including psychology, anthropology and ecology, amongst others. It has provided the basis for the design of participatory social systems, most famously in President Salvador Allende's Chile in the early 1970s (Beer 1981), where electronic communication systems were used to allow workers to participate in the management of their enterprises, and permitted communities to participate in regulating their government. For example, computer models of all factories, enterprises, industries and the whole social economy were made available through an electronic communication system to workers at all levels of the economy, allowing them to see the effects of their contributions, the roles they all played in the total system, and to participate in the continuous development of their particular sphere of concern. This is precisely the quality of responsiveness that is at the heart of the attachment process (see Holmes, Murray, this volume).

Stafford Beer is the British cybernetician who pioneered the application of cybernetics to organisations. He advised the Chilean government in the design of participatory communications systems before its violent overthrow, and he has written extensively on the cybernetics of government. In 'The Cybernetics of National Development' he discusses how, until very recently, developments in communications technology were mainly concerned with one-way communication, or broadcasting. Government's deliberations and decisions are disseminated and dissected continuously by the mass media; people can only respond meaningfully through infrequent elections. In his words:

> Within the theory of a representative democracy, a parliament or congress is a national assembly. But ... the rate of technological development is eroding the traditional system. The mass media disseminate information continuously, whereas the elections occur at long intervals. There is a gross mismatch in the time scales of public awareness and the electoral process. This threatens democracy itself. (Beer 1994, p. 335)

Thus the centralised media, which made democracy possible, now threaten to undermine democracy. Indeed, it is impossible not to notice how politicians' utterances are becoming increasingly for-mulaic. The more the media amplifies the message, the less there seems to be to amplify. Opinion polls and phone-ins, ostensibly offering some kind of feedback mechanism, are misleading because problems are identified by those asking the questions, not those answering. They seem simply to offer opportunities to be patron-ised. However, the marriage of high-speed networks and computer technology now makes it possible for systems to be constructed that can permit the population continuously to provide feedback on their perceptions and feelings about the state of affairs. Beer designed and implemented such a system over 20 years ago in Chile; technology and networks have become much more sophisti-cated since then, and yet there appears to be little discussion, research or experiments on how we can best exploit this technology to extend and improve democracy (see Benington, this volume). Obviously government would be overwhelmed if it attempted to listen to everyone's opinion on all issues; likewise, it would be ridiculous to expect everyone to participate and vote on all issues (government by referendum). But it is possible to design systems that allow people to respond to political debates as they watch them on the news, listen to them on the radio or read them on the internet; and it is possible for this to be captured, aggregated and fed back continuously to those involved in them. This would be as relevant to management in business as to politicians; they could have feedback on their management decisions as they are made, and then could choose to respond or not. At least they would know about their popularity or otherwise, and they would know that the electorate (or workforce) knew that they knew.

Beer devised and tested a small device he called an algedonic meter, which allowed users to move a single dial from 'happy' to 'sad', and anywhere in between. The outputs of these could be aggre-gated into a single output, displayed on a similar device in the man-ager's office, but also in a public place, visible to all. This would simply reflect what Beer calls 'eudemony' (well-being), something like the 'feel good factor', but on a continuous basis. But whereas opinion polls can be structured to get many different answers, this would be completely under the control of those using the device; there would be no question they were being asked, no vote they were participating in. They would simply be indicating how they felt.

Science fiction? Beer was using these devices 20 years ago. I am not suggesting that such devices are appropriate for present-day Britain. What I am suggesting is that ways should be explored in which technology can be used to enable increased feedback and participation, and that imagination is required to design these. Technology has moved on enormously since the Chilean experience and we are rapidly becoming a networked society. We need to explore how we can tell each other, and those we choose to govern, how we feel, what we think of the state of affairs, and how we expect them to respond. We need to move beyond minority governments with parliamentary majorities or, in the case of hung councils, to lowest common denominator politics. Listening to the people has to mean more than listening and then ignoring; it must mean listening and responding, respecting the electorate. We must investigate all means by which this can be achieved, and how technology can be used to support it.

A NEW DEMOCRACY

It has not been my intention to suggest that electronic communications offer a simple solution to societal problems. New technologies offer a new set of tools, and can lead to a new set of problems. What I am arguing for is that the possibilities offered be fully explored. The tools offered are concerned with communication, and focus attention on the communicative act; they can be used to create stable systems, where mutual understanding and collaboration are the norms; or they can be used to amplify the problems we already face. We must act to design systems that lead to the world we want, and not leave the decisions to chance or the marketplace.

People are already exploring the possibilities offered by new communications. Apart from financial, business and academic users, electronic networks are used by a growing and disparate group of enthusiasts, who are busy creating virtual communities based on shared interests. These are invariably fiercely egalitarian, and offer a new context for the setting up of attachments that are not provided for by establishment institutions. At the moment these people are presented as socially deficient, and maybe some are; but this does not detract from the potential the networked society has for creating closer and better relationships between those who previously would have had no contact, especially between government and governed. If the will and imagination were there, those interested in extending democracy and participation would be learning from experiences like those in Chile, and be applying communication technologies to the problems of attachment and identity facing our societies today.

REFERENCES

Beer, S. (1959) *Cybernetics and Management.* London: English Universities Press.
Beer, S. (1981) *The Brain of the Firm.* (2nd edn) London: Wiley.
Beer, S. (1994) 'The Cybernetics of National Development' (The Zaheer Foundation Lecture, New Delhi, 1974) in R. Harnden. and A. Leonard (eds), *How Many Grapes Went into the Wine?* London: Wiley.
Wiener, N. (1948) *Cybernetics.* New York: Wiley.

16 Attachment in Context

Michael Rustin

Attachment theory began its life at a particular historical moment. This was the time at the end of the Second World War when social reconstruction was in everyone's mind. Reparation was directed not only at the damage caused by the war, but also at the social polarisation and impoverishment which had preceded it, and had brought about the conditions in which fascism and Nazism had thrived. In this period of the early 1940s, the Beveridge Report, proposing to slay the 'five giant evils' of Want, Disease, Ignorance, Squalor and Idleness was having its enormous impact, Keynes was imagining a post-war economy of full employment, and reformers were planning initiatives in numerous fields from health, education and town planning, to improved public access to the countryside (Addison 1982). The ideas of an ethical socialism gave a coherence to these different developments, Orwell's representations of the virtues of decency and mutual human respect (1953), Tawney's critique of acquisitive individualism (1921) and Marshall's idea of social citizenship (1963) providing three of the main foundations of this.

The most important social achievement of this period was the development of the welfare state, conceived as a system of comprehensive care for citizens at times of dependency. Titmuss and his colleagues at the London School of Economics provided a policy framework and a justification for its development in terms of ideals of social responsibility, mutual need and equality (Titmuss 1958; 1968). The family, and the social services necessary to support its task, was recognised in this project as a major object of social policy, drawing implicitly on American sociological ideas which theorised society as an organic whole bound by common values. Titmuss' most memorable representation of this ideal was in *The Gift Relationship* (1970), whose account of the blood transfusion system based on altruism and identification metaphorically stands not only for the project of the British National Health Service, but also for a larger idea of moral community.

It was in this context that Bowlby began to write about the damage caused by separation in infancy, and the importance of the primary family unit as the basis for a secure identity (Holmes 1993), providing an important psychological contribution to this broader project of social repair. The development of preventive child and family health services, via the health visitor and child guidance systems, were policy initiatives of the period which reflected these concerns. The elaboration of the insights of attachment theory, both as a research programme in the work of Mary Ainsworth, Mary Main and others (Ainsworth 1982; Main et al. 1985; Main 1991; Main and Goldwyn 1984; Fonagy et al. 1991), and linked by others to broader social issues, have been one of the most fruitful developments of post-war social science, amply illustrated in this volume.

Ideas of attachment are now being discussed at a moment when the individualist counter-revolution of the past 20 years seems finally to be losing its momentum, and some of its sway over public opinion in the Anglo-Saxon world.[1] The question that has to be asked, therefore, is how well do the ideas and approaches developed in the context of the 1940s and 1950s translate to the contemporary situation? Can the 'politics of attachment' form the basis for a new agenda of social relationship and community, or is it in danger of representing a nostalgia for a world we have irretrievably lost?

The difficulties lie in the scope and depth of the social changes that have taken place since the 1950s. So many of the institutions and identities which reparative advocates of attachment could presuppose in the earlier period have been fragmented or transformed. The matrix of identities within a national community, a bounded sense of class membership, an extended family, even a nation, which underpinned the lives of many in Britain after the war, and which had been cemented by the community-in-adversity of the war situation, has now dissolved. Family size has fallen, and divorce now ends one-third of marriages. In a cultural change which seems extraordinary to those who remember the norms of the previous generation, cohabitation before marriage has become common: in 1995 33.9 per cent of babies were born to unmarried couples, although more than half are registered in the name of both parents at the same address. The rates of birth outside marriage were 19.2 per cent in 1985, and 9.2 per cent in 1976 (*Guardian* 11 June 1996). Britain is a multi-ethnic society, and its citizens can, and often must, negotiate many complex trajectories of origin in their own, their families' and their neighbours' lives.

The idea of Britain itself has become problematic (see Taylor, this volume), stretched in one direction by the counter-claims to national identity of the Scots and the Welsh (leaving aside the complexities of Northern Ireland) and in another by identifications with a broader Europe. Class identities, or at least working-class identities, appear to have weakened. They have been undermined by deindustrialisation and the destruction of occupational communities such as those of miners, dockers, fishermen and steelworkers. Working-class membership has been attacked ideologically, in a vigorous anti-collectivism directed at trade unions and welfare provision, and displaced by the appeal of lifestyles which ignore or parody the dimensions of class. Different forms of sexuality have become recognised realities and possibilities in modern society, and now, if not still without difficulties, find their open cultural expression.

Social inequalities have again increased, after 40 years in which they had slowly diminished. The fear of economic insecurity has become nearly universal, with persistently high levels of unemployment, and with 'downsizing' and short-term patterns of employment spreading upwards into white collar, professional and managerial strata from the manual occupations where casual forms of employment had always been a common experience. Rates of crime, now related to this exclusion of significant sections of the population from the possibility of earning a stable living wage, have continuously increased, though official figures are probably exaggerated by the greater ease of reporting crimes as a result of improved communications.

Thus, social identities and moral certitudes which previously existed as an implicit sub-stratum of everyday life, have become problematic, topics for debate and controversy. It was possible for radical writers, like George Orwell (1953), Richard Hoggart (1992) and Raymond Williams (1958), to evoke a sense of community, decency and ordinariness in their work, in ways which now seem anachronistic. What many in British society feel they have lost can be seen in the intense reaction to traumatic crimes, especially those which appear to violate the norms of the family. The theme of the public response to the murder of James Bulger at Kirby, and to the massacre at Dunblane, was: 'How can such things happen here?' Moral panics about child sexual abuse have heaped blame on abusive families, incompetent social workers, and over-intrusive psychiatrists, sometimes in rapid succession, displaying considerable confusion about where the real problem is believed to lie. These fears have had a dire impact on social work with families and children, giving forensic investigation priority over supportive and preventive work with families. In its response to what it perceives to be widespread social anxiety about crime, the government has imported repressive penal programmes developed in the much more violent and racialised social context of the US. Sentencing powers are being removed from a basically conservative judiciary in order to give effect to imputed public cravings for protection from and retribution against persistent criminals. 'New Labour' has been following suit, apparently discounting more thoughtful and compassionate approaches to these problems as only of concern to the liberal middle classes. On all these issues, the role of the popular press is to amplify anxieties and to substitute the projection of rage, self-righteousness and hatred for thought. 'Understanding' is deemed to be synonymous with weakness.

As social ties are felt to be crumbling, hostility is mobilised and directed outwards. Reaction to the outbreak of BSE (or 'mad cow disease') is a symptomatic case, current at the time of writing. Here anxieties about purity and contamination in one sphere – a disease which has crossed first a species barrier in animals, then the species barrier between animals and man – became amazingly converted into virulent nationalist antipathies, as the now-contaminated Roast Beef of Old England is rejected by continental consumers. (Typically, reflecting wider social inequalities of health, the main danger seems to lie in the cheaper cuts.)

In this situation, the problem of who is now to be attached, or re-attached, to whom, and according to what shared norms, becomes difficult to prescribe. It is no wonder that the idea of 'community', which some have sought to place at the centre of a programme of political renewal, seems fatally difficult to define and give effect to. The idea that human beings need a secure attachment from birth, and the security of membership and recognition through their lives, in order to develop fruitfully, is a vital one. But it is one thing to identify this as a problem and to set it out as a desirable goal, and another to say how this is to be effected in modern societies like ours.

'Attachment theory' provides some solid building-blocks at a micro-level for a broader concept of social membership at a macro-level. It provides an explanation for the normal development of secure personalities, capable of developing autonomy and of relating to others with trust. It sets out the conditions in infant life in which this is likely to happen, and identifies supportive structures and interventions which can be put in place when these conditions are precarious. The theoretical foundation of these ideas came in the first instance from biology and especially ethology, in the demonstrated similarities between instinctual behaviours of humans and primates.

These ideas have so far had their most direct practical impact in their focus on the first few years of life. Flourishing research programmes on infant and child development, drawing on several related approaches in psychology and child psychoanalysis, have led to significant recent progress in understanding the preconditions of normal development. Explanatory models of human behaviour based on innate instincts probably have their least contentious applications to the needs of infants. Even so, the gap between the understandings of research programmes and the current priorities of social policy remain extremely wide. The quality of support available to the families of young children remains poor, and nursery education remains largely unfunded, even when increasing proportions of young mothers find themselves obliged to remain in the labour market to make ends meet. But what attachment research has to say about the needs of infants and young children is so consonant with everyday understandings that it ought to be possible to gain public support for a substantial improvement in child support services.

Amitai Etzioni's communitarian movement in the US (1993) responds to a deficit in public frameworks of support with moralistic demands addressed to parents, and especially mothers, to take their responsibilities to children more seriously (see Murray, this volume). It is worrying that this particular version of 'community' should have been so readily taken up by New Labour. Demands made on young parents' and especially women's, sense of responsibility can be a cheap substitute for actions which require different public priorities, and which therefore make demands on everyone.

One risk arising from generalised anxieties about a lost sense of community is that communities will be defined in exclusionary and coercive terms, either at the larger level of the 'national community', or in even more sectional ideological or ethnic terms. When the Home Secretary targets criminals, travellers or 'ravers' for punitive treatment, or when the Shadow Home Secretary targets aggressive beggars, or children on the street at night for 'curfew', we are witnessing the construction of a moral community of the righteous, constituted by imprisoning or segregating those who cannot be accommodated within it. Something similar takes place in the field of immigration policy, where community is being ever more severely defined in racial terms, at the expense even of the rights of entry of political refugees and relatives of residents in Britain. British attitudes to newcomers have never been wholly positive. But in the past, pride was taken in the idea that a free country should welcome victims of oppression, and the concept of Britishness did not end at the English Channel. Counter-communities are constructed in opposition to these prejudicial definitions. These may be defined in terms of racial essence, of religious purity, or even of delinquent rejection of all conventional social norms. A society lacking in the shared ground-rules which should underpin a modern community then breaks up into antagonistic quasi-communities, defined primarily by their hatred of what is deemed to lie outside them (see also Gosling, this volume).

To understand and respond to this situation, we need more theoretical resources than can be provided by attachment theory alone, invaluable as this perspective is. Attachment theory embodies an understanding of the procedures of socialisation, the means by which individuals acquire a capacity to function in secure and co-operative ways in society. This is one fundamental 'micro-sociological' foundation for an understanding of the good society. But an adequate social theory needs, in addition, three other dimensions.

First, we need to understand not only what makes secure personalities develop in the first place, but also what happens when this process fails, and how both individuals and groups respond to situations of high anxiety and threat. This requires that theoretical attention be paid to anti-social forces and drives in human nature, as well as to those instincts or disposition which make for sociability. Second, we need to understand that 'community' and 'relationship' have a symbolic as well as a grounded, matter-of-fact existence, and that in the complex societies of today this symbolic dimension has become more important than before. Third, we need to understand the structural forces which are undermining cohesion and social integration, sometimes thought of as 'globalisation', and sometimes in more old-fashioned terms as the outcome of market forces and the power of capital.

We need ideas which take into account all of these dimensions of what contemporary sociologists describe as 'modernity' (see for example Giddens 1990, 1991, 1994; Beck 1992; Bauman 1992), if we are to respond adequately to the predicaments described in this book. The first two issues have been dealt with most fundamentally within the psychoanalytic tradition; the third within the traditions of political economy.

PSYCHOANALYSIS AND ATTACHMENT THEORY

Contemporary with the development of attachment theory by Bowlby, and closely if sometimes uncomfortably linked with his work at the Tavistock Clinic in the 1950s and 1960s, was the development of a distinctively British tradition in psychoanalysis, often characterised as the 'object-relations tradition'. What distinguished this approach was its rejection of instincts and drives as the core of human behaviour, and its insistence that human beings were from birth related to others, as the 'objects' of desire, love or hate.[2] At their origins, both attachment theory and the 'British school' of psychoanalysis postulated a 'social' view of human nature, against the assumptions of atomistic individualism. But if attachment theory was one reparative approach to the damage brought about by war and violence, Melanie Klein and her colleagues' attention to the innate forces of destructiveness, envy and hatred in the human mind was another. In her work on these negative aspects of the psyche, Klein was developing Freud's key idea of the 'death instinct', proposed by him as the obverse of the 'life instinct '(or libido). Just as the idea of the 'death instinct' had been developed in the atmosphere following the First World War, so one might suppose that Klein's preoccupation with destructiveness and envy, and damage to good objects was also influenced by the climate of disaster surrounding the rise of Nazism and the Second World War. These ideas of innate destructiveness divided the British psychoanalytic community. The principal forum for this debate was the 'Controversial Discussions' of the British Psychoanalytical Society, which took place between 1943 and 1944 (King and Steiner 1991), sometimes literally as the bombs were falling. The contestants were Anna Freud and her supporters, recently arrived from Vienna; Melanie Klein and her group; and a third group which became known as 'the Middle Group', (later 'the Independents'), which included both Bowlby and the paediatrician Donald Winnicott. The debate focused on Klein's view that complex inner life began in infancy almost from birth, much sooner than Freud had proposed, and was based on conflicting feelings of love and hate.

This debate shaped the future development of psychoanalysis in Britain. It gave rise to the three distinct tendencies within the British Psychoanalytical Society on which its organisation has been based ever since. What was remarkable about this moment, as its historian, Riccardo Steiner has explained, is that these differences have remained peaceably contained within the framework of a single institution.[3]

The 'Middle Group', with which John Bowlby was linked, took a pragmatic and moderate position in the fierce discussions between the Kleinians and the Viennese. Sceptical about the 'death instinct', the analysts of this tendency took a more meliorist and environmentalist view of human nature than the Kleinians. From early on, this approach informed Bowlby's active commitment to the formation of preventive family health services within the National Health Service. It also underpinned subsequent campaigns, for example by James and Joyce Robertson (1952), for recognition of the emotional damage caused by unthinking separation of young children from their parents.

The Kleinian interest in destructive forces in the inner world pushed them, on the other hand, to develop psychotherapeutic techniques for working with children. Inasmuch as they held that some developmental difficulties had innate origins, or could not be ascribed simply to environmental shortcomings, they held it necessary and possible to seek clinical remedy for these problems in the consulting room. The development of the professional discipline in the post-war period of psychoanalytic child psychotherapy, and the extension of its interventions to more severe forms of disorder such as childhood psychosis and autism, followed from these clinical discoveries.

Psychoanalysis and attachment theory tended to address a different aspect of the same problem. Attachment theory focused on identifying the causes of maladjustment in separation, 'maternal deprivation', depression, or family breakdown. Those involved in the care of infants and young children should thus be recognised to be providing the emotional foundations of adult life, and be supported in this work.[4] Bowlby was, on the whole, sceptical of the possibilities of psychotherapeutic intervention once severe emotional damage had taken place. The crucial thing, from his perspective, was to prevent the damage being done in the first place.

Those involved in the development of child analysis, mostly in the new profession of psychoanalytic child psychotherapist, sought, on the other hand, to push forward the frontiers of psychoanalysis into the treatment of childhood emotional disorder. They were interested in investigating what could be done once damage had taken place. Work with children and young people suffering from autism, mental handicap, eating and sleeping disorders, and a history of abuse and deprivation, followed from this perspective (see, for example, Tustin 1981, Meltzer et al. 1975, Szur and Miller 1991, Daws 1989, Sinason 1992, Boston and Szur 1983). These interventions were developed at the level of individual psychotherapy, but also in a broader institutional context. It came to be understood that the capacity to provide a good environment for patient or child care could be undermined by unconscious anxiety and psychic pain, and the social defences constructed to ward this off. Isabel Menzies-Lyth's work (1988, 1989) was particularly important in identifying the role of unconscious processes in undermining the conditions of social care. Her argument was that the anxieties engendered by responsibility for suffering patients or for children in institutions needed to be understood by care workers. Only the explicit recognition of the role of unconscious emotion would enable institutions to keep their patients or clients properly in mind. Maintaining the conditions of 'attachment' was seen to depend on an understanding of the forces which pushed individuals and groups towards detachment from what was psychically painful. These ideas found an application in consultation to a variety of institutions – children's homes, schools, day nurseries, prisons. It was found that those working in such institutions could be helped to acknowledge more complex states of mind and feeling by discussion and interpretation (see Miller 1993, Obholzer and Roberts 1994). An alternative to consultation to institutions has been to offer training to care workers, often on a once-weekly basis, in the understanding of the emotional and group dynamics of work situations. Individual members of a professional or institutional staff group can thus be enabled to tolerate and help colleagues to process more of the stress of a work situation, when they return to it.

Underlying these new ideas and practices was the extension of the concept of 'attachment' into the idea of 'containment'. One further theoretical development needs to be noted in order to understand the shift of focus. This is the increased attention given to the development of the mind itself in early life. The emphasis of the British psychoanalytic tradition shifted during the 1950s, as Wilfred Bion, the former army psychiatrist and follower of Melanie Klein, pursued his clinical investigations of the severely damaged mental functions of psychotic patients. Bion (1962) proposed that the ability to hold together the good and bad aspects of the loved person in the mind, which was the basis of emotional integration, depended not just on the toleration of conflicting feelings, but also on the emergence of capacities for thought, or 'linking'. This developmental achievement depended on the functions of 'maternal containment', that is, on the role of the mother-figure in maintaining a climate of feeling that was tolerable for the infant. Winnicott's idea of 'primary maternal preoccupation' (Winnicott 1971) represents a parallel discovery of essentially the same aspect of development. In the mother–baby couple, on this view, the mother is supporting the development of the infant's mind through her own psychic responsiveness to her infant's experience. The experiential method of 'Infant Observation', initiated by Esther Bick in the 1950s, now almost a standard one- or two-year pre-clinical component of most psychoanalytic psychotherapy training programmes, was influenced from the outset by these ideas, and enabled numerous students of psychoanalytic psychotherapy to observe these phenomena of the developing mind of the infant for themselves (Miller et al. 1989).

A remarkable convergence can now be observed between these ideas of mental development derived from the British psychoanalytic tradition, including its practice of infant observation, and recent work by attachment theorists. The stunning correlations achieved between the findings of the Strange Situation Test and the Adult Attachment Interview in identifying the preconditions of pathological infantile development, turn out to revolve around the capacities of mind found, or found to be absent, in parents. A theoretical tradition based initially on ethological analogies between humans and the simpler primates has in the end succeeded in isolating as the precondition of human development the cognitive or mental capacities which have always been regarded as the distinctive attribute of the human species.

These ideas have significant clinical and policy implications. They explain, for example, why such long-term psychological damage can be caused by serious deficits in infant care, and therefore why social support systems for young families are so important. Investigation of psychotic disorders (breakdowns of mind) and the issues of 'containment' necessary to their management in the community, also have implications for what a comprehensive community mental health service needs to provide, in its capacity to absorb and respond thoughtfully to projected emotional and psychic distress.

SYMBOLIC ATTACHMENT

These developments also have a great significance for attachment considered as a social idea. This recognition of the key functions of mind identifies the flexibility and openness of human response as its most important characteristic. It makes it possible to see that 'attachment' in a complex world will always be mediated by symbolic conceptions and representations. Human beings will be related to representations, memories, principles and ideals, and not merely to the quotidian realities of what is presented by direct social experience.

In this respect, psychological theory, in the linked attachment and psychoanalytical perspectives, is able to achieve its own versions of the insights of other discourses of modern (and, according to some, post-modern) society. The idea of a social world constructed by past and present human choices, mediated to individuals by varieties of communications media, and in which face-to-face contact contributes only a part of our knowledge and experience of the world, thus becomes compatible with a psychological model which stresses symbolic capacity and complexity as the key resources of maturity.

We can relate these perspectives to contemporary debates on the nature of 'modernity', 'modernism' and 'post-modernism'. Social theorists such as Anthony Giddens, (1990, 1991, 1994) and Ulrich Beck (1992) theorise 'modernity', following the tradition of classical sociology, as an era of complex, rationalised societies, founded on the transformation of nature by science and technology. Modernity is defined in opposition to traditional society, in which received social and cultural forms are handed down through membership of groups which allow little scope for individual autonomy and choice. This 'modern' social order was a product of rationalising forms of thought, in the natural and the social sciences, which set reason against nature, enlightenment against backwardness, human freedom through understanding against the constraints of tradition and custom. What today characterises 'modernity', in the work of these writers, is the idea of 'reflexiveness', the idea that nature, society and now even human nature are not 'given' realities, but are continually transformed by our own understandings and choices.

Both attachment theory and psychoanalysis can be claimed to belong to this tradition of rational self-understanding, especially in so far as they claim to be 'human sciences' (but not all psychoanalysts now claim them to be so). Each takes an aspect of the natural – the instinctual basis of human behaviour, drives and unconscious forces, respectively – and opens it to understanding and purposeful intervention. But these perspectives preserve the duality of classical rationalist theories, in presupposing a reality and a nature that will always be resistant to understanding. Individual freedom and choice, within these perspectives, is always partial, constrained by the unavoidable limits of human nature and need.

By contrast, we can define as 'post-modernist' those theories which explicitly or implicitly deny such innate limits to freedom.

The view that the world is a product of our own cultural definitions, or is, or can be, constructed largely in accordance with our
wills, represents a critique of the idea of nature and of inherent
constraint. The idea that psychotherapy is a process of constructing
meaningful 'narratives', rather than of discovering or recognising
psychic realities, is an extension of this way of thinking.

The sociologists referred to above see 'modernity' in terms of its
opportunities and challenges of 'reflexiveness', and to that extent
remain committed to an ideal of progress and extended freedom.
But in their writings on psychological questions, there is a contrast
between their positions and both of the traditions being discussed.
They largely reject the idea of biologically or unconsciously-deter-
mined constraints on human freedom, which are basic assumptions
of attachment theory and psychoanalysis. Instead they either celebrate (Giddens) or at least represent as the contemporary modern
condition (Beck) the reality or possibility of total 'self-making'. One
version of this is Giddens' idea of the 'pure relationship', uncon-
strained by anything but the choice of the partners, as a typical or
emerging contemporary state of being. Although Anthony Giddens
defines this as 'modernity', with its new cognitive freedoms, I
think this is best seen as a reflection of a 'post-modern' way of
thinking, in which all idea of constraints or universal limits has
been abandoned.

The distinctive attribute of the psychoanalytical and attachment
theory traditions is, by contrast, their insistence that all limits cannot be transcended. Freedom and well-being, according to these ways
of thinking, is only achieved conditionally, and through recognition
of and respect for the limits posed by 'human nature' and its various
endowments. Or, as Marx put it in a quite different context, men
make history, but not in circumstances of their own choosing.

The emphasis on the symbolic, mediated dimensions of experience of the world makes it possible to think about the conditions
of attachment in modern societies. A number of new dimensions
of social relationship become available to this discussion once the
aspect of symbolic representation is taken into consideration. For
example, 'attachment' becomes an attribute of a state of mind, can
exist 'at a distance' in both space and time, and can change over
the life-course. 'Attachment' is redefined as a disposition or capacity to form and maintain relationships and trust, not necessarily a
fixed state of affairs.

Communities are thus to be understood as symbolic, even
imaginary entities, not merely in their interpersonal, face-to-face
forms. They thus depend on shared forms of communication and

culture for their existence and health, as well as on the immediate human ties they make possible. We can consider 'communities', of meaning, sentiment and values, as more or less able to fulfil the role of containers of the experience and change which occur within their boundaries. How adequate they are will depend in part on the quality of communication they make possible for their members.

In modern societies, these patterns of communication are highly complex. They are mediated for individuals by relations with workplaces, with professionals of various kinds, with the media of mass communications, by crisis services, as well as with friends and family members. In many spheres of life, we can observe efforts to improve and develop the possibility of such understanding, as responses to fragmentation and to the weakening of primary ties. The hospice movement and the large-scale development of ante-natal classes are good examples from opposite ends of the lifecycle, rooted in the voluntary sector. But the state welfare system has been moving mostly in the opposite direction in the past 15 years, under the impact of coercive and finance-driven management styles. It has been substituting aims of higher throughput, and precise behavioural objectives and checklists for forms of work which value relationships with clients and patients, as opposed to measurements, as a core element of therapeutic work.

In its treatment of offenders, the state has been moving away rapidly from any conception of change through self-understanding, to a model of coercion designed only to confine and amplify destructive and vengeful impulses. In education, movement is again regressive. In the schools, an ostensible concern over 'standards' masks a hostility to the developmental objectives and interactive methods of progressive educators. In the universities, the individual and small-group teaching methods which permitted learning through deep-level identification with subjects and their teachers is being made impossible by student–teacher ratios widely approaching 30:1. Throughout the educational system, a culture of institutional competition and the equivalent of funding-by-results is instrumentalising the entire process, destroying the essence of the learning process within a hypocritical rhetoric of 'raising standards'.

It will take time to elaborate the social policies which can adequately meet the needs of complex symbolically-mediated communities. We can note that individuals will be able to cope with different degrees of complexity at different parts of their lifecycle, and in different conditions of advantage or disadvantage. The need for security and membership is such that psychic health may be sought, and even to a degree found, within fragments held together by antagonism to what lies outside their imaginary boundaries. Thus, a gang projects its vulnerabilities on to its victims; privileged groups can project greed or neediness on to the deprived; true believers project uncertainty on to the unconverted or to those holding other beliefs. A complex society is bound to be composed of such sub-cultures. The problem is to ensure that dialogue and movement of individuals between cultures is possible. For this, a society depends on its most public forms of communication – its education system, its politics, its mass media. The health of modern communities, from a psychological as well as a social point of view, depends greatly on their public cultures.

MATERIAL DIMENSIONS

Finally, there is one other precondition of 'community' to consider. This concerns the levels of economic insecurity and inequality now being generated by a deregulated capitalism operating on a global scale. Families will not flourish unless their members earn wages sufficient to support them. If levels of economic inequality continue to grow, understanding and relationship across the social spectrum will break down. The rich will flee the poor from fear and distaste; the poor will avoid the privileged to escape humiliation. Antagonism between classes will surely grow too, though this may gain its displaced expression in modern multi-ethnic societies in racial rather than class terms. Damage to physical and mental health will be widespread in such societies, as a consequence of the lack of basic economic security, even though it will sometimes be represented as their cause, as in those 'culture of poverty' and 'transmitted deprivation' theses, that blame the poor for their own misfortunes.[5]

There *are* material and economic preconditions for secure attachment, within families, neighbourhoods and the larger society. A society which provides the secure attachments which its members need, and which can contain a diversity of communities and cultures in a creative way, is not attainable unless material preconditions as well as moral dimensions are addressed. It is tempting for politicians to say that they are for 'community', and against 'individualism', as a way of not having to say what they will do about the arbitrary and unfettered powers which have undermined communities in the first place. Mrs Thatcher was clear about her moral commitments to individual freedom and inequality, but she was also clear about the means for giving effect to these, by coercive legislation, deregulation, tax policies, privatisation, and all the rest. A New Labour which preaches morality, but intends to leave the Thatcherite arrangements much as they are, is at best unwittingly 'turning a blind eye' to the real problems. At worst, it could become an exercise in calculated hypocrisy.

NOTES

1. Continental European anxieties about social exclusion, and Asian models of capitalism operating with the support of closed family and corporate hierarchies, reflect different cultural traditions, now sometimes identified as alternatives to the Anglo-American model.
2. For clarification of the different meanings of 'object' and 'object-relations' in this context, see Hinshelwood (1989).
3. Steiner attributes this toleration of factional difference, unusual in the international psychoanalytic world, to the civility of British culture. It may be more specifically an effect of the welcome extended by the small group of British analysts to the refugees from Nazism (Steiner 1985).
4. Bowlby's view of the importance of the early mother–infant tie led to much criticism of him later by feminists who defended the benefits to women of working outside the home. Only later did it become clear that attachment theory did not imply that mothers alone should stay at home with their infants for 24 hours a day (see Holmes, this volume).
5. Evidence that within a family, the depression or absence of a parent can have damaging effects on the development of an infant, should not be confused with the idea that poverty is the result of moral failings of the poor. One of the richest societies in the world, the US, nevertheless has high levels of infant mortality, high levels of violent crime, and the highest rate of incarceration of virtually any nation, basically because of the insecurity to which it continually exposes its citizens.

REFERENCES

Addison, P. (1982) *The Road to 1945*. London: Quartet.
Ainsworth, M. (1982) 'Attachment: Retrospect and Prospect' in C.M. Parkes and J. Stevenson-Hinde (eds), *The Place of Attachment in Human Behaviour*. London: Tavistock.
Bauman, Z. (1992) *Intimations of Postmodernity*. London: Routledge.
Beck, U. (1992) *Risk Society*. London: Sage.
Bion, W. (1962) 'A Theory of Thinking' in *Second Thoughts*. London: Heinemann.
Boston, M. and Szur, R. (eds) (1983) *Psychotherapy with Severely Deprived Children*. London: Routledge.

Daws, D. (1989) *Through the Night: Helping Parents and Sleepless Infants*. London: Free Association Books.

Etzioni, A. (1993) *The Spirit of Community*. New York: Simon and Schuster.

Fonagy, P., Steele, M., Steele H., Moran, G. and Higgins, A. (1991) 'The capacity for understanding mental stages: the reflective self in parent and child and its significance for security of attachment', *Infant Mental Health Journal* 12: 201–18.

Giddens, A. (1990) *The Consequences of Modernity*. Cambridge: Polity.

Giddens, A. (1991) *Modernity and Self-identity: Self and Society in the Late Modern Age*. Cambridge: Polity.

Giddens, A. (1994) *Beyond Left and Right*. Oxford: Blackwell.

Hinshelwood, R.D. (1989) *A Dictionary of Kleinian Thought*. London: Free Association Books.

Hoggart, R. (1992) *The Uses of Literacy*. Harmondsworth: Penguin.

Holmes, J. (1993) *John Bowlby and Attachment Theory*. London: Routledge.

King, P. and Steiner, R. (eds) (1991) *The Freud–Klein Controversies 1941–45*. London: Routledge, in association with Institute of Psycho-Analysis, London.

Main, M. (1991) 'Metacognitive knowledge, metacognitive monitoring, and singular (coherent) vs multiple (incoherent) models of attachment: findings and directions for future research' in C.M. Parkes, J. Stevenson-Hinde, and P. Marris (eds), *Attachment across the Life Cycle*. London: Routledge.

Main, M. and Goldwyn, R. (1984) 'Predicting rejection of her infant from mother's representations of her own experience: implications for the abused-abuser intergenerational cycle', *International Journal of Child Abuse and Neglect* 8: 203–17.

Main, M., Kaplan, K., and Cassidy, J. (1985) 'Security in infancy, childhood and adulthood. A move to the level of representation' in I. Bretherton & E. Waters (eds), *Growing Points in Attachment Theory and Research*. Monographs of the Society for Research in Child Development 50: 66–104.

Marshall, T.H. (1963) *Sociology at the Crossroads*. London: Heineman.

Meltzer, D., Bremner, D. Hoxter, S., Weddell, D. and Wittenberg, I. (1975) *Explorations in Autism: a Psychoanalytical Study*. Strath Tay, Perthshire: Clunie Press.

Menzies-Lyth, I. (1988) *Containing Anxiety in Institutions: Selected Essays*, Vol. I. London: Free Association Books.

Menzies-Lyth, I. (1989) *The Dynamics of the Social: Selected Essays*, Vol. II. London: Free Association Books.

Miller, E. (1993) *From Dependency to Autonomy: Studies in Organisation and Change*. London: Free Association Books.

Miller, M., Rustin, M.E., Rustin, M.J. and Shuttleworth, J. (eds) (1989) *Closely Observed Infants*. London: Duckworth.

Obholzer, A. and Roberts, V. (1994) *The Unconscious at Work: Individual and Organizational Stress in the Human Services*. London: Routledge.

Orwell, G. (1953) *England your England, and other Essays*. London: Secker and Warburg.

Robertson, J. (1952) *A Two Year Old Goes to Hospital*. (Film) London: Tavistock.

Sinason, V. (1992) *Mental Handicap and the Human Condition*. London: Free Association Books.

Steiner, R. (1985) 'Some thoughts about tradition and change arising from an examination of the British Psycho-Analytical Society's Controversial Discussions (1943–44)', *International Review of Psycho-Analysis* 12(1): 27–71.

Szur, R., and Miller, S. (1991) *Extending Horizons: Psychoanalytic Psychotherapy with Children, Adolescents and Families*. London: Karnac.

Tawney, R.H. (1921) *The Acquisitive Society*. Brighton: Harvester, 1982.

Titmuss, R.M. (1958) *Essays on the Welfare State*. London: Allen and Unwin.

Titmuss, R.M. (1968) *Commitment to Welfare*. London: Allen and Unwin.

Titmuss, R.M. (1970) *The Gift Relationship*. London: Allen and Unwin.

Tustin, F. (1981) *Autistic States in Children*. London: Routledge.

Williams, R. (1958) 'Culture is Ordinary' in N. MacKenzie (ed.), *Conviction*. London: MacGibbon and Kee.

Winnicott, D.W. (1971) 'The Mirror-role of Mother and Family in Child Development', in *Playing and Reality*. London: Tavistock.

17 Aux Armes, Citoyens!

Helena Kennedy

Like most dutiful daughters living a long way from the parental hearth, I have an established ritual of phoning my mother regularly and 'chewing the fat'. At eighty-something, she is still active, witty and up on current affairs, particularly those of the Royal family, but also those more political. She is my woman on the Clapham omnibus, my touchstone for the likely responses of jurors to my clients' many and varied accounts for their alleged felonious behaviour. As we review the state of the nation – unemployment, Princess Di, crime, social deprivation, the latest political scandal – she invariably ends with her Scottish variant of the Confucius adage, saying: 'Och, we live in terrible times.'

Yet, she is a woman who lived through the Depression and war. She was bombed out of her home on the Clydeside and really has seen some terrible times. She has all her life been a Labour voter and is not, therefore, a disinterested spectator of the political scene. However, for her the horror of the last decade and a half moves beyond the partisanship of party allegiance. She fears the return to a past that she imagined was gone – insecurity in employment, homelessness, rising crime, the removal of hope and chances for the young. In addition, she sees no pulling together for the common good, little of the collective goodwill and shared aspiration which welded her world together. She sees fear for the future on every face in the Glasgow bus queue.

That fear is not irrational. The recent past has seen unemployment on a grand scale and the American economist, Jeremy Rifkin (1995), continues to paint a future scenario of massive job losses from the manufacturing sector, which it will be impossible to replace within one generation. Like other forecasters, he predicts continuing high levels of unemployment into the next millennium. Coupled with the destabilising effects of job insecurity are the uncertainties of a world where old ideologies of the left and new ideologies of the right can no longer be articles of faith. The socialist assumption that

central planning and public ownership were by definition more efficient than market co-ordination has been found wanting and holds
no hopeful vision for those who have witnessed the travesties performed in the name of socialism in the Eastern bloc and elsewhere.
But free market capitalism has failed too. The absence of a vibrant
public domain testifies to that failure. Without the compasses of left
and right as we knew them, the up-coming terrain seems treacherous
and unchartable. But we have to change the political discourse and
anchor ourselves with new definitions and new cornerstones of
thought. While the economics of socialism may be contentious, the
socialist ethic of solidarity and fellowship is as compelling as ever. It
has never been more sorely needed and it is within that ethic that the
roots of citizenship can be nurtured. Uncertainty, exclusion and
failed Government have disabled people. Disillusionment with politics stems from a distrust of those who govern us yet active citizenship only flourishes where there is trust in the political system. The
ideal civic culture would be one in which the political ideas and
values of the citizens fostered political equality and participation, and
where government was seen as trustworthy and acting in the public
interest. However, this is a far cry from our present organisation.

The American sociologist Robert Putnam (1993) undertook a
pioneering study of why certain Italian towns were more economically successful than others. He examined many contributors, finally coming to the surprising conclusion that the factor
which made an overwhelming difference was the development of
what he called social capital, the high level of mutual trust and
reciprocity and the strength of local networks and associations.
Putnam's ideas are now echoed in the work of leading thinkers
around the world, who see that social capital is directly linked
not just with the well-being of civil society, but with economic
performance. Seemingly intangible factors such as networks and
trust are linked with very concrete financial performance (but see
Ormerod, this volume). It is of course out of this recognition
that Tony Blair is developing his stakeholder concept. The idea
recognises that markets are social constructs, shaped and sustained by societies. Markets do not all behave in the same way
or produce the same outcomes. Some are more environmentally
friendly, others more socially cohesive, others more productive.
The simple proposition in stakeholding is that property must
discharge obligations to the wider community as well as to its
owners: that the decisions of a capitalist firm must reflect the
interests of its employees, its suppliers and the localities in
which it operates, as well as those of its shareholders. The idea

may be simple but it engages with the failures of the Thatcher free market experiment, giving texture and nuance to the relationships in a pluralist society. So far there has been a failure by the right and parts of the left to recognise the radicalism of the stakeholder idea and its departure from traditional British shareholder capitalism. It presents the challenge of how we can make the market work for the public good instead of against it.

The current government determinedly insists that globalisation is responsible for our economic ills, and sixties moral decay for our social problems. Those alibis do not withstand close scrutiny. During the Thatcher/Major years, individualism, consumption and self-interest were promoted as not just laudable modes of behaviour, but as the engine of a thrusting economy. The populace was divided into winners and losers, employed and unemployed, successful and unsuccessful, and the measure of success became that of 'value added' and 'cost-effectiveness' and the ugly language of the marketplace. The nation was seduced by the notion that deregulation would let entrepreneurs run free in the marketplace, making us all beneficiaries of trickle-down economics. Instead, the unregulated market, the holy grail of British government since 1979, has been the most significant factor in undermining citizenship. The divisions in our society have become more marked. We have not seen everyone embraced by the benefits of the market but, rather, increasingly excluded.

Anxiety has inevitably been a part of the lives of working-class people, but today the rising tide of casualisation and insecurity buffets the middle classes too. In his book *The State We're In*, Will Hutton (1995) analyses the nervous nineties, showing the impact of downsizing on middle management as part of the 'mean and lean' management philosophy. Companies are finally utilising the power of information technology to reshape or re-engineer how they work, but at the cost of massive job losses and abrupt restraints on incomes. Core activities within corporations are reduced often to the point of under-employment, while short-term contracts are increased so that market uncertainties are borne by the sub-contractor (see Marris, this volume). The irony of such sub-contracting strategies, as at the BBC for example, is that they are sold to people on the basis that self-employment will provide autonomy and freedom, when such 'independence' very often creates a frightening 'dependence' upon the goodwill of the main contractor. The concomitant effect of these changes is that there are fewer people with the money to buy the goods which the businesses are selling, so that companies lose out in the long run. There is also a cost to the state in the form of unemployment entitlements. As Hutton has pointed out, one of the basic social contracts – namely, that between business, employee and society – is breaking down.

The last 15 years have also seen the 'downsizing' of the welfare state. Here too a central social contract – that between citizen and state – is being redrawn. Many old people who looked forward to retirement find themselves on a near-poverty income. Levels of benefit across the board have been reduced. Unemployed school leavers are not entitled to benefit. A whole range of bureaucratic measures have been introduced, which make claiming a frustrating and humiliating exercise. Education grants are being cut, publicly funded dentistry barely exists, state schools and the NHS are being starved of funds, prescription charges are steadily increased. We are seeing middle-class flight into private pensions, health insurance and private education.

Fifty years ago it seemed that poverty, like small pox, might be eradicated with time: now one in three children are born into poverty. We are more socially divided than we have been for a century. As the research for the *Health of the Nation* Report showed (Department of Health 1991), the diet of poor communities is dangerously bereft of nutrition, yet it is not for lack of knowledge that people eat badly, but through lack of money.

Aspects of British life, of which we rightly felt proud, have also been undermined. There has been a denigration of public service so that most of those who chose to work in the fields of education, health care, social work, legal aid, the police, the probation or prison service have been undervalued, deemed to lack the entrepreneurial drive that is so idealised in the present climate. In abandoning our economic destiny to the marketplace we seemed to abandon our moral destiny to it as well. In the face of such uncertainty, there is a growing sense of powerlessness, a disbelief in the ability to effect change of any sort. Young people express little faith in the political process, and have little expectation that things will improve in the future. Their alienation was powerfully demonstrated in the Demos survey, *Freedom's Children* (Wilkinson and Mulgan 1995).

There are good reasons for political disenchantment. The national government is more centralised than at any time over the last 50 years. The executive wields enormous power, unchecked by the legislature or select committees, let alone a proper Bill of Rights or written constitution. Local government has been emasculated. Quangos, of which there is now one for every 10,000 heads of the population according to the Democratic Audit, handle one-third of the total public expenditure budget. Yet they are not democratically elected, their meetings are more often than not held in private and appointments regularly go to friends of those in power.

Because of the behaviour of some politicians, an eminent judge, Lord Nolan, had to be called upon to examine ethical standards in public life. That inquiry was conducted because of public alarm over those who seemed to be abusing their positions for their own financial gain: MPs asking questions in the House on behalf of professional lobbyists if the price was right; newly retired government ministers sliding into incredibly highly paid jobs in the very industries which they had privatised; a government blessing given to boardroom greed. The public service ethic seemed to be abandoned at the same time that we were told there was no such thing as society.

The Scott Report showed that parliament was repeatedly misled over the sale of weapon components to Iraq in breach of a government embargo. In the Matrix Churchill case, on the advice of the Attorney General, politicians signed public interest immunity certificates which might have meant that corroboration of the men's case would not go before the jury. Only one of the ministers expressed any concern that this action might deny three men their defence to a criminal prosecution, which would probably have led to their imprisonment. Liberty is claimed as one of the most precious of the rights we possess, but here we had a case of politicians and civil servants prepared to prevent the truth being told. Was it because disclosure would expose the double standard of maintaining one thing in parliament and doing the opposite in private?

However, the malaise about ethics in public life often takes less dramatic forms with the easy use of lies in public fora and no display of conscience when caught out. No sense of shame when politicians are found profiteering out of the policy on council house sales and a bullish refusal to resign when misbehaviour is exposed or when a contempt for the law has been displayed, such as the deportation of a Zairian refugee in the face of a court injunction, or changing the law on victim compensation without going before parliament, or wasting enormous sums of public money, as in the Pergau Dam affair. We have also seen anti-discriminatory initiatives derided by government as politically correct, and equality of opportunity insidiously pushed off the agenda as an issue of national concern. Lip-service is paid to equal chances for all, but we seem to be shutting our eyes to the damage that injustice and discrimination are doing and the frustration, bitterness and hopelessness that they create in people. Tolerance is now being presented by some public and media figures as only a good thing in small doses, particularly when it comes to refugees. Yet all our historic experience tells us that a just and peaceful society is only possible where there is tolerance and respect for genuine diversity.

Social cohesion is inevitably threatened where there is economic uncertainty: racism thrives, marriages are more likely to break down, wives and children more likely to be abused and young people are much more likely to become involved in crime. Without the rite of passage which was provided by employment or training, young men become marooned in adolescence, and crime is the terrible price we pay for their blighted hopes. Yet the links between unemployment and crime are still denied by government. Public loss of confidence is not confined to our political institutions. The malaise extends to the legal system, the judiciary, the City, the police.

If we are to consider the state of social capital in modern Britain, what we see is a catastrophic civic disengagement. Few people vote, attend public meetings, stand in local elections, want to be an MP, want to do jury service, want to be a school governor, want to run a scout or guide troop, join a political party, join the Territorial Army, become a hospital volunteer, want to be a prison visitor. In fact, each new generation is less actively involved than the one before and a whole tradition of responsible citizenship is gradually falling out of society. The usual suspects are rounded up by right-wing MPs to blame for non-participation and social irresponsibility – bad comprehensive education, left-wing nihilism, working mothers, single parents, the nanny state, self-indulgent sixties hedonism, the rise in crime. Richard Putnam (1993) does acknowledge that lack of will, lack of time and lack of incentive play their part in the unravelling of communities, as does mobility, that is, shifting populations, pressure to work long hours and family breakdown, but he also identifies the role of television. Not only does television occupy many hours but it also promotes a greater passivity and privatisation of our lives. It probably means that one of the few events where the nation comes together in communion is for the National Lottery!

WHAT IS CITIZENSHIP?

If Putnam is right that rebuilding a sense of civic involvement is going to be crucial to our economic as well as social prosperity, then we have to think carefully what we mean by citizenship. As I noted earlier, citizenship only flourishes where there is a vibrant public domain, where civil society is healthy and strong enough to nurture community values of solidarity and citizenship. There also has to be trust in government, and politicians have to be seen to be acting in the public interest. Where, therefore, does one begin?

The state has to have a clear role. It cannot be seen either as bogeyman or wet nurse. There should be such a thing as the benign state, which, like the good parent, provides sustenance when needed, health care, opportunities to learn in the fullest way possible, a shelter if required. It treats its citizen with respect, encourages independent thought. It is not threatened by challenge. It listens. Before this is characterised by the right as the nanny state so denounced by Mrs Thatcher, let us be clear about the kind of parenting we are talking about here. This is not the indulgent mothering which bankrolls the prodigal son lost in the Sahara. This is parenting which says we are always here for you but which encourages independence and self-fulfilment. Just as the securely attached child who has formed a strong healthy parental bond will go on to have good relationships and is likely to be a well-adjusted adult, so, too, the securely attached citizen. Where there is insecure political attachment there is likely to be anomie in all its manifestations: rising crime, anti-social behaviour, dysfunction, intolerance, racial tension, mental illness, the creation of an underclass. The politics of attachment is the politics of citizenship.

One of the claims made for Scottish schools, in which I was happily educated, is that they develop 'democratic intellect', which has to be one of the elements of citizenship. It is about thinking, questioning and refusing to be cowed by others. The mature and confident state is happy to be in dialogue with its citizens.

In his vision of the truly democratic society, Thomas Paine (1792) painted citizenship with three essential strands: memory, imagination and judgement. Experience draws upon memory. It helps us make sense of the past and draw lessons from it. It enables us to understand who we are. But it is important that we recognise that memory depends upon language. Research upon the working of the human brain shows that human experience is more likely to be remembered when articulated. Yet within so many of our communities the recounting of human experience no longer takes place and the narrative of life's events is lost (see Holmes, this volume). Opportunities to meet and discuss and the encouragement to do so are pivotal to community action. Imagination, Paine's second strand, is our place for dreaming the future. It allows us to see that life need not be like this. It presents alternatives. The role of art, music and literature is crucial to this human inventiveness. Judgement, the third strand, draws upon our collective wisdom, enabling us to make choices and move forward. But freedom of information is at the heart of good decision making.

Paine's prescription is a poetic manifesto for change, and one of the mechanisms for its delivery is an agenda of constitutional reform. My own commitment to constitutional change comes from a belief that our political architecture has to be redesigned if we are going to invigorate our political and civic institutions. It is a prerequisite for any genuine sense of citizenship. We can expect duty, commitment and responsibility from our citizens only when they have rights. When Xenophilius the Pythagorean was asked how one could best educate a son in ethical matters, he said: 'Make him the citizen of a state with good laws.' The case for a British Bill of Rights is becoming overwhelming, yet the government steadfastly refuses to do for the people of Britain what it has at last done for the people of Hong Kong. This means that the United Kingdom is now the only nation in Europe or the democratic Commonwealth without an enforceable Bill of Rights. Public support for a Bill of Rights is strong. In a Mori poll, published in the *Independent* in 1991, 79 per cent of respondents agreed that their rights would be most effectively protected if they were written down in a single document. There are few rights within the law of the United Kingdom. Freedom exists in Hobbes' words 'in the silence of the law'. Our laws forbid rather than allow; our freedoms are defined by a complex mixture of statute and common law which is very difficult for any lay person to understand. We have no codified written constitution or Bill of Rights to provide a benchmark, a backdrop of principle, against which all other law is tested. The very complexity in which our rights exist at the moment is a shield for arbitrary power.

This was generally never a source of concern because of the strength of parliamentary democracy, and in particular the regular exchange of power between the two major parties, providing some disciplining power on the overbearing ambitions of the executive. However, recent years have shown major flaws in our democracy: no separation of powers, the executive dominating the legislature, Prime Ministerial patronage, control by the whips, growth of the quangocracy, and the anachronism of the Lord Chancellor's post (sitting in the cabinet, Speaker of the House of Lords, sitting as a judge and appointing all other judges). The voting system leaves a geographically concentrated minority always electing a government. We have an unelected upper chamber with an inbuilt Conservative majority and an unelected head of state. The royal prerogative means that governments can wear the royal mantle and declare war, sign treaties, operate national security provisions without referring to parliament. The European dimension of British politics does not help. The European Commission is deeply undemocratic, with the only democratically elected part of the European Community – Parliament – having the least powers. There is a growing unease that Britain is one of the most secrecy obsessed of the pluralist democracies. Until very recently the BT tower was classified secret!

The need for a Bill of Rights and Right to Know legislation is imperative. Redressing the legal abuses we have seen in recent times – the removal of the right to silence, the interference with the right of assembly and the farcical removal of freedom of speech involved in the broadcasting ban on Sinn Fèin – would radically reform not just the body politic, but the body legal. It would engender greater respect for the law. A Bill of Rights would give people a clearer sense of their rights and their relationship with the courts. They would have a greater purchase on the law, having a better sense of its role and purpose, instead of feeling it belonged to men in long wigs. And it would, of course, be a source of empowerment. Inherent in rights legislation is the concomitant responsibility of respecting the rights of others. In Canada an initial Bill of Rights was introduced, rather in the way that we would incorporate the European Convention of Human Rights. Thereafter a full consultation process with Canadian citizens produced the Charter of Rights which not only commands profound respect in Canada, but throughout the world. That process of listening to the people, having them participate in deciding the content, lent a special authority to the final document. A judge on the Supreme Court of Canada, speaking on how judges interpreted a Bill of Rights, was clear that the popular endorsement of the Charter of Rights gave it a sacrosanct quality which engendered special judicial respect.

That process of real consultation is one which I would like to see replicated here in the creation of our Bill of Rights. Such a process, which it is precisely the purpose of this book to articulate, in itself has an awakening effect and shifts the political culture.

If Tony Blair's stakeholding has meaning, it has to involve the devolution of power not only to the nations and regions of the United Kingdom, but to local communities. In the new South Africa, a concerted effort is going into the establishing of social capital or *ubuntu* (people richness). That is one of the reasons why education is also at the heart of any revitalising project. I am currently chairing a committee for the Further Education Funding Council to look at ways of widening participation in further education. Some of the most interesting projects, which already exist in small pockets of under-privilege, involve the creation of family rooms within schools where parents can come and take classes in basic English or maths or, in some places, computer skills. The start is often an invitation to help children learn through play, and parents are only too keen to do something for their children. Once a little confidence is gained, the direction can turn to parents' own needs. The effect is not only a raising of aspirations for the parent, so that they often go on to courses in local colleges; it brings about more active support for their own child, and the parents become more involved with the school generally, for example in the PTA (Parent Teacher Association).

These efforts may seem small but they all begin to count, so long as people are doing things for themselves, albeit supported. If estates are suffering from neglect, tenants should be drawn into their management. They might pay young people to pick up litter, remove graffiti as soon as it appears, plant out in the open areas. They might design new buildings for themselves, as happens in a growing number of community architecture or self-build schemes. The children could be consulted about improving play areas. Adults might save in a credit union and borrow money at 12 per cent, rather than the 23 per cent charged by credit cards. They might form a co-operative to buy good-quality food at low cost, that is delivered to where they live. They might undertake a drive to ensure that everyone claims their full benefit entitlement. Taking part in a study circle or family literacy project or a jobs club, learning how to build new knowledge and skills, can be the start of greater community involvement. You might see more adults prepared to run a youth club or organise a community event. Each individual action by citizens will be invisible, but a sense of community develops over time. These communities may be based around where people live or work or worship, or around other common needs or interests. What we should never doubt is that community can be rebuilt in large part because it is a human necessity. But community action on its own will not be enough, just as the state on its own falls short of our ideals, but the combination of the two has enormous potential.

These are more or less uncharted waters but the future has to lie in a partnership between government and citizen. Given the role of television in contributing to apathy, it should be challenged to play its part in reactivating civic life. Channel 4 has already experimented with People's Parliaments and Deliberative Polls. In the latter, members of the public from a wide cross-section are asked their views on Europe, for example. Arguments are then presented cogently on both sides and invariably good information changes perceptions (see Liber, this volume). In the US there is a movement called public journalism which has two core themes: the promoting of civic involvement in more overt ways, hosting public forums, promoting volunteering, putting readers' questions to electoral candidates, and framing coverage so that it raises questions and challenges the democratic intellect!

We have lived through an era of failed promises. We are engulfed in social and economic problems. The effect has been a shift in the public mood from cynicism to anger to contempt for many of those in public life. The Conservatives' response to those anxieties is to hark back to basics and a glorious past where there was order and discipline, family values and a strong sense of nation.

We badly need to win back public trust, restore public service, uphold the public interest, but to do this means radical reform. It involves a chain of interconnecting measures, which is why the Charter 88 agenda for constitutional reform cannot be picked over for the cherries which a particular political party likes. A Bill of Rights does link up to the empowering of citizens on estates, as does a Freedom of Information Act; a written constitution would restore checks and balances and in turn help re-establish trust in the political institutions; a new code of ethics for politicians does link to greater responsibility amongst citizens. Reform of the voting system and devolution do engender greater participation. And reform of the House of Lords would remind us that we are living in the late twentieth century where accidents of birth and patronage are unacceptable sources of political power and influence. Members of an organised society need to share common goals and aspirations – what Lord Devlin, one of our great jurists, called 'the invisible bond' which holds society together. We have to find ways of renewing those bonds, and this is our opportunity. To quote the recent Nobel prize winner for literature, Seamus Heaney:

> History says, *Don't hope*
> *On this side of the grave,*
> But then, once in a lifetime
> The longed-for tidal wave
> Of Justice can rise up,
> And hope and history rhyme.

So hope for a great sea-change
On the far side of revenge.
Believe that a further shore
Is reachable from here.
Believe in miracles
And cures and healing wells.

(Heaney 1990)

ACKNOWLEDGEMENTS

This chapter is based on a lecture given at Glasgow University in 1996. It is published by kind permission of the University.

Excerpt from *The Cure at Troy: A Version of Sophocles' Philoctetes* by Seamus Heaney © 1991 Seamus Heaney. Reprinted by permission of Faber & Faber and Farrar, Strauss and Giroux Inc.

REFERENCES

Department of Health (1991) *The Health of the Nation*. London: HMSO.
Heaney, S. (1990) *The Cure at Troy: A Version of Sophocles' Philoctetes*. London: Faber.
Hutton, W. (1995) *The State We're In*. London: Cape.
Paine, T. (1792) *The Rights of Man*. London: J.M. Dent, 1920.
Putnam, R.A. (1993) *Making Democracy Work: Civic Traditions in Modern Italy*. Princeton, NJ: Princeton University Press.
Rifkin, J. (1995) *The End of Work: The Decline of the Global Labour Force and the Dawn of the Post-Market Era*. New York: Putnam.
Wilkinson, H. and Mulgan, G. (1995) *Freedom's Children: Work, Relationships and Politics for 18–34 year olds in Britain Today*. London: Demos.

Afterword

Sebastian Kraemer and Jane Roberts

The processes we describe, though only recently articulated and written about, are hardly new. Everywhere in the world, for thousands of years in countless different cultures, people have been getting attached to each other and to the places they inhabit. For even longer periods our mammalian cousins have been doing so too, and are still at it. Yet the convictions that led us to this project need repeated confirmation, because they so easily disappear in the glare of soundbite and front-page politics, as if that were all there was to political discourse.

The range of contributions might have been different. We could have included chapters on housing, parks, the design and use of public buildings, and other features of everyday life that determine its quality. The details would have varied but the overall theme would not. We have sought to keep in mind the processes which remain central to human experience, and to bring them into the public sphere. Alongside many other possible criticisms, we can imagine being dismissed as too psychological and therefore outside the approved boundaries – that we deal with issues that are entirely private or personal, and which are therefore nothing to do with policy. Yet if politics is simply the struggle for influence between interests, then our aim is to add other interests to the frame. We have taken a leap from what is known about intimate relationships to what could be achieved in political ones.

Index